A Family Of Six At Sea
Crossing The Atlantic On A Cement Boat
By: Werner M. Gysi and Family

Water and Sky open dreams

Dreams of endlessness it seems

Gooly Mooly Publishing
2009

Published by: Gooly Mooly Publishing

Box 978, Enderby, British Columbia

Canada, V0E 1V0   Phone: 250-838-6375

goolymooly@gmail.com   www.gysi.ca

The production of this book has been solely financed by Gooly Mooly Publishing and no public funds or grants have been applied for.

Gooly Mooly Publishing is committed to a sustainable future for all.

Mixed Sources

Cert no. SW-COC-001271
© 1996 FSC

FSC

Front cover: Kristy Nicole drawn by Pascal Gysi

Printed and bound in Canada

Library and Archives Canada Cataloguing in Publication

Gysi, Werner M., 1949-

A family of six at sea : crossing the Atlantic on a
cement boat / by Werner M. Gysi and family.

ISBN 978-1-896424-01-9

1. Gysi, Werner M., 1949- —Travel—Atlantic Ocean.
2. Gysi, Werner M., 1949- —Family. 3. Kristy Nicole (Ship).
4. Atlantic Ocean—Description and travel. 5. Sailing—Atlantic Ocean. 6. Transatlantic voyages. I. Title.

G530.G98 2009   910.91'63   C2009-904615-6

Published by Gooly Mooly Publishing

-Harmonic Farming: Homesteading   ISBN: 978-1-896424-03-3

-Harmonic Farming: Bees   ISBN: 978-1-896424-05-7

-A Family Of Six At Sea Crossing The Atlantic On A Cement Boat
                              ISBN: 978-1-896424-01-9

-A Family Of Six At Sea, CD (compact disc), songs and colour
pictures to complement the book   ISBN: 978-1-896424-02-6

-Harmonic Farming: a love style   ISBN: 1-896424-00-7

Acknowledgements   4

First of all let me say thank you to all the sailors we met along our trip, some that we got to know better, and others we briefly met. We were welcomed in so many places and received so many things, things that made our travels more enjoyable and allowed us to carry on. It still today looks to me as if magic was involved. It's all of you that made this trip a wonderful memory to look back to.

To thank my children for their contribution goes without mentioning, and the support and contribution from my wife was greatly appreciated. She helped me through many valleys, not just those made by the waves, and we somehow managed to go through some very good times and some lesser good times together unscathed. We are now married for over 35 years, and we seem to be happy with that.

Whom I have to thank the most for this book coming together is John, the editor, who had more patience than any person I met before. He has put so much effort and time into this project. When I gave up, he made me start. It made for a very close and great friendship. I hope that John has felt the same.

To get this book printed took a long time; mostly time spent to reflect, to look back, but also focussing on the present life. The children needed education, funds needed to be generated and as a teacher, I had a new professional challenge ahead of me. Now it has all come together to blossom and unfold. I have come to understand that time is not the only thing in life that counts, but it helps to use it wisely.

Heartfelt thanks

About the author

Werner, born in 1949 and educated as an Electronic Engineer in Switzerland, immigrated to Canada in 1981. He published the book Harmonic Farming: a love style in 1995. In the same year he was invited to a one-hour interview on CBC National radio. During his position as a science teacher at a private boarding school in Montreux and being an avid hiker by exploring the nearby mountains, he found enough time to compile this book. Besides playing the guitar and looking after bees, he enjoys sailing.

Table Of Contents

This story is a continuation of the adventures of the Gysi family. Both Werner and Brigitte grew up in Switzerland. Neither felt comfortable in the well ordered lifestyle with neat, green lawns in front of almost every dwelling; they had greener plans. In their search for a Paradise on Earth, they travelled in India and North & South America and, eventually, found such a place in Canada.

They settled on an acreage in the Shuswap area of British Columbia. There they became Canadian Citizens, built up a computer business in the nearby town of Salmon Arm, created a self-sufficient lifestyle on their farm, gave courses in this form of living and wrote a book about Harmonic Farming, ISBN 1-896424-00-7.

Even this Paradise on Earth could not quell the urge to roam. They adapted a van and tent trailer to accommodate the family of seven and drove to Mexico. There, in a tent trailer, parked in a garden on the outskirts of Santiago Ixquintla, their youngest son Pascal was born.

At the time of this sailing adventure the Gysi family consisted of:

Pascal, the mischievous 4 year old. He was not able to keep a diary of his experiences on our journey, but he did contribute some sketches and the drawing of our boat, which appears on the cover of this book.

Carina, the brown haired 9 year old loved animals. With the animals on the farm, she created a little world of her own. For her to go travelling again was fine, but leaving the animals behind would not be so easy to cope with.

Anisha, the artistic 12 year old, spent much of her spare time with her nose buried in a book. A new adventure for her was just the right thing to look forward to, no matter what it was.

Marcel, the 13 year old, energetic outdoors man. Anything was fine with him, as long as there was no homework attached to it. School was really not the thing he adored.

Brigitte (sometimes also referred to as Chäberli), the mother, and Werner, the father. Both dedicated to give their children as much love and care as they possibly could.

Fabian, the 17 year old was in his 2nd year of apprenticing to be a chef in Zermatt, Switzerland. Being so far away from the family was the most difficult thing he had to experience. He was provided with room and board at the hotel where he was undergoing his training.

Thomas, the 19 year old was finishing his third year of apprenticing to be a precision mechanic. He was living with his godfather in Switzerland.

For some time the family had been discussing a trip to Europe. The two oldest sons were both there, and the close-knit family had a desire to be reunited. There was also a wish to turn the trip into something of an adventure. After much discussion, it was decided to drive through the States in search of a sail boat which would be suitable to carry the six of them across the Atlantic. It was in the cold month of November that everything was in place for them to start looking for that boat.

In order to make this book ecologically sound, as well as economical, it was decided to place only a few grayscale pictures per chapter. Readers interested in seeing more pictures (most in colour) can order a CD with more than 160 pictures, sketches and drawings. These pictures are compiled in the same sequence as the chapters in the book and stored in a pdf file format. Included as a bonus are 10 of Werner's songs in an MP3 file format. Ask for the "A Family Of Six At Sea CD, ISBN# 978-1-896424-02-6". Hopefully you will enjoy reading this story. You are most welcome to send your comments and thank you for your support.

Gooly Mooly Publishing

The name Gooly Mooly was coined when we moved onto our acreage in the Shuswap. While clearing some land I encountered a particularly stubborn tree root. As I struggled with it I said, "This is a real Gooly Mooly". The children were delighted with the phrase and the root is still on display at the farm. In Swiss "Guli" means a hole or worse a manure pit; "Muuli" means to argue, to talk back, and in context it meant "arguing out of the stinky hole". In order to pronounce the words properly in English, we decided to write it as Gooly Mooly.

Gooly Mooly

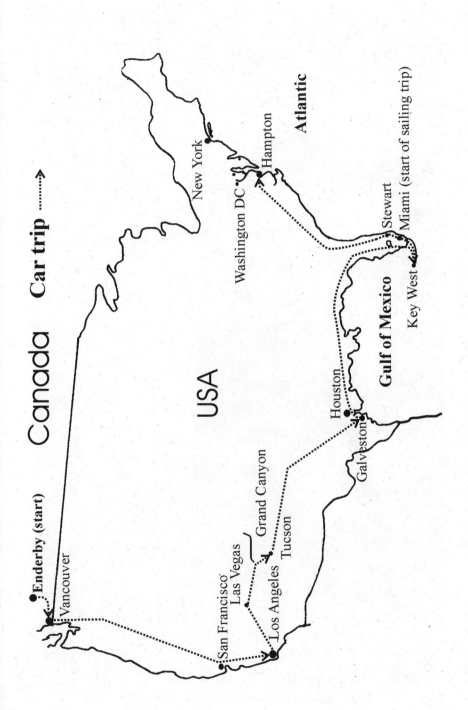

Removing snow before leaving the farm

In Search Of A Sailboat

It was like driving into the unknown of a giant thunderstorm. We had no detailed plans of where we were going or what we were going to do. We were just like a modern day Columbus or a Vasco Da Gama. One last detail to be taken care of was a visit to longtime friends in Vancouver. They were dentists whom we had got to know in our hometown of Enderby. A week-long visit took care of all our dental problems, even if we did not enjoy the experience or the dent it made in our bank account. At least we had a chance to strengthen our friendship.

During our stay in Vancouver we searched out all the boat brokers in the hope of finding a suitable vessel. The prices were, however, too high for our budget which had been set at US $32,000.00. We decided to retrace the coastal route we had taken on our trip to Mexico and try some of the more southerly sources.

The tent trailer was heavily loaded, and we noticed that it had a tendency to swerve sideways, especially when we were slowing down. Since I had replaced the wheel bearings in Enderby, the trailer did not seem to track as well as it had before; I had adjusted them while we were in Vancouver but the problem persisted. I attributed that to the combination of the fact that I had mounted heavier springs and the heavy load we were carrying.

As we travelled south we visited several boat yards but, the more we looked, the more it seemed that our budget might be in need of some adjustment. We made several stops along the beautiful coast of Oregon and eventually reached the State of California. It was there that we were surprised to see the left side trailer wheel race ahead of us while our ears were assailed by a screeching noise from behind. I quickly slowed down, and a glance in the rear-view mirror told the story; the trailer was leaning to one side. It was obvious that something had gone terribly wrong. As luck would have it, we were on a bridge, and I had to pull the trailer another 30 metres or so (about a 100 feet) to clear the bridge and reach an area where I could assess the situation. The wheel had come completely off the hub. All that was left were the remains of the bearings and the lower side of the shaft had been worn flat by rubbing on the pavement. For some obscure reason, the new set of bearings had completely disintegrated and the wheel had broken loose.

We got a tow truck to haul the trailer to Redding, North California. The tow truck driver took us first to the store where we were able to buy a new hub and then to the welder who would weld it on to the axle. We were pleased to see that people were prepared to go the extra mile (as the expression goes) to make things easier for us. American people are rather good that way. It was a rude awakening to see that the new bearings, which fit perfectly, were not the same size as the ones I had installed in Canada. As I remember it was very cold when I did that, and I must have been careless when picking the size of bearing to use. This had caused a loose fitting which had resulted in our coming apart on the bridge. As soon as I realized that, I made another trip to the store to buy new bearings for the other wheel on the trailer. The tools I had brought with us came in very handy at that time. The welder did an excellent job, and we were soon ready to continue with our trip.

We did not spend much time looking at sail boats in San Francisco; the weather had turned rather miserable, so we pressed on southward, along the coastline. A new factor had entered the sail boat purchasing equation; if we purchased a boat on the west coast we would have to sail it through the Panama Canal to reach the Atlantic. The thought of doing so with a new boat and our rusty sailing skills did not appeal to us. As we drew closer to the east coast, the idea of purchasing a boat there started to make more sense.

After having looked at so many boats, I was beginning to get a better sense of what we were looking for. A safe boat, suitably rigged to deal with the Atlantic weather, was, of course, of paramount importance. Comfort, in the form of six berths, ample storage space and a large water tank, was next on the list. In the Los Angeles library, I found a book which showed floor plans for the more common types of boats. These were, for the most part, constructed of fibreglass and gave a good idea of configurations which should be looked for and others which should be avoided. We had noticed that boats which had been built to plans other than the popular ones were, generally speaking, lower priced than the conventionally built ones.

While in Los Angeles we spent Christmas with a close friend. Our children had been encouraged to keep diaries, and Carina had written in hers; "Today is Christmas and I got this diary & some body cream & two beanie babies. I got the diary from mommy & daddy."

We were anxious to head south east, to look at a boat in League City, close to Houston, Texas. The owner had met us in Vancouver and gone into great detail in describing his boat to us.

After leaving Los Angeles we set out for Las Vegas and the nearby Grand Canyon which we were looking forward to seeing. It was raining torrents when we left Los Angeles and, later in the day, we encountered heavy winds. We noticed that the traffic flowing in our direction soon died to a trickle. Later on, in the town of Primadonna, we learned that a big truck had been blown over on the road behind us and that explained the reduction in traffic.

The wind continued to blow all day and into the night; we were unable to set up our tent trailer and had to sleep in the van. Because of the wind we were not able to ride on the huge roller coaster located in the fair grounds but did have fun roaming through the casino after dark. Even 4 year old Pascal enjoyed the glitter, lights, sounds and free rides on a train connecting a couple of the buildings. What a change of worlds for our children. They were used to finding enjoyment in the woods around our farm. We retired early that night as we were keen to carry on to the city we had talked about so much over the past weeks.

Las Vegas was indeed a fun city for the kids. Several factories such as a marshmallow factory, a chocolate factory and a clown museum, where they made all kinds of figures and puppets, offered free tours. The last was the favourite. We also had free rides on a merry-go-round.

In the evening we bought the children rides on the roller coaster, and there was free entertainment in the casinos. A street show depicted a battle between two pirate ships. This got me to thinking about our plans for a boat. Ships seem to fascinate and nurture peoples' imaginations. It was well into the night before we returned to our van in the nearby campground.

The next day we set off for the Grand Canyon and arrived just as the sun was setting. Freshly fallen snow made it resemble a huge cake with frosting sprinkled over it; how beautiful it all looked. We had thought to spend the night there, but once the sun had set, it became clear that it would be too cold and the two or so inches of snow on the ground were not very inviting.

We packed up the tent trailer and headed off to Flagstaff where we spent our first night so far on our trip in a motel. We were glad to have the luxury of the heater with which it was equipped.

The next day the van windows were iced over on the outside rather than the inside, as had happened on a previous night while we were sleeping in the van. The sky was a clear blue, with a wonderful sun warming up the morning air.

We visited the Petrified Forest National Park while on our way to Tucson, Arizona. Chäberli seemed to come down with a bit of a cold, and the others did not feel well either, so we stopped off at the Picacho State Camp Ground which is quite close to Tuscon. At least we did not experience any snow there, and Marcel, the outdoors kid, was convinced that he could finally take off the string on the back tire of his bike. He had installed it as a "snow chain" while still up at the farm. It took him quite some time, but later on I saw him zooming along the road enjoying a ride. Being used to ride the bike through the forests, Marcel used the small paths leading around the area in the park. However, it didn't take long before he was back at our camp site. He was very disappointed, and with a sad face he showed the bike to me. Both tires were flat. After close inspection I noticed small spines sticking out from the tires. They were obviously from cacti. The small bushes along the ground had spikes which were strong enough to push through the tires. Obviously he must have left the path at some point. After we had both tubes patched up, they looked just like someone recuperating from the measles. Once placed inside the tire, however, they worked just fine. It was time to buy a new tire repair kit, as all the patching material had been used up. Marcel was off again, a happy kid riding his bike, but careful about choosing his path.

With the weather being so cold, it was rather difficult to keep warm in our trailer and van. Chäberli's condition got worse, so we phoned

Removing winter gear from tire

a friend we had made there a couple of years previously, on our way to Mexico. She was glad to hear from us and invited us into her home.

I have often thought about how big a difference people like that make to the lives of those around them. We were looked after so well that we found it difficult to adequately express our thanks. As it turned out, we were very fortunate in having found substantial shelter. The Flagstaff area was hit by a blizzard the day after we had left, and the snowploughs were barely able to keep the roads open. The following day, the road to Houston was made impassable by poor weather and ice. We were most fortunate in having been delayed by the flu at the right time and in a place where we had found such a warm welcome. The illness lasted for about a week. Fortunately I managed to avoid catching it.

It'd been a while since we'd left the farm. I can't really pin down what it was that I missed the most from home, but maybe it was the familiar environment, my comfy bed, the quietness around the house, and the possibility of playing outside whenever I wanted to. Not that travelling with the car wasn't fun. On the contrary, it was actually pretty fun, and I easily fell into the routine of sitting in the back seat with Carina, talking a lot, which invariably led to arguments that ended in "I'm never gonna play with you again!" and then started all over again after a few minutes of pouting and stony silence. Of course, there were also the odd fights about who had to clean up the cards that we'd played a while ago (the winner or the loser?), or the toy animals that were spread on the floor. Most of the time, though, I could be found reading one of my favourite pastimes.

On January 20th, I wrote, in a letter to a friend of mine in Canada:

"We are staying at a campground right now. We are in Austin, Texas, but it sure is cold down here. Almost every night I have to have an extra blanket over me so I don't get cold. I heard there is quite a bit of snow up there. In Flagstaff it was so cold we had to sleep in a motel. That was when we started to get the flu and the cold. After Flagstaff we stayed at a friend's place close to a city called Tucson. We stayed there for about six days, first of all because the roads ahead of us were bad, all icy and slippery, and second of all because we were still a little sick. Afterwards the roads and us were all better and we headed out again."

It was beginning to look as if we would only be able to realize our sailing desires in our dreams; things were not going as we had planned them. We had great hopes that the boat Whimsy, in League City, would change our luck. It had been taken out of the water a few years previously and had since been stored in the back yard. It was a 12 metre (39 foot) C&C boat which had been built in Canada in the early seventies. We had seen several pictures of it, but it was still difficult to visualize the exact dimensions of the interior from them.

On our way east, we encountered strong headwinds. There were sometimes trees along the road, and the wide motorway stretched itself over a fairly flat countryside. We had been moving along just fine when the motor started to sputter. We slowed down and had no other choice but to pull over to the side of the road. The motor stopped all together. What was going on now I wondered. I stepped out of the van, into the cold blowing wind, and opened the hood. There was a pipe, covered entirely with ice. It was the supply pipe for the propane and had frozen right up. This had happened to us once before. We just had to wait till the heat from the engine would warm up the area where that pipe was mounted. The strong, cold wind must have prevented the heat from the motor travelling up to that spot where the propane feed pipe was. Relieved to know that it was nothing more serious this time, we waited out the freeze. A propane-driven vehicle seemed to have its own little glitches.

Houston, like any other city, impressed us with the tall, glassy towers of office buildings. The weather was wonderful, and flowers were starting to bloom everywhere.

We arrived in League City in the second half of January and came face-to-face with Whimsy. She sat, on a slightly canted cradle, under some large trees. The deck was covered with a gray film of decayed leaves, and the bottom showed the remains of the many barnacles which had once coated the hull. It did not look too bad, but it was quite clear that much TLC would be required to restore it to a pristine condition. As we went inside, we were assailed by the mixture of stale air and dampness which is peculiar to boats. There is nothing actually wrong with the smell, but it takes a bit of getting used to, particularly for land lubbers like us. The interior of the boat was well laid out, but there was a noticeable shortage of storage space. The V-shaped hull was designed to give the boat speed rather than comfortable living space. It was clear that this was not to be the boat for us. The couple we met this way had been such helpful people that we felt sorry that we could not make use of their boat but did know that we had found some new friends.

With their help we checked the boat brokers in the area and rejected quite a few boats which were offered before we found one which looked promising. It was located in Key West, an island at the southernmost tip of Florida. The boat had been built to the plans for an 11 metre (36 foot) Bruce Roberts design and had an asking price of US $32,000.00. Before the end of January we had signed a purchase agreement with the broker with an offer of US $27,000.00, subject to inspection and a sea trial.

We were able to leave our trailer behind, in order to travel faster, as we crossed the States of Louisiana, Mississippi and Alabama on our way to Key West. It took us two and a half days to complete the journey. On the way, however, we had some trouble with the van. I noticed that the front brakes were making a squeaking noise, indicating that the brake pads should be replaced. I bought new pads and parked in front of a 24-hour shopping mall in the town of Homestead, Florida.

Unfortunately the brake cylinders had seized up, and I could not get them to open. Because the front wheels were off the van, I had to hitch hike back to the automotive store to buy new cylinders and then thumb a ride back to the stranded van and family. Darkness had fallen before the repairs were completed, so supper was late that night.

We had placed a box between the front seats in the van and used that as a table for our propane burner when preparing meals. That evening we had soup, accompanied by bread and tuna. The contents of our meals had changed quite a bit since we had started travelling. The rich pallet of fresh food from the farm had vanished and we had become dependant on the retail stores for our food. All we had left from the produce of our farm was a small quantity of dried fruit and some grain which we would grind into flour. We could no longer walk out into our garden and harvest whatever fruits or vegetables happened to be in season. Fresh apples were what I missed the most.

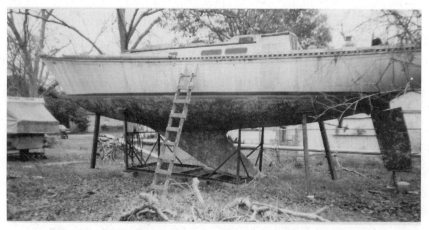

Whimsy in the back yard, to the left the Pop-up trailer

Organic food was available in some places but at prices which we could not afford. To locate farmers who would have sold wholesome food would have taken up too much time. We had given up one of our most valuable resources in maintaining good health, namely clean, healthy food.

As we were preparing the above meal, we had a visit from the local police. Their car pulled up in front of our van, and we were blinded by their spot lights. They used a loudspeaker and called to the driver, me, to step out of the van with my hands raised. One of the officers then slowly approached to check for weapons and asked to see our papers. After carefully inspecting the contents of our van and learning that we were on our way to Key West but too tired to travel further that night, he became more relaxed and wished us good luck. We were not pleased with this high-handed approach to keeping the peace. I had another similar experience while travelling by Greyhound bus to Miami. The police searched all the passengers and baggage and became quite rude when one of the passengers objected to such treatment. We soon began to understand that Florida, and Miami in particular, is one big security jungle. It seemed to me that there were more people employed in the security business than in productive ventures. Fences and protected enclosures seemed to be the norm. I wondered if these barriers were there to keep me out or the residents in. We were later twice checked by the police while on our boat. They were then known as Water Police, but all Water Police, Sheriffs and the Coast Guard were there to provide security for some from others. There will be more about this need-for-security in later chapters. We were not impressed with this side of Florida.

Most of the time we stopped at pumps or shopping malls. One evening things went a bit off schedule. My Dad was busy repairing the brakes and found more wrong than anticipated. We were in the parking lot till dark and decided to stay put. We drove the van to a lot at the side a bit to prepare for the long awaited supper. I was really hungry and there had been no choice of eating till then. We had to do things at the same time to lessen the amount of getting in and out of the car. Dad must have been tired and his hands were full of grease when he finally emerged from underneath our van. I was amazed how well the van actually drove. Hardly ever did we have a problem. I remember travelling across Canada a few years before with it. We got quite used to this routine, and the van had never given us any problems.

I remember, it was a nice fresh evening; a slight breeze kept us enjoying the stay. The interior of the van was just at a cosy temperature, and Mom was setting up the one-plate propane camping stove in front on top of the blue box, to prepare a soup. We were all seated in our spot, ready for the meal. That blue box was about the only flat surface in the van, bridging the gap just level with the two front seats. Daddy was opening a can of tuna, and as usual, we joined in when he started the little poem we got used to saying together on such occasions once the can was open: "Mission completed, the juice is deleted and now we can open the can". Deleting the juice referred to the task, when Daddy dumped the surplus liquid out, holding the lid on the can safely while turning it around. Just as we were having a good time, all of a sudden the front screen got all very bright and as I looked towards the stove, I saw two very bright lights bang into my eyes, blinding me so I was not able to make out anything else. I first was afraid the stove was about to explode when I heard some loud speakers calling the driver to step out of the car, hands-up. I for sure was totally petrified and could not understand what was going on. Still blinded from these lights, I tried to look to the side but could not make out anything. My heart was racing, and I started to shiver. A moment later, my dad opened the door. Now Daddy stepped out of the car putting his hands above his head. He looked like a criminal, would I not have known that he was my Dad. From the back I could just see the silhouette of his body and the hands in the air. There was now a policeman checking his body, but I could not make out exactly what he did. I could hear some demanding voices. Dad lowered his hands and stepped towards the car again, asking mom for the car papers. Now I understood what was happening. It was a police patrol, but how scary. After Dad talked to the policeman, he demanded to see the inside of the van. It must have taken another hour before the scene was over. At least that is how long it felt. Nothing really was wrong. Apparently someone had reported our suspicious activity in the parking lot. Finally we were ready for our well-deserved supper. It had been a scary moment with a satisfying outcome. We did not have to pay for entertainment tonight, and adrenaline was flowing in plenty.

We enjoyed the drive to Key West, a real tourist oriented town. The place had been rebuilt a couple of times, due to storm damage. It had, however, retained its old-style glamour and is well known as the most southerly part of mainland USA. Because the Keys are a chain of islands, there are many bridges linking them together.

The man who was trying to sell the boat was expecting us and had prepared a small cottage for us to stay in. After a quick inspection, we had the boat hauled out so that we could check out the hull before taking it for a trial sail.

Feb. 4th. We might buy a boat called Dawn Treader; it is a very nice boat. We were thinking of giving it a different name. Today we took the boat out of the water and pressure washed it to see if it had any blisters. It didn't have any (that's good).

Several things which we considered basic to the boat were missing, so we felt it necessary to reconsider our offer. We put the boat back in the water and took it for a sail. Unfortunately there was little wind, and this made it difficult to judge the strengths or weaknesses of the boat when under sail. With what new information we had, I decided to reduce our offer to US $25,000.00, but the owner did not seem interested. I asked him to give us a clear decision by the next day.

While awaiting the above decision, we toured the town and enjoyed the interesting sights and functions which included a free public swimming pool. In the evening we watched the street actors down by the wharf. There were fire eaters, men who managed to escape from being chained (just like Houdini), one-wheel bicycle acrobats, theatres, pantomimes, music etc. etc. in a seemingly endless panoply of entertainment. The children enjoyed it immensely.

We had moved out of the cottage and were sleeping in our van down by the wharf, close to the Dawn Treader. The owner had rented it out to some people who were living on it, so we were not able to look through it. That evening, however, I met one of the people who were renting the boat, and he gave me the key so that I could inspect it at my leisure.

The interior was simple, no water storage tank, no sink or table and only a small fuel tank. I knew that the boat had once run aground on a reef and wanted to have another look at the bilge for any signs of damage. I could see nothing wrong with the bilge but did hear a strange noise. It sounded as if a battery was being charged, with gas bubbles bursting as they rose to the surface. I wondered if some metal part of the boat was forming an electrolytic exchange with the salt water but could not pin point the source of the sound. This new knowledge, on top of my original doubts, made me less interested in buying the boat, but our offer was still on the table.

The next day the owner said that he was not prepared to lower his price any further than he already had, so the deal fell through. With a lighter heart on the one side and a concerned look on the other, we parted company.

Much later, during our travels, we found out what had caused the strange sound in the bilge. Small fish were eating the algae off the boat. The hull was acting like a sounding board and amplifying the sound so that it could be clearly heard inside the boat. We experienced this phenomena several times later that year.

One inconvenience of travelling was the public washroom problem. I remember in one town, there was a bizarre automatic washroom type thing. It was really a rather unfortunate incident that took place in there that day. We'd stopped purposely for me to go to the washroom, although I'm sure the others were glad to stretch their legs as well. I went into that washroom, and on my way in, I forgot to lock the door behind me (this being something we rarely did at home). So when I was washing my hands, Mummy opened the door, thinking that I wasn't in there anymore (after all, it wasn't locked), but seeing me, she closed it again. Now, this being one of those high-tech washroom facilities, every time the door had opened twice (once to go in, and once when the person leaves), there was a spray mechanism to wash down the floor, walls, toilet, etc. The problem was that even though the door had opened, I was still inside, and proceeded to be sprayed down along with the floor, walls, toilet,

etc. Needless to say, I was quite upset and very wary of public washrooms from then on.

 At 9 years of age I felt quite happy to just follow the crowd. After all, every day there was something exciting going on. Sleeping in the van, however, was one of the things I did not feel comfortable with. On the shelf in the back of the van rested a plywood sheet as wide as the inside of the van, covering the full length of the van and resting on the seat's backrests below. It ended at the two front seat's back rest. Across the front seats was Marcel's place to sleep. Then underneath the plywood on the back seat was Anisha. I was stowed away, so to speak, lying across the next seat in the back of the van. I had a sleeping bag and my dolls to comfort me, but it was a bit of a confined space to be in. I could only get out once both swing doors of the van were opened. In order to get out, I could squeeze between the water tank resting on a board at the end of my seat and the forward row seat while climbing over another water tank on the floor. The said shelf in the back provided enough room for Pascal, and my parents were lying on the said plywood sheet. They had thin insulation mats, maybe 10mm (0.5 inch) thick, to at least cushion it a bit. Sometimes Pascal crawled forward and cuddled in with mom or dad. There was not much headroom for them, but it seemed to work out fine. It was a great way to just stop and sleep wherever we were. Of course the trailer was a much more comfortable place to sleep but could not always be set up. All my personal stuff was stored right next to me under the forward seat. Shoes, if not worn, were left on the car's floor. Each of us had a box the size of about 3 shoe cartons to store our personal belongings and clothes. As it was, we were happy to reach the warmer weather on the way down south. When stopped I could be mostly outside and play. I had brought some of my toys along. Many stuffed animals and then a lot of books. I love animals and had always enjoyed the cats and the dog, back at the farm. I missed them. It was always nice to be with the dog. I sometimes rested my head on its belly and fell asleep. To fill the void, I found more time to play with Anisha. Sometimes that worked well, but other times we just could not get along too well. It was mostly due to the fact that now everything was so close together. Sometimes I wished to have my own four walls. With so little space, it was

certainly important that each of us kept it all nice and tidy, else we were not finding our stuff anymore.

I still remember stopping along the way, looking at many sailboats. But more so I remember stopping at the Amusement Park and Casino with Campground in Primadonna, where we were going to stay for a day. It was quite a treat for my brothers, sister, and me. I'd never been in such a large amusement park as this one before. We went bowling, played arcade games, watched a circus show, ate out for early breakfast, and were just plain spoiled! After that we went to visit a chocolate factory, clown museum, and we watched a pirate show in Treasure Island. After all the excitement, we needed a bit of a breather, so we viewed the Grand Canyon, a petrified forest, the Painted Desert, and an old meteor crater.

Eventually we went on to the Everglades, Florida, where we saw a lot of alligators and birds. We then went to Key West, Florida, to look at an 11 metre long (36 feet) boat that was over-priced and ugly. The owner was desperate, though, and even let us stay in his spare house in the middle of Key West. While we were being tourists, Dad looked around for a better boat, which he finally found.

A quick stop along the route

A Boat For All Of Us

Once again we were left wondering if we would ever find a boat to suit us or if we should just have to head back to the farm and put our dream on hold. With such thoughts running through our heads, we decided to head northwards to Fort Lauderdale, which was supposed to be the sailboat capital of Florida. In the same direction but further north was Annapolis, the sailboat capital of Maryland.

While we were stopped at a gas station, my interest was piqued by a magazine with "Boats for Sale" blazoned across the cover. It was quite inexpensive, so I figured that we did not have much to lose by buying it. One of the first craft which caught our attention was a ferro-cement boat. Such boats were, I believe, turned out in large numbers during the second World War, as they were easy to build and inexpensive freighters. The price seemed quite reasonable at US $28,000.00. We made several calls to the listed number as we continued to travel towards Miami and were eventually successful

FLORIDA SAILBOAT TRADER February 14   Issue 6

4' Sloop
S, VHS,
aft wheel,
er heater,
key, ac,
sheets,
, $35,000

Due to illness must sell or trade, SAMSON FERRO Cement Ketch Cutte Center Cockpit 36', 42' overall, profes sionally built equip. for cruising, o owner, launch 1982, great boat, call more info., asking $28,000, 305-

Original Ad

and received a friendly, "Hello!" My blunt response was, "Hi, this is Werner, I would like to buy your boat". There was silence on the other end, so I filled in with, "Where can we see it?" After some discussion about the seriousness of our interest and our location, the owner agreed to meet us in an hour or so. He turned out to be a congenial, elderly man with some whitish, gray hair showing from below his sailor cap. After brief introductions, we followed his car to the boat's berth.

There were several fine-looking boats berthed here, and all looked well cared for. It was like a dream come true when we stepped on to the most outstanding one of the group. There it was, a beautiful boat, resting in its slip with the two masts, painted light green, making it more noticeable than the others. The matching hull and white painted cabin top, hatches and vent pipes gave it an inviting look, and the good supply of windows promised a well-lit interior. The central cockpit, and the entrance to the boat, were covered by a dodger, a hood which covered the cockpit to protect it from the rain and wind. Aft of the cockpit, a seat was attached to the stainless steel railing which bordered the deck from stern to mid ship. The cockpit was small but functional. A 1.2 metre (four foot) bowsprit with its stainless steel rail provided safety and also support for the stay to the jib sail. The stay for the stay-sail was located further aft and ran up to the main mast. By the bow there was space for two anchors to be placed in preparation for dropping them and a hand winch conveniently located for retrieving them. The owner had taken great care in maintaining the boat; everything was in its place and working or, perhaps, I should say, ship shape and Bristol fashion.

The interior of the boat was equally well thought-out and cared for. There was a 700 litre (200 gallon) water tank built into the floor. A 320 litre (90 gallon) fuel tank was housed under the benches. The U-shaped hull and the layout provided enough space to move around in but also left ample room for cupboards. There was also an electric fridge and a propane oven suitable for baking bread. Not only was there a double sink in the galley but a small basin had been hooked up to a foot pump in the head. The only thing we could think of adding would be a plywood shelf across the foot of the aft cabin to provide sleeping space for Pascal.

I knew that the hydraulic steering, if properly set up, would be more reliable than any mechanical device. A 30 hp engine was located in the centre of the boat. Because the boat was made, mostly, of cement and iron bars, the latter giving it the name ferro-cement, it weighed close to 18 tons when fully loaded. We thought that the 30 hp motor would be just strong enough to allow us to manoeuvre the boat (for further specifications please see Appendix B).

There were so many extras on that boat that it took us quite some time to appreciate them all. There was even a small dinghy, complete with an outboard motor, as part of the deal. We looked over the boat for several hours, asking the owner all kinds of questions; he must have been exhausted by the end of the day. All this diligence, in the end, paid off. We were delighted with the boat and offered to buy it subject, of course, to a satisfactory sea trial. We paid a deposit of $500.00 as a bond of good faith. It was almost too good to be true. The respect I had already developed for the owner made me feel that this boat had been waiting for us and uneasy about attempting to bargain over the price. The sea trial was a success, and shortly thereafter, I arranged payment in full via the bank.

The boat's bottom had been redone a couple of years previously, and we saw several pictures of the finished work. With this knowledge and the satisfactory sea trial, we did not think it necessary to haul the boat out of the water; there would, at least, be no blisters on the cement hull, something to watch out for on fibreglass boats. We were also happy about the fact that our new house would not be just a fibreglass hull but made of cement. In addition to that, the interior walls, ceilings and floors were all of wood; it felt just like home. We all agreed to keep the name the boat already had.

In a letter dated March 23rd, I wrote to my brothers in Switzerland: "Hi, Fabian and Thomas. We bought a boat! The boat's name is Kristy Nicole. It is pretty fun on the boat, even though sometimes it is kind of boring because I have read all the books we have, twice already.

Carina and me share the V-berth, Marcel sleeps on the bench by the table, Mommy and Daddy sleep in the back room, it is called the aft cabin. Daddy built a little bed for Pascal to sleep in. It is pretty cute when Pascal is sleeping in it. The first few days he fell out of it onto Mommy's and Daddy's feet. But now Daddy put a net so Pascal doesn't fall out of bed at night.

We are anchored close to a marina, and Marcel has fun driving the dinghy to shore and back using the motor. There is a pool on shore, and we go swimming there very often. We went to a sports store called the Sports Authority and bought flippers (fins) for Carina and Marcel. We did not buy fins for me because there were already some fins and a snorkel on the boat. We also bought snorkels for Marcel and Carina, and diving masks for all of us.

Marcel and me bought our own cross-stitch patterns and have been doing a lot of it lately. Marcel does it more than me but his is also harder. Carina got some toy horses for her birthday, and she lets me play with them quite a lot. It seems there are more Dollar Stores here than anything else. I bought a wind-up tractor and trailer at the Dollar Store for Pascal's birthday.

The boat is a cutter-rigged ketch which means it has 2 masts and an extra sail in the front. The back sail is called the mizzen, the middle sail is called the main, the small front sail is called the stay sail and the sail in the very front is called the genoa (or jenny)."

As the month of March drew to a close, it became necessary for us to move the boat or renew the slip lease for another month. The former owner helped us with the move, and we motored for several hours through waterways till we reached the North Bay Landings Marina located at 79th Street. In the course of that trip we had passed several swing bridges which had to be opened to let us through. We stayed at anchor in North Bay for about a month and used that time to take care of all the necessary paper work. We had to have a temporary registration under the Canadian flag and a cruising permit. This, of course, created further expenses and, all in all, our bank account took quite a beating. At the same time we stopped receiving the monthly payments from the person who was buying our computer business in Salmon Arm. I contacted her by phone and was assured that we would soon receive those missing funds.

In preparation for our bid to cross the Atlantic, we felt that there were several improvements we should make to Kristy Nicole. First we bought a $2,500.00, eight-person life raft and mounted it on the deck.

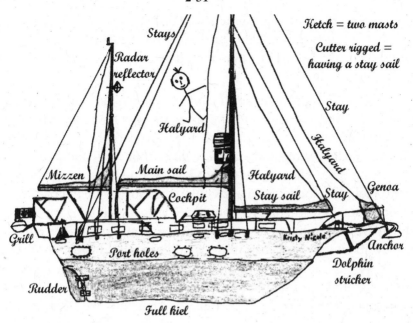

Some of Kristy Nicole's parts

As with all forms of insurance, we hoped that we would never have need of it. A bilge pump was installed in the chain locker, under the V-berth and a hand-operated water maker, which changes salt water to drinkable water by the process of osmosis and an EPIRB (Electronic Position Indicator Radio Beacon) completed our emergency equipment needs. The EPIRB would send an SOS signal to air traffic, should the need arise.

I installed several plywood partitions in order to make better use of the storage space available. The size of the saloon table was increased so that we would all be able to sit at it together. All of the plywood used was recycled from the box I had built for the roof of our van. The contents of that box were now all aboard Kristy Nicole, so we no longer had a need for it. We soon learned how to move around the boat without getting any boat bites; a descriptive phrase learned from a long-time sailor. We experienced our first 35 knots of wind while still at anchor and the boat handled it well. We also learned to measure wind or boat speed in knots, a measurement used in the boat world. A knot refers to about 1.9km/h speed and for ease of reading the following chapters will refer to knots whenever wind or boat speed is expressed. The 16kg (35lb) anchor seemed to be quite adequate. Hardly any noise could be heard below deck; it was a cozy place to be.

One day, after a great supper, I came up on deck to find the dinghy gone. Someone had stolen it. I swam ashore and asked a person with a motor boat to help me search the surrounding waters for the missing boat. Darkness had already fallen, but we found it, tied to a rail about three kilometres (two miles) away. Unfortunately all the gear, including the motor, oars, cooler and tools, were gone. It was a good lesson to learn, that we should not leave anything in the dinghy when we were not using it. At least we would no longer have to worry about the motor being stolen, and we would be forced to use the more environmentally-friendly oars in the future. Rowing was a good way to keep fit, although we later bought an electric motor to help where the current was strong. In Annapolis we modified the dinghy so that it could be used under sail (more about that later).

At the end of March, we sailed back to Texas, in order to sell the trailer and to gain the necessary off shore sailing experience before attempting to cross the Atlantic. The hurricane season could be expected to start in July. It would be a tight schedule, but we thought it would be possible.

 *On the 9th of February, we stopped at a gas pump to fill up with propane. Stations which sold propane were not easy to find. It was there that Werner noticed a rather low-priced ferro-cement boat listed in a boat magazine. That was when the ball got rolling to acquire our sailboat. I was not so sure if it was not just one more of these lousy things we had so far seen in the lower price range. Werner was, however, determined to give it one more try. In this case, things turned out much better than I had expected.*

In less than a week, my parents would arrive in Orlando. They had booked a flight from Switzerland to explore Florida and to meet up with us. I spent many hours with them, and, of course, they were keen to see the boat, but firstly, we did some sight-seeing tours in Fort Myers and the Everglades. I left Werner, Marcel and Anisha with the boat while the rest of us went on the tours. There were many things

that Werner wanted to change in the boat and this arrangement left him free to do them. I measured the inside walls of the boat in order to make some hanging pouches to store things in.

My parents stayed in a motel and we met up every day while the boat's papers were being arranged, a life raft bought and secured, and dinghy blocks installed. It kept Werner busy, and I took care of the children. It was quite nice to use the pool at the hotel. We had to pay a small fee to anchor and use their facility. It was a great arrangement. My parents stayed for almost four weeks, and I was very happy to have seen them again.

On March 15th we celebrated Carina's birthday. We wrapped the few gifts we had in paper towels, for lack of wrapping paper. She got a large pony from Marcel and Anisha. It matched the three smaller ones she already had. I bought her a watch from the dollar store. It even had the date and worked just fine. Most of her gifts were given ahead of time, particularly the ones from her grandparents.

I was kept busy stitching lee-cloths, to keep the kids in their berths. Not an easy job. The first trial for Marcel's berth in the saloon came apart at the seams on the first test. During the same time, Werner replaced the automatic bilge pump, which was causing intermittent problems. Once installed, he asked Marcel to look overboard and see if water was indeed coming out over the side, and where. It didn't take Marcel long to find out. The pump worked well and gushed its filthy bilge water, right into the dinghy which was sitting alongside.

The paperwork for the boat seemed to take forever, but we did manage to have everything ready in time for the first trip. I made a bread dough. For lack of a scale, I just put things together as I knew from experience. We were tied up to the dock for a day, in order to stock up, and then it was time to go on anchor again. I handled the dock lines while the rest of the crew handled the boat side of the operation. I then jumped into the dinghy and motored out, after the boat. Half way out, the motor sputtered and I came to a halt. I tried to pull-start it, but nothing moved. I noticed a plastic bag stuck around the screw. Once I had loosened it, I was able to do the rest of the trip and rejoin the crew. On the boat I noticed the bread dough hanging over the bowl. It was high time to get it into the oven! It sure smelled and tasted good when we took it out.

Our new boat was in good shape, and the price was pretty low, for one in such good condition. The owner had to sell because he couldn't go sailing anymore because of an operation he'd had in his stomach which would irritate him badly when he went out on the water. Nevertheless, he came with us on a little boat test, and for him, farewell trip which he and my dad really enjoyed. That's when we decided to buy. Since we could not bring our van to his place because of the lack of space and the fact that it was a closed-up subdivision, we stayed at a campground about 6 kilometres (3-4 miles) from Bruce's living area. That's when my Mami's parents decided to come down for a visit, and they treated us to the wonders of two museums: a Kids Museum, and the Edison & Ford Museum. Then my parents and grandparents decided that while Dad, Marcel, and Anisha got things moved onto the boat, Mami, my grandparents, Pascal, and I would get out of the way on a little trip to the Everglades, Florida, where I saw an intriguing selection of alligators and birds. After seeing a lot of interesting things and staying in a few motels, we went straight on to Miami where my dad and older siblings waited with the boat. We stayed anchored there for a month. We dropped my grandparents off at the airport and took life easy for some time, swimming in the marina's public pool that was also part of a hotel. The pool was four stories up and quite nice.

The weather was so nice that I slept on the deck of the boat. It was awesome to sleep out under the stars surrounded by water which, though not exactly clean, was fun to swim in during the day, so we would throw on life jackets and swim a bit. But the water did not seem so attractive to us after our first mouthfuls of the bitter salty water. We spent my birthday, Pascal's birthday, and my dad's birthday in Miami that year, all birthdays in March. That's around when we heard from Switzerland. My second oldest brother, Fabian, had broken his ankle trying a stunt known as the "Gysi Flip", on his roller blades. He'd sent me pictures before the accident which I treasured for a long time after, and his accident scared me quite a bit. Soon after that, on the 28th of March, we finally left Miami to take a trip over the Gulf of Mexico towards Houston, Texas. And with us we had the skipper of Whimsy, the person we had visited to see his

*boat some time before. He was now trying to teach my dad how to
sail. And that's when all the sailing actually started.*

Pascal's impression

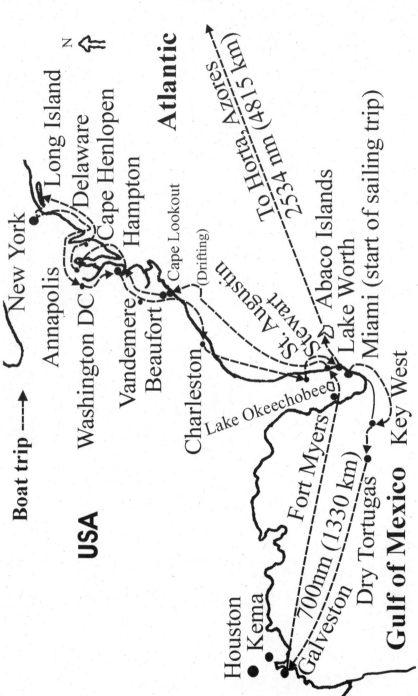

Boat trip ⟶

N

New York

USA

Annapolis

Long Island

Washington DC

Delaware

Cape Henlepen

Vandemere

Hampton

Beaufort

Cape Lookout

Charleston

(Drifting)

St. Augustin

Stewart

Atlantic

To Horta, Azores
2534 nm (4815 km)

Abaco Islands

Lake Worth

Miami (start of sailing trip)

Lake Okeechobee

Fort Myers

Key West

700nm (1330 km)

Galveston

Dry Tortugas

Houston

Kema

Gulf of Mexico

The First Trip

We realised that we had no experience in handling a boat the size of Kristy Nicole in the open water and asked our newly-made sailor friend in League City to be our skipper and sail with us. He had previously offered such assistance, and we undertook to pay for his flight out and to treat him royally. The trip to Galveston (near League City) was expected to take about twelve days. I hoped that this shake-down cruise would help me convert the book knowledge I had accumulated over the past few years into practical experience.

When talking to our skipper on the phone, I had difficulty, due to my limited knowledge, in giving an accurate description of our boat. When he arrived he was not even sure that the boat would be safe to sail in. I was relieved when, after a careful inspection, a large smile creased his face, and he said, "This boat really fits you". A more detailed investigation merited a comment to the effect that we had bought a "handsome boat", the skipper's ultimate level of praise. The fact that we had a snow shovel and gardening tools on board did give him cause for concern, but he agreed to cast off the next day regardless. Our first stop was a free pier in down-town Miami in order to pick up the appropriate charts. The course we had plotted would take us to Key West, the Dry Tortugas and then across the Gulf of Mexico to Galveston. We left our van parked at the marina, although we had no idea of when we would be able to return to pick it up.

The excitement was rising. Nobody really knew exactly what to expect, but everyone was preparing for the unknown. We made a few more trips back and forth with the dinghy for showers and shopping. Then the skipper arrived. He wanted to make sure that there was ample food on board before we pulled the anchor, so he asked me if I had enough food on board for the next two or even three weeks. I said I did and then he asked me what I had. I had got canned vegetables, beans, tuna, rice, pasta, and flour to make bread, fresh salad for the first few days and cabbage and carrots for later. We also had some cereals and I had found milk that would keep for a month called Parmalat. There were still a lot of grapefruits in the

net. The Skipper wanted a few more things that I had not thought of. He had sailed before and knew exactly what he wanted. So off we went to get more things like canned beef (spam), oatmeal for porridge and other things which I no longer remember. We also got some things to snack on between meals. The skipper told us that, when one is seasick, it is good to have salty snacks to nibble on (and we really needed that; it was a very good thing that he thought about it). We did not use all the food we had with us. We ate a lot less than what we would have eaten normally, mainly because of the seasickness.

With spirits high and our eyes constantly on the depth sounder, we followed the channel which would take us through downtown Miami and, eventually, to the open sea. We had to pass several bridges and just managed to squeeze under some; others were too low and had to be opened for us. Bruce had shown me how to signal for a bridge to be opened. It was fun to see those heavy bridges open just for us, a small sailboat and crew headed out to who-knows-what kind of adventures.

The charts and GPS (Global Positioning System) were used to plot our course, and our skipper noticed that the speed log did not seem to record the actual distance travelled. He was not keen on the idea of having to rely entirely on the GPS to tell us where we were. With the boat at anchor I dove down to ensure that the impeller, which drove the speed log, was free. In the murky waters of Miami harbour this was no easy task, but after several dives, all seemed to be in order. We then tested it against the "one nautical mile" markers which are set up along the main channel. The readings still did not agree with the GPS information, but the difference was, at least, constant. Much later I found out that the GPS readings were in land miles which are shorter than the nautical miles used by the speed log. With readings from the GPS, the depth sounder and sighting of shore lights, which were described in our navigation books, we were able to keep track of where we were. I practised taking compass readings of two distant lights or objects to determine our position and compared that with our speed and the course we had been following. The GPS readings were used as a further confirmation.

This was the first time that we had travelled at night, and our skipper explained to us the kind and meaning of all the different lights. Close attention was also paid to the charts to warn us of what might lie ahead of us in the water. There were more than a few things to learn. The greatest dangers were the barges being towed by a tugboat which could be as much as a kilometre (0.6 miles) ahead of it. The cable stretched between them could remain invisible until we were right on top of it.

The shipping lanes were quite busy, and we learned the different signals to be given as we passed other vessels. In spite of all the challenges, we safely reached Key West.

The art of docking was a fresh challenge which had to be dealt with. At first we approached this unknown with uncertainty and much concentration. After a few successful berthings we became more relaxed and realized that it was not the monster it had seemed to be. One peculiarity which had to be dealt with was that Kristy Nicole, because of her full keel, would not back up in a straight line. The rotation of the screw would make her turn to the left. Slowly we managed to master the various skills required to persuade the boat to go where we wanted it to go.

We decided to top up our fuel tank to ensure that we would be able to use the motor if the winds failed us. We were told that the engine would use 1.8 litres (half a gallon) per hour to push the boat through calm water at a speed of 4 knots or about 7.6km/h. This would give us a range of about 720 nautical miles (1370km). On our first trip the winds were more than cooperative.

Our next stop was the Dry Tortugas. The old fort had been used by the U. S. Government as a prison. The buildings, though still intact, had been abandoned. The island was a fine spot at which to take a short break. While at anchor we noticed that, for the first time, the water was as clear as glass. The seabed, about 3 metres (10 feet) down, was clearly visible. We dove off the boat and swam around until we noticed a barracuda resting beneath our keel. Our skipper assured us that there was no need to worry; even though it was a good sized fish, of about 2 to 3 metres (10 feet) in length, it seemed to have no interest in us. Perhaps it was just enjoying the shade cast by our boat.

At anchor in crystal waters during our stay in the Dry Tortugas

Towards evening the weather changed and a strong wind blew in from the open water. The skipper and I agreed that the crowded anchorage was no place to be in such a blow. We hoisted our anchor and headed off into a strengthening wind and mounting waves. A boat which had started to follow us was soon out of sight, and we wondered if it had run aground or turned back. We had no time to dwell on their fate as our minds and hands were soon focussed on our own well-being. It was not long till everyone, except the skipper, was suffering from *mal de mere*. This was the first time in our lives that we had experienced seasickness; it was no fun. Four year old Pascal suffered the most. Such a small body could easily become dehydrated, so we took great pains to make him drink whatever he could. He could not understand why he was so sick. In desperation he said, "I don't like myself anymore". We did, however, manage to survive. It took me 3 days to adjust and the remainder of the 7-day trip across the Gulf of Mexico was both bearable and eventful.

One such event was that the toilet became plugged; in desperation we cut a hole in the seat which was attached to the outboard side of the rail at the stern. It was strategically placed to avoid fouling the side of the boat and proved to be very useful during the rest of our trip. I have it, on good authority, that this was a common practice in the past.

Our first encounter with rough weather had shown that our steering equipment did not function properly. The skipper felt that we should carry as much sail as possible, so the autopilot had more than its share of correcting to do as the boat zigzagged through the water. I did not feel comfortable with the manner in which the boat moved. When I checked the mountings at the back of the boat, my worst fears were confirmed. One of the bolts which held the RAM, a cylinder which controls the movement of the rudder, had been sheared off, and the other bolt was working itself loose. With so much loose play, it was no wonder that the autopilot was having problems. We had no spare bolt of sufficient length to replace the severed one, so I had to cut threads into a stainless steel rod, cut to the proper size, and use nuts to secure it. The fact that I was still suffering from seasickness did not make matters easy. I frequently had to stop work from sheer exhaustion as my body tried to vomit, even when my stomach was empty. Eventually I got the bolt mounted, and the autopilot was able to steer better. I made a mental note that another brace should be mounted opposite the rudder post to improve the effectiveness of the RAM. I was sure glad that I had purchased several lengths of different-diameter stainless steel rods as spare parts or this repair could not have been done. The next thing would have been to install the emergency tiller, a much more inconvenient solution.

On the first clear night to follow the storm, we received an unexpected bonus. We were fortunate enough to witness an exciting sight which occurs only once in every 4200 years. It was the comet Hale-Bob which is visible for just a few days as it passes planet Earth. It appeared to our right and seemed to be heading towards our destination. It was easy to imagine that it had been sent just for us as a reminder that we should not forget our dreams and continue to explore the beautiful world around us. When I found out that the comet was about 150 million kilometres (94 million miles) away from us, it underlined the fact that time and distance are unimportant factors. We saw Hale-Bob a few more times before a fresh onslaught of bad weather obscured our view.

This time the weather system came at us from the North-West. It blew over the starboard side and the wind was stronger. The skipper was not impressed and could not, or would not, calculate the strength of the wind. A few land birds landed on our boat in search of refuge from the boisterous wind. They must have been taken by surprise and blown off the shore which we calculated to be over 320 kilometres (200 miles) from our boat. The children were delighted to have some pets which were, at first, very tame. In a few days the birds recovered their strength and left us.

 *I wrote in my diary, Saturday, April 5th (fifth day out on the Gulf of Mexico). Fortunately the wind has dropped. The night sailing was very fast, and we felt uneasy. Seasickness has made Pascal throw up again, and I do not feel very well either. The waves are about 3m (10 feet) high, and the boat continues to swoop up and down. Around noon 4 birds joined us. I am the Cook. Werni is the Captain-to-be and also the one who has to repair the many things which need to be repaired, whether he likes it or not. The skipper and Werni took a shower in the heavy rain, and I used the water which ran off the mainsail to wash my hair.*

For the night of the 6th to the 7th of April, I described the journey as follows: We again had strong winds. The boat was heeling more than usual, and I could not get to sleep. Werni slept on the floor, in the head, where rolling was limited by space. It was a very fast journey but made me feel unhappy. At 6 o'clock a.m. I should have started my watch but did not want to. The waves were coming over the boat and everything was flying around below decks like never before. At 7 o'clock I woke Werni and asked him to take my watch. I resolved never to go on the boat again and went below to sleep.

We still had the Genoa up, believing that it would give us the best speed possible. Eventually the winds eased up a bit and the seas calmed down somewhat. A few lights appeared ahead of us and soon became a host of beacons. This was puzzling till the skipper explained that, for the next couple of days, we would be sailing through a field of oil rigs. We were careful to steer well clear of these rigs, as several would have various obstacles in their vicinity. The lights could be confusing as some of the brighter ones were actually further away than some of the dimmer ones. It was also interesting to note how the pattern of lights changed as we progressed through the field. At least we now knew where the birds had flown to; I wondered how they knew that the rigs were so close. According to the weather forecasts, another storm was about to hit us with even stronger winds, this time from the North.

This was the first time in my life, that I was travelling on open water. The first part of the trip was exciting, since seasickness hadn't yet made its presence felt. We sailed during the night and saw all the lights along the shore sparkling like a long string of shiny beads. For the first time in my life I could see all the stars in the sky. I watched them and dreamed of home, of my soft, dry, warm bed. It felt like a long time since we had left the farm. My thoughts still wandered home at times, even during the excitement of a new boat suspended in water. On the boat there was just not as much room to do things. I was certainly very happy to have my beanie babies with me; they were the newest fad with us kids on the boat, and we collected them with just a touch of competition. Together with Anisha, we told each other stories about the lives of these creatures and played with them as if they were living. We were getting good at using our vivid imaginations and making up stories.

When the new day broke we arrived in Key West. I recognized the shore line again, where the jugglers had been showing off their amazing skills, some even juggling bowling balls. I looked forward to the Dry Tortugas, which has now become a National Park and is made up of several islands, about 110 kilometres (70 miles) from Key West. I hoped to see some marine life and was specially interested in the dolphins. The islands were in Spanish hands around 1513, and as Florida was handed over to the US, a fort was built for protection of the waterways. It later served as a military prison. Many of the inmates were once wiped out by yellow fever. Our stay was rather short. We arrived early in the morning with the sun rising into a blue sky and left in the evening with a thunderstorm in the making. We toured most of the fort, and played tag around the hallways. We even took a swim, but I did not see much marine life apart from some sea cucumbers which I found rather disreputable. At least I was able to use the flippers and mask I had got for my birthday. It was fun to swim in the crystal clear water, even though it was salty, and every now and then I would manage to gag on a mouthful.

The trip across the Gulf of Mexico was pretty rough. I very well remember the skipper and Mami were the only ones not to get sea sick, and I was very glad when we reached Galveston, near Houston, Texas, alive! I did not make any entries into my diary about the journey; in fact, my entries once we started sailing became very few as I was busy being sick or sleeping. The only trip I can remember that was worse was much later on the Atlantic; and by then we were used to a rowdy sea.

April 10th. We have just finished our first 7-day crossing of the Gulf of Mexico from Dry Tortugas to Houston. I did not like it too much, first of all because it was so much up and down, up and down that we all got seasick and had to throw up. Secondly we had to strap everything down so that it would not fall over-board. Once there was such a big wave that everything went flying.

We arrived in Kema, near League City, in the evening of April 7th. What an event it was when we reached the marina there; it was close to our skipper's home in a suburb of Houston. I felt happy and tired at the same time. We were unable to walk properly on land but had a great feeling of achievement. We had spent 7 consecutive days on the water and come out of it impressed but fine. A passing sailor was surprised to see us arrive in such bad weather and mentioned that the winds were that day in the 45 knot range. We had not thought it was that bad and were glad to have survived such an experience.

Once we had the boat properly secured to the pier, we had a very good night's rest; the sun was high in the sky before we awoke. We placed our boat in a slip, paid for a one-month stay, and then proceeded to enjoy the amenities of the marina. The improvements we hoped to make to the boat, and the time spent with the skipper and his wife, would make short work of the allotted month.

The strengthening of the rudder post was the most important work to be done. I had stainless steel braces made and mounted them in such a way as to keep the post from flexing. This reduced the play on the steering. Working on the boat was much more easy to do in the slip than it had been on the tossing water (not to mention the lack of seasickness).

The skipper thought that the rudder might not be big enough to steer the boat and suggested that I should design a larger one. A phone conversation with the former owner, on the other hand, told me that changing sail would achieve the same result. He gave me clear instructions as to which sails should be changed and at which wind speeds to make the changes. We decided to leave the rudder as it was and looked forward to testing the sail changes. The strengthening of the steering system was, undoubtedly, a worthwhile improvement.

One day we were invited to sail in a boat race and, of course, asked our friend and skipper to join us. As total greenhorns we had a horrible time just getting out of the marina. It was very difficult to make left hand turns with Kristy Nicole, but we soon learned that we could make tight-radius right hand turns.

During our "Training on the job" experimentation, we barely managed to avoid several collisions, so our skipper once more took control of the wheel and got us out of the mess and into the bay where the race was to take place.

 *April 12th. Today we went on a sail boat race called a regatta and we came in 23rd place out of 27 racers. We decided that we would not go on the race tomorrow mainly because we had so much trouble getting out of our slip today.*

April 14th. Today Carina and me found a fort. The fort is in grass that is taller than me. It is a pretty big fort. There are rooms in it, and the room I claimed is very small but has a secret room in it. The rooms are just little bushels of grass growing around a little open patch on the ground and a little grass pushed aside for a doorway.

I have a friend already. Her name is Sara. She lives on a boat on Pier 12, at the very end on the right hand side. Marcel has 2 friends too. They made a fort in a bamboo bush. It is a cool fort. I say it is better than Carina's and mine, but Carina thinks ours is better. The two boys Marcel made friends with are twins.

We all knew that the weather would turn very hot soon and started to make plans to repaint the bottom of our boat. We made contact with a marina in Galveston, which turned out to be the same one where the former owner stayed, to build the cabin top for Kristy Nicole.

The sails were inspected and repaired as needed. Weak spots where reinforced with black patches. At first the black patches on the tanbark-coloured sails looked a little funny, but we soon got used to them. A large black patch was sewn on to both sides of the mainsail where it would touch the backstay of the mast when we were on a down wind tack. This would prevent any chafing to the sail proper.

A small window was installed in the cockpit cover so that we could see the wind indicator which had been mounted on top of the mast. Marcel had enjoyed being hauled up in the bosun's chair, attached to the main halyard, in order to drill holes in the mast, and Anisha enjoyed the ride up the mast in order to install the device. We were thus able to have a much better understanding of the varying wind directions. An extra red/green navigation light was installed at the bowsprit because the ones on the sides had been partly covered by the dinghy we had stored on the deck. It was then time to test our alterations with a day long cruise.

By trial and error we became familiar with manoeuvring the boat in tight quarters and allowing for the torque of the propeller when backing up. On our return to the marina, we developed a plan to return to our slip like seasoned salts. Marcel was to jump off the bow of the boat and secure the fore and aft lines to the bollards as we entered the slip, while I controlled the engine and steered. Marcel did a perfect job, but I, unfortunately, put the engine in forward gear instead of reverse. The boat surged forward with such vigour that it was way too late to put it in reverse. The wooden boards placed along the concrete pier split with a loud crack as the boat tried to climb over the concrete wall. The dolphin striker, (which is normally a straight, vertical pipe), became a convoluted U-shaped contraption and the attached chain and mount were ripped from the hull. By then I had the engine under control and moved the boat back into the water. For a moment chaos reigned before we could determine if water would pour in through the hole in the bow and sink us. Fortunately the hole was above the water line and quite small, so there was no immediate danger.

As Captain of the boat it was, of course, my duty to report the incident to the Marina Manager. They handled it with good humour, and felt that we had received punishment enough with the humiliation of being watched by all the people who had come to investigate the unusual noise. We never did receive a bill for the repairs to the pier but had a couple of new items to add to our own repair list.

I must say, the best thing to happen to me during this trip was, that there was little room to do home schooling. Done quite intensively at home, since our trip with the car, the books were hard to get at. Of course it wasn't just that, activities otherwise were plenty and I did not see any problem with getting by without the kind of schooling my parents thought of or even worse, the public school was providing, remembering stuff my older brothers told me about. They were only briefly in public school, and I preferred the home schooling as it was. I never liked to study from books, but to learn things by doing them. Travelling had, so far, provided that for me. There were so many new things to learn for me and, thank God, the books stayed nicely tucked away in a cupboard somewhere on the boat.

I asked Daddy if we could find some fishing gear. Together we bought some line and the required hooks, floaters and such for this area. We didn't bother with a rod. For lack of worms or those bugs called hellgrammites, which we found under rocks along river beds when fishing in BC, I used bread. Most of it, however, fell off rather fast and I had no luck. Cheese worked way better. After some trial and error I caught the first fish while we were at anchor. It wasn't a big fish but a big event. We thought it was a catfish, but were not so sure at all. When Daddy was about to kill it, he got hurt by it between his thumb and the pointing finger. It must have hurt him a lot. The whole day he had his hand in a sling, the hurt area patched up with a Band Aid. We all enjoyed the taste of fish, and from then on I was not just first mate, but also the fisherman. I got myself a booklet about the different fish and what hooks to use. Other than that, I just tried out what I thought was best. I used the winch from the mizzen mast to secure the line. It also acted as a clutch, to release some line if the pull was strong enough. It was my responsibility to watch that the line did not run out in such cases. Soon I was skilled enough to catch more fish. It was mostly Mom who cleaned the fish, while I was watching. We sometimes prepared them on the grill mounted in the back of the rail. That is how I liked it the most.

My quarters in the saloon were not very private. I stuck my pillow and sleeping bag into the cupboard just behind my berth, located under the VHF and tape deck unit. The VHF-radio got a lot of attention from me. I was told how to use it and what to do when someone called. As it was just next to my berth I had ample opportunity to answer calls and to turn the dials and to listen into other sailor's conversations. We also had a hand-held unit, which we could use from shore, to call the boat. This was all quite exciting for me, and I became a well-trained radio operator. I stopped listening to other's messages, if they were none of my business.

The next attractive thing for me was the dinghy, and in particular the motor on it. It was so much fun to drive that thing and to pick up stuff ashore. It was just the right toy for me. I learned how to start it, check for problems and clean the spark plug, if it did not start. The great fun was to zoom through the waves and splash the water to the side. Of course sometimes water came overboard, as waves mounted. Dad and I built a dodger on the peak, by cutting up some tarp. It never really did help and was mostly in the way. We soon removed it again. I remember it to be a very sad moment when I one day heard that the dinghy was gone. We found the dinghy again but the motor was gone. It was now muscle power we had to show. It worked, but was half the fun. Daddy promised that one day we would make a sailing dinghy out of it. I could live with that thought and concentrated on other things.

Once the skipper arrived, Anisha, Carina and I were told how to change the jib and what to do when tacking. Wow, it was exciting to work with that stuff. The girls did not show that much interest, particularly Carina who had other thoughts. She was mostly dreaming of animals, specially horses and was always kind of in the way. With Anisha it worked quite well, and we became a trained crew. The skipper seemed to know his stuff, and he was very strict about how things would have to be done. For a tack we had to wait for the skipper to shout "ready about?" and respond with "ready" once we were in position. Then the skipper shouted "helm's alee". In real life the stuff we had just learned became quite a challenge. Out on the gulf of Mexico, when we had to climb the foredeck in poor weather, we did not like it as much anymore. Then, wearing life jackets, we were tied down to lifelines run on either side of the deck. That did not make it any easier. But we did change the Jib or set the stay-sail at times, especially later on, all on our own. It was on us to get out in case sudden winds started to pop up. Daddy was happy to see everyone of us pitch in. This way we each had things to do and the trip, for me, became quite challenging and fun.

One less memorable occasion was when we rammed the pier. I was told to jump off the boat as we gently glided along the pier and to tie the back line to the cleat. I was eager to jump and all went well. I had the line along with me and tied it to the back cleat, giving it plenty line. Then Mom threw the front line to me. I noticed the boat still moving rather fast. When I was about to secure the front line to the cleat, I heard a weird cracking noise coming from the front of the boat. I looked up and saw with dismay how the front of our boat had run through the wooden dock and then climbed the concrete wall behind. I was shocked and started to cry. What was going wrong now I thought. Was it all my fault? What had happened? Of course there was a beehive of activity around the boat, and onlookers were gathering. It was one of the most embarrassing moments I can remember. Only after some time I could grasp the facts, when Daddy repeatedly told me, about his error using the wrong gear. That was a great relief to me but I was sad to see the boat I had come to enjoy so much, being crumbled up like that. Amazingly enough, my parents later on fixed it up just like new.

Don't Chase The Wind

1. The time will come
This world will be gone
And you will be alone
Why don't you come
Ref: But don't try to chase the wind   (3 times)
2. They say
That some people will stay
And some will find
Their way (ref:)
3. So close your eyes
At death's surprise
For spirits made out of crystals
Will never die
4. So close your eyes
At death's surprise
For spirits made out of diamonds
Will always survive
5. So close your eyes
At death's surprise
For spirits made out of jewels
Have eternal life (ref:)
(Voice and Guitar by Werner M. Gysi)

A CD with colour pictures and songs can be ordered.

Dry Docking The Boat, The 4th Dimension

Our bank account had shrunk from little to nothing. The promised monthly payments from the Salmon Arm computer business, which we had sold, had not been forthcoming. We did receive the rent payments from our house, but that had already been factored into our budget. We had nothing to replace the monthly payments we had been promised by the new computer business owner. That money had been budgeted as insurance against unexpected health or boat costs. We had incurred the extra boat costs but the "insurance" had vanished. I toyed with the idea of flying to Salmon Arm to find out what the problem was, but we did not have enough money for such a flight and there were no guarantees that it would restart the flow of cash. Some money had been sent to Switzerland to finance the holiday we had hoped to have when we got there but we were now forced to transfer it into our depleted account. We rationalized that we were on holiday, even if it was not in Switzerland.

On May 21st we sold our cherished tent trailer. It had served us well for several years and been the birth place for Pascal. We could not make up our minds if it should be called the " holey", "holy", or "wholey" trailer. The well-worn canvas certainly had many holes in it. As the birth place for our youngest son, it had a certain consecrated aura for us. It had served us so well in so many ways that it was looked upon as a whole or complete entity in itself. The emphasis had been on the word holy.

A reasonably-priced dry dock was located about a day's journey away from the marina. We chose a fine day to make the trip and motored most of the way there. The channel into the dry dock area was not very deep, and we barely made it over a couple of sandbars. We had to wait for about an hour before the travel lift pulled Kristy Nicole out of the water and placed her on the six supports in the dry dock. That was the first time that we had seen the bottom of our home. Climbing a ladder to get into the boat was another new experience. When bedded down at night we could feel the boat flex and vibrate in the wind. It was an odd feeling to know that the stability of our 18 ton (gross) boat was dependent on half a dozen metal stands. On our trip across the Gulf of Mexico we had found out how delicate our balance in life could become and now had to rely on six crutches as much as in our faith, a fine balance indeed.

Bright and early the next morning we got down to the task of servicing the boat. We first used a pressure washer to clean the hull and then everybody got busy scraping, scrubbing, sanding, rubbing and scooping off the many barnacles which had settled on the body of Kristy Nicole. I used a chisel to remove the damaged material around where the

Damage to the boat at the waterline

chain for the dolphin striker had been mounted.

There were a few spots on the rudder which needed to be fibre glassed and the sides, above the waterline, had a few hairline cracks which I repaired with a special filler. We were more than glad to be able to use the showers after a hard day's work - work that covered us with dust from head to toe. The sculpting tools and skills I had received from a friend of mine back at the farm came in very handy for repairing the damage to the bow. Sculpting on a sailboat was certainly a new experience, highlighted by the knowledge that this was our house, our home, our transportation, and the bulwark which would protect us from the sometimes merciless weather.

Tired, but with a good feeling of accomplishment, we spent the nights sleeping in the landlocked boat. It took a small adjustment to live on land once more; we had become accustomed to the ritual of getting ashore before we could go anywhere. This interval in the dry dock also gave us time to reflect on our trip across the Gulf of Mexico. The days of plain sailing, the comet, the visiting birds, the excitement of navigating, and the many ups and downs, both in the water and ourselves. None of us had enjoyed the rough parts of the trip, and we were glad to realize that being anchored in cosy coves would be more common than enduring stormy crossings.

Seasickness was one demon which would have to be dealt with. The homeopathic remedies we had taken with us had not helped. We did find some new homeopathic drops which promised to be of help but, just to be on the safe side, we also purchased some chemically based drugs. If necessary we would test the potency of these medications on our return trip to Florida.

I spent most of my time repairing the bow of the boat so the privilege of scraping, cleaning the bottom of the boat and painting it landed on the shoulders of Brigitte and the two older children, Marcel and Anisha. They did a great job; there was not a blemish on the paint and the boat looked as if it were new. It was, indeed, a wonderful boat.

Bottom, after painting

All the repairs and planned additions had been completed, and we had managed to unplug the toilet (the cause of which will never be revealed), added navigation lights on the bowsprit, a wind vane, a rudder indicator, (which showed how much the rudder was set against the sails), and several other details. It was a well-equipped and fine-looking boat. We had considered adding a couple of 23kg (50lb) anchors to our selection of one16kg (35lb), one 10kg (20lb), and one 7kg (15lb) Danford anchors. Because of our shrunken budget and the fact that such heavy anchors would not be required either on the open ocean or in a sheltered marina, we decided to defer this purchase.

With the work in the dry dock completed, we returned to the marina and offered to help our friends in League City do some work on their house. By then we knew that it would be imprudent to attempt a crossing of the Atlantic before July because of the threat of hurricanes. Instead we decided to eventually sail northward towards New York. After a week or so of sawing, hammering, and painting our friends' home, it was time for us to leave. On May 29th they paid for our stay at the marina, gave us a friendly send-off, and we were on our way back to Florida.

Sailing is much as I would imagine war to be: short periods of intense activity and long periods of relative calm. During such periods of calm, I would have ample opportunity to reflect on the meaning of life itself and the place of my family in the Grand Scheme of Things. It was easy, while sitting at the stern of the boat, and rocking to the swell of the waves in a seemingly endless ocean, to believe myself to be part of this majestic universe. Simultaneously I felt quite alone in the vast expanse of water but also at one with nature. It was easy to conceive myself being connected to the boundless ocean, the unseen land mass, and the distant stars. I was no longer a separate entity but an integral part of the limitless energy from which this universe had been created. Time and distance appeared not to exist. This allowed

me to understand that it did not matter if we went to Europe this year, next year, or never. All that mattered was to enjoy the journey.

We now had time to be land lubbers again. I actually enjoyed our stays on land immensely. Living on the boat at the marina in Kema, near Galveston, was just fine with me. We had our little house in the water along the pier and could step off whenever we wanted. There were so many other more attractive things to do. I sometimes went off to the boatyard to investigate. There was a big dumpster and, with some luck, I could find some canvas and sticks to enhance the fort we had built in the reeds. Soon Marcel and Anisha were keen to come along dumpster diving, and soon our new dwelling had all the necessities of a playhouse. The canvas protected us more from the sun than the rain. Most of the time we had nice and warm weather, except when a big rain squall flooded the marina. It was yet more fun for us, as we then could run around in the knee deep water. At night we played tag with the flash lights, dashing through the receding water.

Soon we made friends with other kids in the marina and used the pool a lot, in spite of the ducks who already lived there. I had a great time, except once in a while, when I had to go along to help clean the yard or do other chores my parents asked me to do. I hated to do that kind of work and hid as best I could if we were going to visit. If I had to go along, I was mostly found inside the house in front of the TV watching a show, from where I was then ordered outside to continue my shirked job. Of course Marcel and Anisha had to pitch in too and I think Marcel didn't mind as much as me. We had some good food while visiting them and that compensated a lot. They also had an ugly little dog that I made friends with. It was fun to have an animal around but it could not at all replace my dog, Jeffro.

A cross-stitching session in the cockpit

On Our Own

What a strange feeling it was to be on our own. This was the first trip on Kristy Nicole with only our four children as a crew. We intended to head for Fort Myers, Florida, a trip of about 1100 kilometres (700 miles) from Galveston, Texas. On the eve of our departure we anchored in the wide channel which connects the port of Galveston to the Gulf of Mexico so that we could have an early start the following day. We had selected an area which was shown as a designated anchorage on our charts, but I was surprised to find that the water was some 14 metres (45 feet) in depth. This mystery was soon cleared up when I received instructions by radio to move a few hundred metres (yards) inshore, as the area we were in was reserved for freighters only. We quickly recovered the 40 metres (125 feet) of rope plus another 30 metres (100 feet) of chain and the anchor as we leapt to follow instructions.

The forecast was for good weather with moderate winds. The boat had been well provisioned with food, water and fuel and every movable item on board had been well secured. We knew well enough what could happen to loose cargo if the weather turned bad. It was a great feeling to know that we would not be required to spend any more money for some time to come and that the boat was "ship shape and Bristol fashion".

In the shallow anchorage the waves coming in from the Gulf of Mexico rocked the boat quite a bit, and Anisha became seasick. The sea bands she had on did not seem to help, and she complained that it hurt to wear them. To add to her troubles the boat was permeated with a very unpleasant smell. Eventually we managed to sniff the source of the problem out; our supply of potatoes, which was stored in nets above the bunks, had gone bad. Getting rid of the offending tubers did clear the air a bit, although it did nothing to still the motion of the boat. After some interrupted sleep due, for the most part, to excitement, we were ready at first light to start on our trip to Florida.

In spite of Anisha's bad experience with the sea bands, we all wore them in the hope that they would work for most of us. The wind picked up and filled our sails nicely. Unfortunately it also increased the size of the waves and, in short order, Carina and Pascal fell foul of the dreaded *mal de mere*.

The homeopathic remedy we had brought had a strong odour, and in their distressed state, they were not keen to try it, so we were forced to resort to some Dramamine for them. My tummy started to feel funny, and I soon found myself hanging over the side of the boat. The experience, this time, was not as bad as it had been on the first bout, but that was, I think, due to the fact that the waves were of only moderate size. Chäberli took some of the homeopathic medication, and it seemed to work for her so I followed suite. Marcel ate some ginger and had no problems at all.

Our friend and skipper was no longer with us, so a new watch routine had to be worked out and the following is what we came up with: Anisha & Marcel from 20:00 to 22:00 hrs, Werner from 22:00 to 24:00 hrs, Chäberli from 24:00 to 02:00 hrs, then again Anisha & Marcel 02:00 to 04:00 hrs, Werner 04:00 to 06:00 hrs and Chäberli from 06:00 to 08:00 hrs. Carina and Pascal had no watches assigned to them.

The Dramamine had worked well on Pascal, and he was all over the boat, mostly, it seemed, in someone else's space. This caused quite a few squabbles and served to drive home the point that space was limited. When we were all in the cockpit there was enough room for each person to have a seat, but no-one could stretch out. It was like a glorified version of a long car trip where the children are crying out, "Mommy! Jimmy just put his colouring book in my space." etc. etc.

After two days of good sailing, the wind died to a whisper, and our tanbark-coloured sails started to flap like old rags hung on a washing line. To get rid of the annoying noise, we had to furl them and start up the engine to glide across the mirror-like surface of the Gulf of Mexico. All worries about seasickness had passed; what a wonderful feeling that was. On our trip to Houston, not so long ago, we had seen the Gulf as wild as a fountain. On this trip we were able to take pictures of ourselves looking over the sides at our reflections, mirrored on the calm surface of the water. In those peaceful surroundings all, except for Pascal and I, took up cross-stitching. We would often scan the water around us and were soon able to notice any changes in the surface of it. On one occasion we spotted some funny-looking objects bobbing on the surface, just off our starboard bow. We shut the engine off and glided into the midst of a group of large sea turtles. It was exciting to watch these creatures swoop up and down in the clear water, breaching the surface every so often for a breath of air. We all felt privileged to have had such an experience.

Several days passed with just light winds. We thought that sailing could not have been any better, even though we could not get better than 2 knots when under sail. On the days with very light winds, we used the motor. The odd group of dolphins would join us and seemed to enjoy crisscrossing our bow; they were much faster in the water than we were. What a lovely feeling for all of us; we felt well cared for and the children were able to wander about the deck as they pleased; only Pascal was made to wear his life jacket at all times. With the trip to Galveston in the back of our minds, it was hard to believe that we could have such an easy crossing this time.

Every night I would listen on the portable short-wave radio for news of any weather system which might be coming our way. On June 4th a tropical storm over the Virgin Islands was reported to be moving northward. The wind picked up and we moved along at a pleasant

Trying to spot the dolphins

4 knots. Out of nowhere three pelicans appeared and joined us for a day. They tried to land on the top of our mizzenmast, but the oscillating tip of the mast would not permit a bird of that size to touch down. We were amused by their repeated attempts. Eventually they landed on the water for short spells or watched us from the air as we watched them, full of curiosity about what they would try next. After some time, they gave up and we lost sight of them. The following day two smaller white birds, with long yellow legs, landed on our bowsprit and stayed with us for a few days. They left when land hove into sight. We were not able to decide what kind of birds they were but were not sorry to see them leave, as they had been putting their marks all over our boat. It was exactly 7 days from the time we had left Galveston till the time we approached the first marker to navigate the entrance to Fort Meyers, Florida. The wind was still fairly good but against us, so we used the motor to get up the channel to Fort Meyers and the anchorage.

Our attempt to moor alongside a dock under windy conditions was like something out of a Keystone Cops movie. A lady was waiting on the dock to receive our lines. It seemed to me that it would be best to approach the dock from the windward side; this was an assumption I would live to regret. The engine purred with a throaty grumble and all 30 horsepower was put in reverse to slow the boat as it bore down on the jetty and the unsuspecting lady. Kristy Nicole stopped at the right spot but, because of her full keel and the fact that she was starting to reverse, the stern swung away from the dock. We were able to throw the bow line and the lady secured it to the dock but the stern swung round in a 180 degree arc and brought our side with no fenders against the dock, a full boat-length away from the spot we had been aiming for. Fortunately neither the boat nor the dock sustained any damage. We were all relieved to be able to step ashore, but then we suffered from our seven days at sea; the solid land seemed to be very unstable. We must have looked like a bunch of drunken sailors returning from a 48-hour leave on shore. Undoubtedly any bystanders would have had an amusing story to tell that evening.

After the trouble it had taken us to become secured to the dock, we were dismayed to learn that it was not the proper dock for refuelling or replenishing our water supply. We had to untie ourselves and make a fresh attempt on the adjacent dock. This time I approached upwind, and we managed to get berthed without a hitch. It required 160 litres (45 gallons) to top up our fuel, about half of the tank's capacity. I calculated that we had motored for about 360 nautical miles (680km), so this would give us a range of about 700 nautical miles (1330km) on a full tank of diesel fuel, a handy thing to confirm.

With our fuel and water tanks refilled, we left the fuelling dock and headed for the anchorage. It took a few tries before we managed to manouevre between the anchored boats and drop our hook in the appropriate spot. Once the boat was securely anchored and the engine was shut down, we felt that we had accomplished a great deal, for a bunch of landlubbers.

There was a fresh breeze blowing over the choppy water. It was difficult to row ashore with a heavy load, and we decided that I go ashore alone in our dinghy in order to replenish our food supply. One "luxury" item I bought was a block of ice cream, which everyone enjoyed.

We had no plans to stay in Fort Meyers but would head out the next day into the Okeechobee waterway which would, eventually, take us to the east coast. Preparations for this leg of our journey were quite simple. The engine had performed well on our trip across the Gulf of Mexico, so we felt confident that it would get us through the Florida waterway where sailing would be rather tricky. The sails were covered with the ready-made green covers which would protect them from the sun. Heavy, 19mm (¾") docking lines were prepared and hung along the boat's rails in preparation for passing through locks. When in the locks, it would be necessary to secure both sides of the boat to the sides of the locks, or so we thought. The charts indicated that the distance across the Florida peninsula was 224 kilometres (140 miles), so we estimated 4 or 5 days of easy travel.

One possible problem could be the 15 metre (49 foot) high railway bridge which crossed the waterway near the Port Mayaca lock. Our boat, fully loaded, was about 15 metres (49' 2") tall, including the radio antenna. We hoped that the 15-metre bridge measurement had been taken at high water and the fact that we were now in fresh water would give us an inch or two to spare; otherwise we might need to get a new radio antenna.

I had been more than curious to get going. That first trip had been a bit of a "shake down" as they had said. It did shake me down. I had no clue what was in store for me when we set out for the first time. When the skipper was in charge of the boat, we had better listen to him. He never got sea sick. I, however, felt more than sick. On top of it, we had to learn how to set sails out front. Geared up with life jackets we must have looked like comical actors. Carina and I were trying to get the genoa attached to the forestay. We had been instructed while we were still at anchor, but this was like day and night. Now the boat was jumping up and down like a crazy horse, and I was busy hanging on for dear life. Having no hand left, it became an impossibility to do just the simplest of things like attaching the hanks to the sail and the stay. Somehow we did manage, but no longer had much control over our body's need to empty the stomach. As a matter of fact, all of the crew got miserably sea sick for the first few days. It was a great relief when we were dismissed from our duty of doing any work on the foredeck.

But now, on the way back over the Gulf of Mexico, I could not believe that we were actually going over the same waters. The ocean, remembered as such a confused mass of water, lay in front of me like a mirror. Not a ripple. It was one big sheet of glass, broken only by the bow of our boat, making two almost symmetrical curls on each side. It was actually nice to watch the many eddies and curls the water made, before passing along the side of the boat. In the back a trail of foam was all that was left. At night it became a trail of glowing plankton, something so bizarre-looking but at the same time magical. It brought up memories of stories my Dad had told me about faraway places. These little lights had that inspiring glow to make me ponder over things in the past. There was a lot of time to just have my thoughts wander, and this was one such moment. With the seat in the back of the boat, it was convenient to just sit there and gaze into the warm air. It also provided extra space to stretch out and be on your own, at least in such nice weather as it was. Every day was clear and sunny. It gave me a tan, something I realized only later, when mom had to put sun tan lotion on the red parts of my body. These calm days later on changed to some windier ones, but we did not experience any bad weather.

The animals that visited us during this trip kept me occupied with thoughts. I liked the turtles the most. Their movement through the water was so gracious, even though they looked clumsy to me. They could, however, move fast, carrying their large shell with them. When our boat approached the many heads that were poking through the shiny surface of the water, they quickly disappeared to surface again in another spot. We were able to watch them move underwater, using their legs to push themselves through the crystal-clear water. Only the movement of their feet caused the surface to be disturbed. Eventually we moved so slowly that we were very close to them, almost able to touch them. Their bodies were immense. For me it was almost unbelievable, because I had seen turtles before, in the pond across from our home in Canada,but the ones here had bodies the size of mine,while those in the pond back home fit nicely into my hands.Carina and I had sometimes played with them.

It was with a certain relief that we saw land again, approaching Fort Myers. I was glad not to have been sea sick, and the trip was actually enjoyable. I still remember the celebration of our first trip on our own when Dad brought some real ice cream to the boat at anchor. I felt at home again.

Calm

1. A mirror image strikes the eye
The boat moves almost as if shy
Towards an endless sky
You can hardly hear a fly
Ref: We sail over the open seas
Waiting for a gentle breeze (2 times)

2. The sun reflects its silver rays
Like an island our boat just stays
Further away we see the dolphins play
Jumping and making their own spray
Ref: 2 times

3. We are out in the Gulf of Mexico
We know where we would like to go
The sun's setting with a real red glow
With awe we admire a perfect show
Ref: 2 times
Voice and guitar by Werner M. Gysi

A CD with colour pictures and songs can be ordered.

The Okeechobee Waterway

It was early morning when we brought the dinghy on deck and pulled the hook. We had organized the necessary charts while still in Texas, and I again studied them carefully. They showed us all the bridges and where they were, just like a street map. After passing through Fort Myers and under several bridges, some of which had to be opened for us, we followed the Caloosahatchee River. We reached the Franklin lock, the first lock out of three to bring us up to lake Okeechobee. There was a red light to let us know that the lock was not ready for us. We tried to contact the lock engineer to confirm this but could not get any response. As it was easier to drop the anchor than trying to manoeuver the boat in the confined area before the lock, we did so and shut off the motor until the light got green. To our surprise we did an excellent docking and secured the boat with the two lines received from the lockmaster. Shortly after we left the lock we anchored along the side of the river, close to a small marina. A large 3-masted sailboat was docked along the only pier, and we asked the person on it where we could dock our dinghy to go ashore. A lengthy chat evolved, as is usual with boaters, to tell each other the latest seafaring experiences. The girls got ready for a swim, but someone from the marina mentioned to us that there were alligators in this river, something we had not thought about, but gladly took as good advice!

Another boater came alongside and offered to share his fresh caught fish with us. The grill, clamped to the back of the railing was loaded with coal and fired up. The fish were cleaned. Then an aluminium foil was placed on the grill and covered with some butter and lots of spices. Several of the cleaned small fish were then placed on the grill and sprinkled with onions followed by another layer of fish and herbs. This made it ready to be wrapped into the remaining foil. The whole package was left on the grill for an hour or so and those many small sized fish sure tasted wonderful when cooked like that. It was late when everybody went to bed.

We got up in the later part of the next morning, and our travels took us on an easy ride along the river, enjoying all the green vegetation mixed in with the odd house and many citrus orchards. Cypress, mangrove thickets, palms, live oaks, pines, and plenty of lush vegetation bordered the river along the route. The odd tree stump along shore showed the remains of trees that had once bordered the channel but had given way to erosion or some other challenge.

It felt quite good to know that we moved along with our house and belongings. It made me always feel right-at-home no matter where we stopped. Travelling inland also brought back the memories of when we had been driving along the highways with the van. Now that land-lubber feeling came back again, seeing shorelines so close on both sides. Surely our pace gave us another sense of going places. It reminded me of stories told about the olden days, stories I heard about people moving around with horses and wagons. Certainly, we did not go any faster and with the sunshine out everyday there was no concern to rush it either. Still, there was the gentle pressure about moving north to avoid any hurricanes or tornados, and it was that which kept us moving on, if not north, then at least eastwards for a while.

We went past several inviting landings along the way, lined with great-looking sailboats with their flags flying, some revealing that the owners were from another country, just like us. I felt happy about being able to show our Canadian flag on the stern. We were always well received and had some great and positive encounters. To others, Canada seemed to present itself as a stable and attractive country with no extreme political or other views. Being Canadian myself has become something I cherish. It's the place that has given me the opportunity to fulfill my dreams, dreams that otherwise could not have come true. If our two older sons were not living in Switzerland, we would not have considered going there for a visit. There would certainly be no sailing grounds such as these and what would we do there anyway? If I had longed for anything else at all now, it would have been for the farm, the fruit trees in particular and with all the other things about, the sense of living in paradise. However, experiencing this new way of living, steering our house through these channels and travelling on water for some time now, gave us a sense of great satisfaction and compensation. Being together as a family was great too. The kids enjoyed the freedom of learning about new things along the way rather than solving questions from the home-schooling material we had brought along. It was the sheer weight of all these books we carried on the boat, rather than their contents, that helped us now, by lowering the waterline slightly. This meant we would have a better chance to pass under the 15-metre (49 foot) bridge which was not far ahead. The books certainly did not get used as originally anticipated, and schooling became more a matter of learning about what we saw and did along the way.

We passed through two more locks, Ortona and More Haven, before reaching at the same elevation as lake Okeechobee. Throughout our channel passage, Chäberli and Marcel dealt with the lines and were doing an excellent job. Marcel was usually a bit nervous, always trying to do a perfect job. At age fourteen he also enjoyed steering the boat while going along in the channels. It gave me some extra time to just sit in the back of the boat, on the inviting seat extending over the back railings, and doing nothing but watch "the world go by". With the arrangement of the cockpit in the centre of the boat, the back became something like an outdoor living room, and when travelling in calm waters such as these or at anchor, it was the place where we enjoyed many meals together. A green canvas cover provided the necessary shade. However, when we left the second lock, a drizzle started to make things a bit dull, and when it turned into rain we decided to anchor, not far from the lock we had just passed. There were a few mosquitoes around, but it didn't seem to be serious, and we had nothing to worry about. All our opening hatches, four of them plus the companionway, had removable screens mounted. The hatch screens were hinged on one side and could be closed with a locking bolt on the other. The rain soon stopped, and we could open the hatch covers to cool off the inside somewhat. It became a bit stuffy, and a cool breeze was a welcome thing. We had an early supper and retired early. However it was far from retiring. Mysteriously there always seemed to be some mosquitoes trying to sting us. Once eliminated, they would be replaced by more coming after us. All the hatches were locked tight. It became very annoying, and it was impossible to fall asleep. It just became unbearable, and I got up in order to find out how these mosquitoes were finding their way in. It was unbelievable to see a black cloud of humming wings over each hatch. Mosquitoes everywhere were desperately trying to squeeze between the mounted screen and the hatch frame. There were so many of them on the outside that the screen appeared to be darkened up with paint, and it looked as if they would be able to push themselves through any remaining gap on the hatches. I became a bit grumpy about the nasty beasts and got to work. With the drill I placed two more holes into the screen frames, so the spacing between the hinges and the locking bolts was cut in half. Then I placed some self-cutting screws and tightened the screens against the frames. I was wet with sweat but, after we had killed the remaining mosquitoes inside the cabin, things quieted down. I was relieved and looked forward to a good night's sleep.

Daylight broke and we approached Lake Okeechobee. With the highest hills around the lake only little more than 90m (300 feet) above sea level, it looked just like a pretty flat country. Florida in general is not very hilly, with the highest point, a hill in the panhandle, at 105 metres (345 feet) above sea level. With the lake having a shallow shore some ways out into the open, a channel had been dredged for some ways out to deeper water of at least 2 metres (7 feet). There we pulled up sails and rode across the lake with a good breeze from the side. The water was choppy and the girls and Pascal got sick. They each took a pill and soon fell asleep.

Eventually we reached Mayaca lock, the 4th lock, situated right at the shore of the lake. The lock was open and we could motor right through it, approaching the low bridge. We could see it from afar. It was an old railroad bridge, and it looked like a very low opening. We were not sure what would happen next and approached the opening carefully. It was impossible to tell wether we would fit under or not. After we passed through, without a hitch, we were all relieved. It had been almost too easy to be true.

We carried on for a while, admiring the scenery along the way. During our overnight stop, rain washed the deck of the boat, and when I climbed on deck I noticed that the boat had moved out into the channel a bit. We had two anchors, one in the back and one in front. The back anchor had not held very well and, with the wind during the night, had come loose, holding the boat just with its weight.

Soon we were on our way again heading towards St. Lucie lock. We dropped about 4 metres (13 feet) to reach the level close to that of the Atlantic Ocean. We were back on the East coast of the USA again.

The reception was a bumpy one. With the 1.83 metre (6-foot) draft of our ocean-going boat we, for the first time, touched ground more than once. Several times the boat ground over something, slowing down slightly. It felt like soft sandy ripples were pushing Kristy Nicole's keel up. These were some scary moments for all of us. So far we had never touched ground or felt a jolt like that, and the thought of getting stuck was terrifying. First we thought we were outside the channel, as the markers were far apart, and with the river widening a lot, there was no way to tell if we were in the place we were supposed to be. With the momentum of the boat and the engine at full throttle, we jittered over a few more ripples before the water got deep again.

Another opening bridge had to be passed, after which a marina was located. We were now in Stuart. After these four hot and sometimes rainy days, we all felt the need to take a break and have a shower. We radioed the marina and asked for directions to approach their dock and managed a more or less perfect landing on the fuel dock to fill in 61 litres (17 gallons) of diesel. Considering that we had moved our whole house across the State, 61 litres didn't sound like much. That amount of fuel brought us across Florida from west to east, mostly under motor power. After filling up we entered a slip without any great problems and felt happy to have become more skilled in manoeuvring the boat in tight corners. By now we also learned that the rather small engine's power had to be used with perfect timing in relation to the boat's movement in order to manouevre the heavy boat correctly. With no currents or winds, it became an easy task.

It was time to check on the money situation, to make sure that we still would have enough funds to continue. I tried to reach the caretaker on our property, who was in charge of situations such as rental payment delays, but was unable to reach him. The next day, however, I was successful, and he mentioned that there were some problems between the renter of our house and him, but that he had been able to settle things and that the check was in the mail. The payments for the business loan, however, were still not forthcoming, and I was not able to reach the owner. Eventually I asked a friend to check up on the owner and to persuade her to pay. We just had to make do with what was left on our two MasterCard accounts. We also understood that we could not afford to stay on in a marina such as this, which charged $36.00 per day. For the last time we enjoyed the swimming pool and the hot showers the following morning and made the boat ready to leave. We found out that the anchorage for small boats was just across the water from us, about 30 minutes using the motor. It was a nice, quite open area but a rather long ride with the dinghy to shore. We definitely felt that a dinghy motor would have been a very helpful tool, and we agreed to buy an electric one. We decided to use the starter battery from the engine of Kristy Nicole to power it. With two banks installed as house batteries that ran all the stuff in the boat, we could always make sure that one of the banks was charged.

Our van, sitting in Miami with a "For Sale" sign on it, had to be picked up if it had not been sold. I planned to take the Greyhound bus the next day and, if needed, bring the van back with me. We would then have to leap-frog with the boat and the van as we headed north. We would have to sit down and plan a route north along the east coast in order to find out where we could drop the van off.

A shopping mall, close to the dinghy landing, made stocking up with food easy, and a bus stop wasn't much further from the mall. The following day I went off, heading towards Miami. The bus ride was comfortable but ended with some discomfort of another nature. Just when we arrived in Miami, three civil policemen entered the bus, showing their ID's and asked everyone to hand over their bags for a search. Whatever they were looking for I never found out, but one passenger felt quite annoyed about the whole thing and a big argument started until the policemen asked him to repeat his insults, while another policeman stood by. The words the policeman used were not at all appropriate, but after some more quarrels the traveller gave in to the demand to show his bags as otherwise the policeman would have arrested him. I was glad to leave the bus. It was the second time that I had been confronted by aggressive, unkind police while in Florida. Florida to me appeared like it was governed by police. I changed buses and rode on a city bus to reach 79th. Here the van was still parked sound and safe, the "For Sale" sign barely hanging on the remaining string of still sticky tape used to mount it. I assumed that the inside must have become quite hot at some point and melted the glue on the tape. Checking with the marina for any calls on the car was a negative. Starting the car did not work at first, as the battery had become drained, due to the clock which had been running all along. Help was quickly at hand from a kind person parked close by who noticed my troubles and helped me out. The van started very quickly and off I went. It was time to visit the former owner we bought Kristy Nicole from and share with him our seafaring experiences as well as to pick up some of our mail that had been sent there. I was invited to stay there overnight. He was very pleased to see me and to know that we were very happy with the boat and its performance. So far the weak link while travelling with Kristy Nicole appeared to be the crew. The next day I drove back to Stuart, glad to leave Miami, a busy but not-too-inviting place. On the way out I picked up an electric outboard motor for the dinghy. It looked like an oversized hand blender to me, and I was not sure if it would be strong enough to do the job. Only experience would tell, I thought, and grabbed it. It certainly was cheap and an environmentally clean option and with very little noise pollution. These were criteria I still appreciated and tried to adopt as much as was possible.

 Sailing on our own now was indeed much more fun. I did not like it at all to be told what to do and certainly was not a happy camper to be ordered to set sails. I had little sympathy for the skipper that taught us a bit about sailing, as he always called me the princess, she who wanted things served on a silver dining plate and other such names. Everyone else seemed to support that idea about me. There was, however, little space left for me to be just the way I wanted to be. Maybe therefore I did not show much interest in what was going on around me until we were in the Okeechobee waterway and anchored in what appeared to me to be one particularly uninhabitable place.

The day went by just as usual. I spent it playing with my beanie babies with, sometimes, Anisha joining in. We had them spread out all over the V-berth and the adjoining saloon, playing with them as if they were alive and happy. On other occasions, it was my teddy bear that could place me into another world. He was my best companion on this trip. Always at my side and well looked after. It was this

imagination that kept me happy on the boat. I did not bother much about the passage at all. Wherever we were was fine with me. After all I had my little dolphin hanging around my neck to protect me from all bad things. But this night became a bit too close to comfort and made me realize more of what was around me.

It got darker and some light rain made the inside feel moist. The hatch in our room was under the dinghy and could be left open to get some fresh air inside. I guess the sun must have set a while ago, when mosquitoes started to get my attention. We were all about to go to bed when some of us got stung. We had screens on all the hatches. However the companionway was open, and we thought that some had found a way in through that opening. Daddy then closed it up tight. Of course like that more heat stayed in the boat and the air became very moist and sticky. It made things worse. There seemed to be actually more mosquitoes around as time passed on. Closing the hatches entirely would certainly have created a sauna inside the boat. Eventually Daddy had to work on the screens to the hatches in order to make them tighter. I saw him all wet from sweating while doing the work. It did help to keep any more mosquitoes out, but by then I was stung all over my arms and legs, like a pin cushion. It was painful. I scratched myself and caused some of the stings to get infected and bleed. I hardly could sleep. It was not till the morning, when mom put some cream on the infected stings, that the pain decreased. This was pretty much all I remembered from the Okeechobee waterway.

Carina, with her teddy bear and safety gear

Heading North

When I arrived back in Stuart I found the dinghy tied up on the pier which formed the edge of the little park, where the kids usually played. I could not, however, see them anywhere so I placed the few things I had brought along into the dinghy and waited for their arrival. Not much later they all came running towards me, happy to see the van and the new motor for the dinghy. We installed it and picked up the battery from the boat. The motor pushed us all along quite well but not too fast. Helping with the oars was possible, and it helped save some battery power. We all felt happy with the solution. Having the van again allowed us to drive to a restaurant to dine out. It had been a long time since we all had been able to do that, so it was something very special for us.

We were now seriously thinking about where, and when, to travel further north. Our stop here was enjoyable but not far enough to consider it safe from bad weather. We decided to do an outside passage directly to Beaufort N.C., about a four-day trip. From there we would follow the Intra Coastal Waterway (ICW) up to Hampton, VA. We decided that I would bring the van up to Hampton and leave it there. It meant I would have to drive the van up the Florida east coast, then through Georgia, South Carolina and North Carolina in order to reach Hampton, about 1400km (875 miles) further north. I set out early the next day, with a full tank of propane. Along the way I picked up a hitchhiker in his twenties and the conversation cut out a bit of the drag of driving on the freeways. He was very happy to talk. His life centred around travelling the coast to make a living. He was happy to hear that other places did exist. He had been going up and down the coast for the past 5 or so years, he said, and had never thought of going anywhere else.

I was very lucky to always find propane along the route and arrived in Hampton in the late afternoon the following day, sleeping at a rest stop along the road. The people we had tried to reach by phone over the previous week were not at home, so I decided to park the van at a marina. I found a place where they agreed to let me park at no cost. I left the car and took the next bus back to Stuart in the evening. It didn't take long, and I fell sound asleep on the ride back. The bus reached Stuart early in the afternoon, and I went to the dinghy park where Kristy Nicole junior, as we sometimes called the dinghy, was docked. I sat down on a bench and waited for the crew. When they arrived, they were surprised to see me back so quickly. Once on the boat I listened to the marine weather forecast, and it sounded as if there would be some decent weather for the next few days. We made the decision to leave the next day to reach Fort Pierce. After fuelling up we had an easy trip north, along the Intra Coastal Waterway. It was evening when we reached Fort Pierce. Originally we had planned to drop the hook and sail early the next morning. However, with the weather so nice, we decided to continue and set out to sea just before dark. The first day was a bit rough with the sea fairly bumpy, but no one got sick. We had all sails set and went at a good speed of 6 knots. The next day we had to use the engine to keep moving. However, we soon got carried along by the Gulf Stream, running at about 1.5 knots, which took us a bit off-course. This we didn't notice until plotting our course on the chart. We were drifting quite a bit east while under sail. Some course correction was needed in order to point towards Cape Lookout, the entrance we chose to join the ICW again, and then following it to Beaufort harbor. Four days later we arrived in the early afternoon. Anchoring was a bit tight. There were many boaters here, but we were helped by the others and found a spot to drop the hook. Beaufort was a very inviting place. With its maritime museum it became a real attraction. The museum was free and so was a courtesy car to be used for shopping, which was provided by the staff. We made good use of that opportunity. We made friends with other boaters in the anchorage such as the skipper and his sister on Rhiannon, who were also on the way north on a small wooden boat. We invited them for supper one night and had a barbecue. A few days later a catamaran, sailing under the German flag, called BonBon, pulled in. The owner had sailed it across the Atlantic, with a crew member. He joined his wife and children, who had flown across, on arrival in the Caribbean. We became good friends and so did the children. We shared several meals together before they departed, on their way up north, where, by chance, we met again. I had a lot of questions for the owner about the crossing of the Atlantic. He agreed with the idea not to do it earlier than late April to avoid cold fronts developing in the north that could still spread quite far south. It was the 24th of June then. In my mind I quickly calculated the time left to do our crossing. Ten more months ahead of us, I figured, and with it plenty of time to get used to the boat, the water and to explore more of the east coast.

The following night, for some unknown reason, gnats also known as "noseeums" invaded the boat (as we had experienced when travelling in Mexico) and it became difficult to sleep. The children were all very grumpy the following day and had bites all over. We stayed another night, covering the mosquito screens with dish washing cloth because the gnats could easily pass through the mesh of the mosquito screen. It helped keep the bugs away, but it also stayed fairly warm during the whole night. It was time to move on, taking the ICW north to Norfolk. We again needed to navigate the channel, something we already knew well, we thought. After a first overnight stop, we were about to enter the Pamlico River. Marcel was on the wheel, and I took a bit of time to enjoy the sun. We were just about half way through a long drawn-out right-hand bend in the channel. Marcel had not noticed that the wind was continuously pushing the boat to the right, and all of a sudden we came to an abrupt stop. The engine was running but the boat did not go anywhere. I realized that we had run solidly aground. The boat would not move at all. Reversing the engine did not generate enough power to free the boat. The 30 horsepower Yanmar engine was just not powerful enough to do that. The boat leaned slightly to the left and Marcel and I quickly got busy launching the dinghy and loading the small anchor. To launch the dinghy took a bit of time, and we were all alarmed about the tide going down and making things worse. There was no time to study the tide table for that particular location. We first had to untie the dinghy from the deck, hook it up to the mainsail halyard in order to pull it up and then, as with a crane, swing it onto the railing. It needed two people, and Marcel was already used to this kind of work. However everything had to go fast this time. Once the dinghy was resting upside down on the railing, we gave it a good flip, out and around to get it in the water. The anchor and line were loaded, and I boarded as fast as I could. Using the oars I brought out the line to cover a distance of about 46 metres (150 feet) away from the boat and off to the side. The rope uncoiled itself as I slid over the ripples of the water until I had only the anchor left in the dinghy. I dropped the anchor with a big splash. The crew brought the line through the back scupper, then around the mainsail winch and started to ratchet while I returned with the dinghy and climbed aboard again. I took over the wheel and put the engine in reverse at full power. I could hear the clicking of the ratchet, which indicated that there was a lot of pressure on its parts. I hoped that everything would take the load. I could hear the water wash along the sides of the boat. The crew was busy taking in rope, and after some precious minutes the boat started to slide back out and to the side as expected, away from whatever we sat on. We were free again. With some manoeuvring we managed to get the anchor out and were under way again. What a relief to know that we were floating again. One more experience gained, I thought. After all it wasn't that hard to do and now I knew that the port winch was mounted very well and able to take the extra stress. However, we made sure to watch out for the channel with a bit more care. We caught up to a boat whose crew had offered to help as we sat aground. At that point we were almost free and did not need help, but were happy to see some support. As we were passing them in the channel, later on, they cheered, congratulating us for the great rescue operation. It made us feel better again.

The evening came fast and we found another nice spot to stay for the night. With an early start the next morning we navigated Alligator River, crossed Albemarle Sound and entered into North River. Just before it got narrow again we slowly left the channel a good distance to the right and dropped the hook. Here the water had a really brown colour as if it was a moor or similar and we took a good swim in it. It did not feel dirty and was not salty either. We had some great fun jumping off the bow or swinging out with the main halyard. Before dark some thunderclouds pulled in, and we decided to dry out before we got wet from above. After a great dinner we climbed into our beds. A quite strong wind picked up, the water got choppy and the rain clouds were soon over us. Kristy Nicole held nicely on her 16kg (35lb) anchor.

Rain still was falling lightly when we were ready to start the new day's journey. The usual routine glance at the ammeter, to check for battery charging current, showed a zero reading. We had this problem before, and it was normally due to a loose or broken belt. It was time for me to get out the tools from underneath the settee in the saloon and to find the trouble. The belt was fine, but still there was no charge coming forth from the alternator. When the former owner sold us the boat he left a spare alternator on board. I dug it out and mounted it instead. "Oh great," I thought and relaxed, it was charging again. The old alternator did not do its work anymore. We were glad to have a spare one on board, as otherwise we could not have continued for too long without power. There was the fridge that took the bulk of it, but also the lights and electronics such as the depth sounder, the radio and the GPS were hooked up to the batteries. The latter we used in addition to the charts when navigating the channels in open areas such as in the Albemarle Sound. It was still our wish to install a wind generator to charge the batteries, but money was tight, so we had to do with what was available. Off we went, soon crossing the state line into Virginia, following the rest of the channel to Norfolk and arriving just before visibility was overtaken by the approach of night.

As soon as darkness set in, the City lights, in their full glamour, surrounded us. We were amazed to see so much electrical power squandered to illuminate thousands of lights, which enhanced advertising signs, tall buildings and other fancy-looking shapes, while we were trying to use the least amount of electricity on the boat to save engine-running time. We understood that we lived in another world. Music could be heard over the water from the nearby city pier and, with the many lights along the edge of the water, we could watch people going to and fro along the promenade.

After three days of travel through remote areas we had arrived in a heavily-populated area again. We didn't intend to stay here. Setting out the following morning we passed the many military ships and submarines stationed in Norfolk. We crossed Hampton roads and then navigated the approach to Hampton. As soon as we approached the anchorage, I recognized the area from my earlier visit with the van. The place was small and now a barge was also placed in the anchorage in order to dredge the channel. We found a spot along the channel and put both anchors out to avoid swinging around. With the protection of the houses and trees so close on both sides, we did not need to worry about strong winds. The anchorage was a pleasant place and the harbor-master more then willing to help. For a dollar we could take a shower, and the nearby shops provided shopping facilities. On top of it all, we now had the convenience of a car again. It came in handy but we knew that, sooner or later, we would have to sell it. The problem was to find someone willing to buy it. Propane was not a common fuel, particularly in the USA, and we would have needed to advertise it in a paper. Furthermore, selling it in the US would have caused a lot of paper work, something I hated to do. For sure, once again, I regretted having bought a propane fuelled van.

A drive to a McDonald's restaurant made the kids happy. Then a visit to a block party that was under way downtown, where we looked at all the wares displayed. There were also jugglers, clowns and musicians, and in a nearby park different music groups gave their best. The following day we visited the Bluebird Gap Farm, a small zoo. Everyone had a good time, and it reminded us a lot of our farm at home, especially the goats and their babies.

Back at the boat we noticed that we were sitting on the mud. The tide was very low and had caused us to touch bottom. It was funny to walk on the boat and not sense that ever-so-gentle rocking under the feet. It just didn't feel right, and we decided to move the boat at the next best chance and find another free spot with deeper water. We spent another day with more sight-seeing, this time visiting the Space Center located nearby. Back at the boat we noticed the boat still sitting in mud. Marcel and I thought about pulling the back anchor a bit tighter so the boat would move a bit more towards the deeper water. We started out fine and pulled the boat out of the mud. But all of a sudden, the current from the river moved the boat in the other direction, and before we could secure the anchor line, we lost the bitter end (a sailor's expression of the line's end) and the boat was back in the mud. Forty-five metres(!) (150 feet) of line, with the small anchor attached, had gone. I couldn't bear the thought of having lost the line and made myself ready to jump into the murky water. The digging by the barge hadn't made it any better. It was almost impossible to see anything 0.6m (2 feet) underwater. About 1.2m (6 feet) down I had to blindly feel through the mud to discover whatever was there. After a few tries I was successful and safely recovered the line and anchor. "Enough playing around," I thought, and sometime later, as the tide allowed, we moved the boat to a deeper spot in the anchorage. By now the barge had left and with that we had some more room and a good spot to drop the hook.

I located a store selling car parts and accessories and found a spare alternator for our boat. It was actually the same unit, and I was able to trade the old one in. I felt quite happy to know that there was a spare one on board again. There was still a long way to go, and who knew if something like that could have been found again. Just to be sure, the new one was mounted right away to find out if it worked. And as usual with thing such as these, Murphy's Law (a law that states that if something can go wrong it most likely will) played its tricks. The connections were not in the same place and the wires could not reach. Another trip to the store rectified this. The enclosure could be mounted in two ways, but to change it required a special tool, else it would not have aligned the enclosure properly. Back at the boat all worked out fine, and the alternator worked just as expected.

The films we had dropped off earlier in the week for development at a major US supermarket chain store were not yet ready, and they said that we would have to wait three more days. We bought some other necessary items and the first Bikini for Anisha. We really wanted to leave the following day and enter the Chesapeake Bay but now were forced to stay until our films were developed. Carina and Marcel spent time fishing in the anchorage, and they were both successful.

Another boat, sailing under the Swiss flag, pulled into the anchorage. The owners of Tonaria, a couple with their small child, had built the boat in Lucerne and had it trucked to Basel, where they launched the boat into the Rhine, the starting point of their voyage. According to what they said it sounded as if it would be difficult to leave the boat on anchorage or at a marina in or near Basel, so we abandoned the thought of doing so. We considered the idea of sailing up the French canals, but were not able to glean much information about them. The following day, BonBon, the catamaran belonging to the German Family we had met in Beaufort, pulled into the anchorage and we had some more time to chat with them. The 4th of July approached, US Independence Day, and we were looking forward to the fireworks planned for the evening at the nearby Fort Monroe. It was indeed a spectacular fireworks display. It lasted for more than a half an hour, and the children enjoyed it a lot. We thought that all we had to do before setting out was to make one more trip to pick up the films at the supermarket the following day. The pictures, however, were still not ready so the staff promised to do them for free by Monday, yet another two days away.

A plan for our future travels had to be made. We could not leave the van in Hampton, and selling it there seemed unlikely. Our idea was to drive it up to Toronto, Ontario, and to sell it there to avoid much paper work. We had an address of a friend there and were sure she would help us. This time it would be Chäberli's turn to drive the car about 1000km (625 miles) and to organize the sale.

When we returned to the boat we heard that a couple from Canada had just arrived. Another boater told them about our van for sale and they showed interest in buying it. They were pleased with the look and feel of the car as well as with the price and we had a deal, if ownership could be transferred. A couple of calls to the insurance company in BC confirmed this and they had arranged a transfer paper to be sent by courier. Just like a miracle, we had sold our van. In a way we felt sad but also happy. Happy because we knew that no more driving was needed and that we had some extra cash in our pockets. Of course a 15 year old Dodge van was not the newest thing on the market anymore, and we were glad to receive US $750.00 for it. Payments from the sale of the computer store still hadn't materialized, and we were glad to have this extra money.

A wire that had broken off on the brace to correct Marcel's upper teeth needed replacement and the wire on the bottom also needed tightening up. We thought that it would be an expensive repair but had to pay only US $50.00 for all of it. The dentist must have felt sorry for Marcel being in such a situation and at the same time enjoyed hearing from him about his adventures on the boat. We were very happy about the way it all unfolded. It just makes you feel funny to see how things take shape sometimes. For example, the delay caused by the supermarket's film development staff provided the opportunity to sell the car, get the films done for free and the urgent dental repairs done. It was already the 14th of July when we finally left Hampton, a place we had really liked a lot.

It was good to know that we could leave these stubborn gnats behind and for that it was great to leave Beaufort, Even though it was a great place to anchor. We met kids from other boats and became friends, saw a very good maritime museum and visited the town and its shops.

I enjoyed the life on the boat, and steering it was what I enjoyed the most. I became quite good in keeping the boat in the middle of the channel and with it felt very confident. But, on one occasion, I had to navigate through an open space, with markers farther apart than usual. This was not an environment I was familiar with at all. The sun was out, and it was a nice warm day. No other boats around or obstructions to keep an eye on, so I sat back a bit and enjoyed myself behind the wheel. The boat glided ever so gently through the water, and I did not bother checking the depth sounder. Things were going so smoothly when, suddenly, the top part of my body abruptly moved forward and bent right over the wheel. I could not figure out what was happening. The motor was still running, and I could not remember if we were stopped or were still under way. I straightened myself out and noticed that the boat was no longer gliding gently and that it was sitting on something very firm. It didn't take long and Dad came running from the back and asked me to put the motor into neutral. We were solidly stuck on a sandbank. How could that have happened to me? I was very puzzled but had no time to think about it. I had to help Dad to launch the dinghy, after he had failed to pull the boat out by using the reverse gear. He quickly had an anchor set out and we started to pull in the line over the port winch. It took some good strength to turn that winch and soon we had to take turns to keep the line moving. It got very tight. I could hear the cord scrape on the back scupper as it slowly passed through it. Mom was on the winch now and she had to put all her weight into that winch handle in order to get it to turn. By that time Daddy was on board again. The tension was high, not only in the rope but in all of us. I was standing there like on coals looking at the wide open water all around us wondering how in the world a shallow spot like this could have moved here just for me. The grinding of the rope was clearly heard. The anchor seemed to hold pretty good. It was one of those Danforth ones. They are good for the sandy bottoms, Daddy had explained. It sure proved the fact now. Finally, with the motor in reverse, the boat started to move and I noticed the rope slackening. The boat moved back and to the side a bit. We were free again. I was sure glad it went over so smoothly. I now left the wheel to Daddy who explained to me how it all happened. Doing a light right turn, the wind had blown from the port side and moved the boat, ever so gently, to the side and out of the marked channel. Of course none of us had noticed it until we came to a standstill.

Later in the day we stopped off the channel where we were the only boat far and wide. The water was deep enough for us to leave the channel markers for quite a distance. The sun was still above the horizon and Daddy took a swim in the water. We all followed and soon we jumped off the boat doing front and back flips, trying to compete with each other. We took one of the halyards and swung ourselves way out into the air before dropping off into the water. It was great fun and another day to remember. A small storm over-night kept me waking up, and at one time I had a short look out to see if our boat was still in about the same place. I thought it was strange to depend on this rather small anchor and line for survival, but it worked.

Eventually we arrived in Hampton. Carina and I took out the fishing gear and went off with the dinghy to try our luck. We used our home-made bread as a bait. The weather was cloudy and a few drops of rain came along here and there. We put on our rain gear. Not far away from the boat in a small bay, we tried our luck. We watched our floats like the main figure on a computer screen. From time to time we rolled in the line and cast anew. It paid off. First Carina caught a fish and sometime later I had one as well. Carina in the meantime caught another one, and we decided to quit. They were small, maybe a foot long at best, but it was good enough for a meal. We were very proud to present our catch to mom. She asked us to clean them out. This dampened our enthusiasm somewhat and fortunately mom seeing it, decided to do it herself. The supper was excellent and everybody cheered us on our luck as fisherman-women.

Along the ICW

Exploring The Chesapeake

Because of its size, a full description of this area is almost impossible, and there are many books that explain the Chesapeake in great detail, including stories galore about sailing in this area. Protected from the sea, it can still be a dangerous place to sail, but always provides the opportunity of finding a safe anchorage. Planning trips with the two-day weather forecast in mind was a safe and sound way for us to avoid bad weather, or so we thought.

Our first interest was to see the many sunken ferro-cement war ships, which were set up as a harbor wall. They were located a few hours away by boat and across the bottom of the Chesapeake Bay at Kiptopeke Beach. These boats were used in the Second World War but then after the war were found to be of no further use. With their heavy hulls they now made a good wall to break the waves and gave good shelter for sailors such as us. The view, however, was not pleasing to the eye. Because the wrecks were only half submerged, the decks were well above the water line and covered with various types of vegetation, exposing large red cracks and holes and revealing a mess of rusted steel rebar in several places. Birds used these and other places to nest. The nice sandy beach that the wall protected was a great blessing for us all, and we enjoyed the short stay. We sailed off the next day and with some decent wind made it to Deltaville, a pleasant and cozy anchorage. Big heavy rain clouds started to cover the remaining blue sky, and it looked as if a big storm was coming our way. Just then Tonaria, the Swiss boat and her crew that we met earlier in Hampton, pulled into the anchorage. We once more gathered and celebrated our journeys with a good roast chicken dinner until later in the night when a light rain started to sprinkle onto our boats. We said farewell to each other, each of us eager to continue our trip up to Annapolis the following day.

At 7 a.m. we pulled out of the bay and headed towards Solomons (MD), our next stop. We rounded Smith Point and entered Maryland State at about noon. The tropical storm Claudette, on July 15th located about 320km (200 miles) off Cape Hatteras, had moved out to the Atlantic and seemed to be no threat to us. It made us uncertain when we heard about these storms close by, because in the past they

Solomons museum, lighthouse and replica

had, on occasion, reached Annapolis. Our two anchors were just not large enough to hold our boat in real heavy winds. We had been lucky so far, because the worst blow while we were at anchor was a 35-knot wind, and our anchors had coped well with that. We arrived in Solomons in the evening.

Solomons had once been a fishing town, especially for mussels. Since the mussel beds had dwindled in size the industry had shrunk, but the town had become a tourist attraction. The local museum shows the history quite well. One fishery is still in operation and offers tours to tourists. A replica of a 17th century sailboat was docked beside the museum and open for visits. We enjoyed seeing and comparing with our boat the way sails had to be set and controlled. It was the first time we had looked at a boat this size, and it was very impressive to see how hard it had been to do this in the olden times. Certainly not easy for a crew like we were! Of course it was a schooner about 60-foot long, and therefore almost twice the size of our boat. For easier manoeuverability the replica featured a powerful engine. The sheer cost of maintaining such a big boat, especially one constructed of wood, made me appreciate living on Kristy Nicole.

There was one more very unique service to the tourists in this town that was much appreciated by the boaters. The local grocery store had a bus running frequently to and from the harbor, and you could ride it for free. Stops were plenty and for a boater this was a welcome help, especially when time came to stock up on food and other necessary items and to get to and from the laundry with many garbage bags, filled to capacity with clothing.

The two bicycles which we had brought along on the van, from Enderby, BC, had been sitting on deck in the back of the boat since we had left Texas. They were unloaded but needed quite a bit of servicing to get them in working order. I had sprayed all the moving parts with the famous oil spray, WD40, when we left Texas and once in a while during the trip. In spite of that, the chains had rusted solid because, I suppose, of all the saltwater spray. It was amazing to see how everything was hard to move, even the cables in the sleeves, the pedals, the gear levers and so on. All exposed steel such as the saddle post, the spokes, the many scratches on the handlebars and the pedal-arms had turned a rusty colour. After applying plenty of oil into every nook and cranny, the parts started to turn freely, and we were able to use the bicycles to explore the town. With the chain still stiff in some places, it was not possible to pedal backwards without the chain coming off the gears. Every time the chain passed the gear switch mechanism, mounted on the back axle, a clicking noise was heard. The back wheel brake still did not work because of the cable being stuck in its sleeve. We hoped that, with more use, it would start to loosen up.

We were sure glad that most parts on Kristy Nicole were made from stainless steel, aluminum, fibre glass or wood. Only the 30 or so metres (100 feet) of anchor chain started to turn a rusty brown now and with it the front deck had turned from white to a light brownish tone. We used Ospho, a cleaning liquid we had bought while in Galveston, designed to remove rust stains. It seemed to clean the deck, without damaging anything else, and bring it back to its original colour without much effort.

A small hole in the take-off exhaust pipe, mounted right after the motor block, had been temporarily plugged with epoxy. Except for that, oil, and filter changes, not much maintenance had been required to keep things shipshape. Everything had held well together. It was great to know that, for now, no more money would have to be spent on the boat. We decided not to buy new parts until we reached Annapolis, where we hoped to find some good deals on anchors. There I could also follow up on the outstanding payments from the store in Salmon Arm. We wanted a wind generator, to make sure that we would not be dependent on the engine only for electricity. The thought about making the dinghy into a sailing dinghy was still fresh in Marcel's mind. We were only a day trip away from Annapolis and eager to move on and explore new grounds.

The following day the boat was ready and after filling up with water and fuel, we left in the early part of the day. Sailing with just the light winds we faced out on the bay was difficult, and we used the motor for most of the trip to move at about 5 knots. It was a routine passage of about 80 kilometres (about 40 nautical miles) through the calm waters of the Chesapeake. Most of the time the boat just went along under the control of the autopilot. The crew was busy looking around and enjoying the scenery or doing some cross-stitching. We arrived in Annapolis later in the evening and decided to enter Back Creek, which was the smaller of the two main water accesses close to downtown Annapolis. We moved the boat to a nice spot further up the creek, close to a marina and the dinghy dock. After a couple of turns around other boats already at anchor we dropped ours. We then got busy, rolling the sails and making the boat ready for a longer stay. This meant mounting all the sail covers, unloading the dinghy, putting away navigation aids such as the GPS, charts, binoculars and other small items. The cockpit was covered up with the extra board to create a nice flat area to sit on. The dodger's front window got covered up with an extra piece of cloth, to protect the clear material from the sun and eventual scratches by the crew while dealing with things on the boat. The hammock we had purchased in Mexico came in handy now and was hung between the front stay and the mast, a distance just wide enough to provide a cozy place to rest and swing ever so gently with the rocking of the boat. The many vivid colours of the hammock made for a good contrast between the green sail covers and the boat's turquoise green hull and masts. The dominant feature of the boat remained the same: the green masts by which we could always distinguish our boat from the many others in the creek.

To the southeast, fairly close to the water, we could see a large water tower on top of a hill. This was part of a small park, bordering the creek. On the east side of it was a marina and on the other side the dinghy dock. Adjacent to that was a big boat yard and another marina. It felt like a boater's world only. Across on the opposite side of the creek were some buildings several stories high. I sometimes called these large apartment buildings people silos, not because they didn't look nice but because of the fact that so many people lived in them. A small private dock had been built to serve the boaters living there. Adjacent to that was another slightly larger dock, with a few boats moored to it, belonging to the people living near by. It all appeared open and inviting. This first impression certainly did not replicate the fences and security measures we had faced in Miami, Florida. This still came to my mind very vividly every time I saw city dwellings. Annapolis, however, presented itself as a very inviting and friendly place to be. We thought that we may want to stay for a while.

I also had the daunting task of following up on the situation of not getting payments from the business in Salmon Arm. The person I had sold the business to had not been able to pay for it in full. I had agreed to accept a down payment with the promise of further monthly payments till the full purchase price had been paid. We were relying on those monthly payments to cover our living expenses. Only the first few payments had been deposited to our bank account. This was a difficult situation at best. I hated to follow up on it but it needed to be done in order to know how we would finance our future travels. It felt terrible to think about the loss of the payments and with it the constant worry about how we would finance our trip. Whenever I phoned the store I was assured that payments would soon be made but nothing came. My friend in Salmon Arm assured me that the business was still open but he too got only promises. Eventually I had difficulty getting hold of the store owner, she always seemed to have been somewhere else. Not having a phone on the boat was another handicap. I could not be called back.

The heat of the day slowly was replaced with some cooler air blowing through the area. On the longest day of the year we sat down to have supper while still enjoying daylight. It was then that it really sank into me about how beautiful it was to travel on a boat. We were able to stop along the coast wherever we felt invited. We had our "house" with us, independent and on our own. No hotel bills to pay and our transportation costs were minimal. For a family the size of ours, these were important criteria to look at. Here we were, right in the centre of a beautiful city. Neighbouring boaters came and went. The change of neighbours brought with it the making of new friends, and we never met a boater who was not inviting and willing to share stories about their sailing adventures and what had made them choose this way of life.

There was a man for example, a war veteran from the Vietnam War. He had lived, he said, on his small boat, Sol del Mar, for the past 27 years. A person with many stories to tell backed up with pictures of the boats he had served on while at sea. Or there was the lady from St. Meloris, an 8 metre (26 foot) wooden boat originating from England. She had bought it in the Caribbean. Many hours of sharing made our trip very special, and a feeling of great respect for these people came to the surface just from these kinds of encounters. Of course there were all the boaters with children that we had most of the contact with, especially here in Annapolis. Many get-togethers were organized and much food shared.

As mentioned earlier, we needed to follow up on several things. Chäberli had relatives in nearby Rockville whom we wanted to meet up with. They had some of our mail which had been rerouted from Canada. On the way to the food store, I located a Yanmar dealer and ordered a replacement for the exhaust pipe which turned out to be a one hundred dollar item. We unloaded our bikes again. They came in quite handy when shopping. I wanted some pieces of old fire hose from the city fire department. We used short pieces of fire hose to prevent chafing on the mooring lines or the nylon anchor line, but we had run out of them. We also had to call a person we knew who was setting up a contracting business and who might need a hand in doing some renovations. Of course we all also wanted to explore Annapolis and visit several other places.

The museum in Solomons was a nice experience even for the little ones. There was an extra room for them and our children had lots of fun dressing up in clothes from long ago. There were games for them to learn all about the sea animals and the sea shore.

It was really good to be able to use the bus that the grocery store offered. They even let me use it to go do the laundry. With two full garbage bags full of clothes it was not so easy to move around. I'm sure glad we don't have to wear the clothes which were worn in olden times, that would have added to the pile of wash. I am also glad that there were washing machines, even if I had to go to them. It was always good to be able to do the shopping with a ride back to the boat. We were not able to do it every day, and so we usually had a lot of things to carry. We did a lot of walking when we went on land, not everything was close by. The children sometimes did a lot of complaining when they had to walk so far, but they were getting better at it.

Time on the boat was usually spent with lots of reading. In the marinas they had shelves of books where we exchanged the books we had read for others. We also exchanged children's books with other boaters. In one box we found a book entitled, "Martin the Warrior". I was the first one to read it and then told the children to read it. It was about a mouse and his adventures. They did read it and loved it. Anisha now has the whole series of these Redwall books. Marcel never was a big reader, but we did get him to read as well; there was not too much else to do. He read his first whole book on the boat.

We had all taken up cross-stitching in Texas. We were looking for a present for a friend and found a cross-stitch picture of a clown with the saying on it "Colour your day happy". We liked it so much that we all did a picture of it to give away. After we were all in to it, I bought a cross-stitch book and then the cross-stitching started in earnest. That was what I did the most besides reading. I stitched lots of pictures. Some I still have and others became nice presents. We played games together as well; we had brought a selection of them with us. Marcel got a laptop computer when we were in Kema from a friendly person in a computer store in the marina. It was a 14th birthday present. This is his best friend now. He played games all the time. Marcel also started a very hard cross-stitch of a mother snow leopard and two small ones. (He did not finish it while on the trip, but later during his stay at the farm in Enderby.)

Taking it easy while at anchor

Machine drawn by Pascal during the trip

One Month In Annapolis

Anisha and Carina soon made friends with a girl who lived in the nearby marina. We were invited to meet her parents and enjoy a cool swim in the pool. All our kids loved to take such an opportunity and had great fun swimming in the pool. It was there that Pascal, aged 5, learned to swim. Being guests of the marina allowed us to use the marina's facilities now and again. This was pure luxury when compared to the modified garden sprayer we used, which was designed to spray insects on trees. We used it on the deck of our boat as a shower. The converted sprayer was a practical device and worked well with the black bag, placed in the sun, providing hot water. It could not, however, compete with the unlimited hot water and facilities at the marina.

Marcel had started to build a model catamaran sailboat, using, for the most part, throwaway items. It looked really cool but was not buoyant enough to sail properly. I suggested that he use some of the Styrofoam insulation which was lying around in the boat yard, across the channel. He cut two pieces to the proper length and hollowed them out in such a way that they clamped neatly on to the wooden hulls. The catamaran then floated quite well, and he spent many more hours improving the sail plan and other details so that it could head into the wind, if needed.

Many boats came and left the anchorage during our stay there. One day a boat, Cool Change, arrived with two children on board. As they were about the same age as Anisha, they quickly made friends with each other and we parents got together to share food and experiences. There never was a dull moment. There was, of course, the odd moment when our kids got into arguing and Anisha summed it up in her diary like this:

"July 24th. Marcel and Carina are being quite grumpy and 'fighty' today. It started this morning when Marcel decided to make this day 'pick on Carina day'. Anyway, it is quite annoying."

There was a public phone on the corner of the building facing the pool of the above-mentioned marina. For several days I made use of it, trying to follow up on the state of my business in Salmon Arm. It did not look good at all. The phone in the computer store in Salmon Arm had been disconnected, and all I was left with was a cell phone number at which I had previously reached the owner. Eventually I got through and reached a person called Nigel (or something like that). I was unable to find out who he was, nor was he willing to tell me. He explained that the owner of the store would be unable to continue making payments. At least the message was clear. I would have to rethink our whole trip. Was it time to quit? Should I fly back to rescue what was still left of the store? Perhaps some of the tools, some inventory or furniture was still there. Could I find the owner and help her re-establish the business? Or should we just "bite the bullet" and take the huge loss?

We didn't think we had much chance of recovering much, so we decided to make do with what we had left. It was certainly a very tight budget. No frivolous expenditures could be considered. We were even thinking about taking on some work during our stay in Annapolis. On our travels we had made contact with a couple who were touring on their sailboat. They lived in Annapolis and had given us their address and telephone number. I contacted them and, the friendliness of sailors being what it was, we were invited to visit them for supper the next day. The husband ran a small home improvement business but the holiday season was on and not much renovation was being done. When we got together, we all enjoyed sharing our sailing experiences. During the conversation it turned out that there would be a slight chance of getting some work to do later, during the boat show. We wanted to be back in Annapolis for the boat show anyway and left it at that.

There were other things we wanted to find out about Annapolis. We were helped a great deal by the couple who told us where the stores were to inquire about the prices of anchors, something we were still in need of. They also gave us a sail from an old surfboard as well as some pipes that we thought would be useful when refitting our dinghy. The possibility of making it a sailing dinghy was one step closer to reality.

I checked out the local fire department in order to find some "out of use" fire hose. The guys were very happy to hear about the perfect use for their old fire hose, and I picked up a full length. It had imprinted on it: Fire Dept. Annapolis. I almost changed my mind and wanted to keep it as a souvenir. At first I was unable to mount it on the bicycle due to its weight. However, after I found some more tie downs, it seemed to work, and I was even able to sit on the saddle and carefully pedal along, at a slow pace. Where the back tire touched the road it was squeezed together like a flat sheet of rubber and, where the road surface was a bit uneven, I could sometimes feel a bump through the frame as the valve touched the ground. The bicycle tube held up and did not start to leak. I was able to share this material with many other sailors who required some chafing proof material.

The spare part for the motor arrived, and I got to work exchanging it. The thread that connected the old elbow to the motor block was so tight that I had to heat the outer part. The piece expanded and loosened up enough to be moved. I was then able to unscrew the bolts. It all came together nicely, and the engine was soon emitting its original sound.

One day, when I visited one of the boat stores, I saw a big Danforth anchor sitting at the entrance of the store. It had a for-sale tag with $200 on it. I could not believe it at first. The anchor was brand new and weighed 32kg (70lb). We had intended to buy a plow anchor, which the Danforth isn't, but the price was right so I decided to buy it. A plow anchor would be bought as the 2nd anchor later on. I asked the owner of the store if, for that price, he would deliver it to the marina where we were anchored. He did not mind at all, and the deal was made. We finally had one good, strong anchor for our boat and, after some work, had it placed in the bow of the boat, with the shank resting on one of the two bow rollers. It fit in nicely with the rest of the hardware. It would be, of course, a bit heavier to pull up than the 11kg (25lb) anchor which it replaced, but the peace of mind I got from knowing that this anchor would hold the boat in some strong winds made up for that many times over.

During the same week I found a reasonably-priced rudder for the dinghy and a new rubber dinghy for only $80 at a used parts sale organized by the boaters. It served us well while we were in marinas. It also came in very handy to have an extra tender when we were installing the well for the centerboard in our dinghy. I wasn't sure where exactly to place the well for the centerboard so just made a guess. As we found out later it worked well. We placed the dinghy on the dock, and I got to work. I still had some half-inch plywood left from the roof carrier which had been on our van. This material was just perfectly suited to build the well. Another sailor gave us a large, heavier piece of plywood for the centerboard. This determined the length of the well. There were no power plugs on the dock, so our hand-driven tools came in very handy. I cut the slot in the bottom of our dinghy and used fibreglass to fit the boards together, forming the well. Marcel hauled the necessary tools ashore, while I was busy on the dinghy. Our design allowed the short mast to pass through a hole drilled into the existing front box of the dinghy's peak. The bottom of the mast was fastened with a U-bolt to the partition making up the box. The triangle-shaped sail we had been given was the left over from a lost surfboard. It was held between two aluminum pipes connected to each other at right angles. The bottom pipe was heavier and acted as the boom, and the pipe was raised up the mast, similar to a gaff rig. A U-bolt attached the boom to the mast. With it the sail could be pulled up easily and extended quite a bit above the mast. It was great to see it all come together and a great satisfaction to actually see it work. We now had a perfect sailing dinghy. The children were very happy and quickly learned how to sail it and explore their surroundings. I found out, later on, that it was possible to load up a bicycle, a child and myself and still be able to tack.

A week later Chäberli called her relatives in Rockville near Washington. We arranged to see them and were received very openly and with lots of care. They offered us the use of one of their cars during some of our time in Annapolis, and we gladly accepted the offer. We then had 4 wheeled transportation and could make some sight-seeing trips. Shopping for goods became easy, and we stocked up as much as we could. We were also invited to visit their home and enjoyed a wonderful meal there. We had much to share as we recounted our latest experiences. Mail from the past few months had been shipped to their house and the children were eager to read up on the latest happenings back home in Canada.

One of the letters was from the Canadian Ships Registry Office. We still had to fill in one more form to attest to the fact that the boat was

Under sail with Anisha and a bike

marked according to standards. This meant that we had to buy some self-adhesive, large lettering and mark the boat with the words "Vancouver BC" on the back, the ship's name on each side of the bow and carve the ship's registration number into a structural piece of wood inside the boat. The work would then have to be inspected by a local authority.

After we had done all the above, I paid a visit to the US coast guard office and was told to wait for an officer to come by. During the next two weeks I made a couple of more visits to their office. Each time they promised that someone would come to see us, but nothing happened. Memories of living in India came back to me; would we be obliged to bribe an officer in order to get his services? We were glad to see it come together without any such intervention. Eventually an officer did appear, approved our work, and signed the necessary papers. Kristy Nicole was "up to scratch". No more paper-work would be required and the boat was officially sailing under the Canadian flag.

We had a lot of time to explore Annapolis, and I took the opportunity to approach several health food and bookstores to offer and, in some cases, sell some of my Harmonic Farming books. There was a Starbucks café nearby, and it was fun to take the dinghy ashore and then walk about 15 minutes to get there and indulge in one of their strong coffees. At one time I actually sailed the dinghy out the creek and around the shore right to the café shop. It took me almost an hour, and it was a bit tiring but lots of fun and still easier than using the oars. Once a week the boaters came together for a barbeque in the nearby park, and many stories of sailing adventures were told. Twice we used the car to visit another park, Quiet Waters Park, where we listened to some excellent free concerts. Some other sailors came along as well. A couple from Switzerland, sailing on Sufra, arrived at the park later with their bikes. They had just arrived in the anchorage, and we shared some time with them. I was keen to know how they had sailed the canals of France. One concern I had was our draft of 1.8 metres (6 feet). With the canals often being shallow on the sides, I wondered if there would be places for our boat to anchor or lay ashore. Unfortunately they had not used the canals I was interested in.

During our stay at anchor, things were usually quiet. One evening a thunderstorm brought some life into the place, when lightning hit the nearby water tower. We could smell ozone, and the noise of the thunder triggered a heavy downpour. It scared the wits out of me. At the same time it offered a perfect chance to take a shower and then climb into the dry cabin and prepare some coffee. On another occasion the police were chasing a delinquent who was trying to escape by swimming out to a sailboat to find refuge. After an exchange of words, shouted across the water, the person tried to swim across the creek to the other side in order to escape, but eventually was intercepted by police and taken into custody.

In no time it was August 19th. We met with our relatives for the last time to hand back the car and to once more socialize while sharing food. We were ready to take off and to do our last bits of shopping. We said good-bye to all the boaters we had met during our stay and pulled up to the fuel dock to fill up with fuel and water. We were surprised to see that the 700 litres (200 US gallons) of water had lasted us for more than 4 weeks and there was still some left!

For some time I had not been sure what to make out of this trip. We were going from place to place and stayed nowhere for any length of time. The friends we made were lost as fast as found. I had a difficult time adjusting to that. Compared to life at the marina in Galveston, everything was now changing almost daily. I can vividly remember the socializing we did with the friends we found in Kema near Galveston, and I was glad when Daddy announced that we would stay in Annapolis for some time. We stayed for a whole month. On top of that we planned to return for my birthday. It didn't take long before I made friends with a girl, the daughter of a family whose boat was berthed in the marina, just across from ours. It was not as convenient, however, to visit as it had been in Galveston, where we could hop off the boat at any given moment. Being at anchor was a different story. We always had to time the use of our only dinghy in order to give everyone a chance to go ashore. The portable VHF helped a bit, but it was never as convenient as when we stayed at the marina in Galveston. About a week into our stay, Daddy arrived with a rubber dinghy which had been on sale. It was one of the cheap ones, but it had a couple of aluminum oars with removable plastic ends and could carry us kids without any problem. What better could I have wished for? It was a sort of early birthday present from Mom and Dad. We were mobile and could take off for visits as we pleased. And so we did. Having another boat, Cool Change, with children aboard and anchored right next to us, we did not get bored anymore. There was some time where the other kids had to do their school work, mostly in the morning. That actually got us interested in doing the same thing, and I remember doing some of my studies. I had my own schedule and learning was fairly easy. That, however, was not half as much fun as meeting up with our friends.

Peeking out of the V-berth

On The Way To New York

Our first day out on the Chesapeake went without a hitch. A gray sky covered the sun and, from time to time, it started to drizzle. Heading north we reached Betterton on the south shore of the Sassafras River in the evening and had enough light left to prepare for the coming day. We went to bed early in order to be ready to leave at first light. Had we known what was in store for us, we would have waited out the weather.

Chäberli was up at 5:30 a.m. and made coffee. We sat in the cockpit and waited for the light to break while listening to the radio. The forecast was for 100% rain. There was no further mention of any winds or similar problems, so we decided to put up with the rain and, around 6:30 a.m., pulled up the hook. The kids were still sleeping. Not much later a light rain took away some of the visibility. The front window of the dodger was covered with rain drops which would slowly accumulate on the sloped surface and then swiftly roll down. For us it was great to be able to sit under the cockpit cover while the boat motored through the water. There was almost no wind and soon we entered the C&D canal leading to the upper part of the Delaware.

The Delaware in this area is a wide river that runs southeast, with a wider opening into Delaware Bay and then into the Atlantic Ocean. It was about 11 a.m. when we entered the upper part of the Delaware channel near Delaware City, which lay just to the north. The river was wide, but there were many shallow spots, and therefore a marked channel was laid out leading safely to the ocean. The wind picked up, and we were glad to be able to set sail. The rain also got a bit stronger, but there was no need to change into foul weather gear as it appeared to be just some light rain. We were sailing at about 3.5 knots, hard into the wind, but on course when we arrived at the first knee of the canal. To the left were 3 large cooling towers resembling an atomic power plant. There was a notation on the chart indicating that the magnetic field might be distorted in this area. Great help, I thought, but with our position given by the GPS, it didn't concern me much. With the change of course we now faced the wind head on. We had to take the sails down altogether and use our motor. We were not moving much faster but were, at least, again on course. The three large towers, now behind us, dominated the landscape for quite some time. They never seemed to get smaller, as their huge size distorted any estimation of distance by sight.

I checked the back of the boat to see if we were towing something with us that would slow us down. And so it was. A piece of fishing net was dragging behind our boat, most probably caught by the rudder. It was frustrating to see this. There was nothing we could do about it. For the next hour and a half we covered only about 7km (3.5 nautical miles). In the meantime the rain and wind had picked up and visibility became quite low. At least it was still possible to see a fair distance and navigate the buoys by eyesight or with the binoculars. The time marked in the logbook said 3:48 p.m., about an hour later, when the reading for speed over ground on the GPS dropped. We could hardly maintain a speed over 2.5 knots. Checking the position on the chart confirmed the speed. It was a relief to notice that we were still in the channel, because now it was impossible to see the buoys until we were right up to them. The GPS told us our approximate position and speed. In the narrow channel this was not an accurate enough way to navigate. Radar would have come in handy. With the readings taken from the depth sounder, we could assume that we were still inside the channel so we kept a constant eye on it. We knew, however, that it could easily mislead us. If we had veered off, into one of the dead ends that branched off at a slight angle and was about the same depth as the channel, we would not have noticed it until marking our position from the GPS onto the chart. By then many things could have gone wrong. The Delaware Channel itself had plenty of depth, but in some spots the sides got shallow fairly quickly, especially around the shoals that we were about to pass. Ahead on the left was Arnolt Point Shoal followed by Ship Point Shoal and on the right Bombay Hook Point Shoal. To complicate matters, the winds picked up and the rain was coming down like pellets.

My original intention was to cover the 76km (40 n.m.) of the Delaware in about 8 hours, averaging 5 knots, while using the outgoing tide to help us along. Our boat could go 6 knots under motor and normal conditions, and I thought that I had calculated on the conservative side of things. With this in mind we should have reached Cape May Canal, our planned destination, about an hour after the tide had started to rise again, or around 7 p.m. The whole trip would have been during daylight hours.

Fate had turned against us. There we sat, moving ever so slowly, inside the dredged channel. Visibility had become so poor that it was hard to see the bow of the boat. The outgoing tide and the oncoming wind made for some choppy, big waves and a lot of spray. The boat moved up and down like a horse in an obstacle race. The big difference was that we were making no headway. Here was a boat with a crew, soaked by the rain, not knowing if the boat was still moving forward and, if so, in what direction. Oncoming ship traffic, including large commercial freighters, were visible only once they were right on top of us. With all these sudden changes, I became physically sick. The rain quickly cleaned the stuff away, but, at the same time, I felt tears running down my cheeks, mixed in with the rainwater which had leaked through the cockpit cover. I remembered that I had been sick before, on our trip across the Gulf of Mexico, but it had not affected my sense of judgement. Now I had, for the first time, lost confidence and traded it for fear. I was not sure if I could master the situation. Pictures appeared in my mind of the boat sinking. I saw my family floating, struggling in the water. It became all very real. An earlier vision about how I travelled through the water, squeezing between spaces of molecules now revealed itself as a terribly dangerous flood of water that engulfed me and slowly took me down to the bottom of the canal. I had to bring myself back to reality. There were things to do and, all of a sudden, I remembered my experience when capsized on Shuswap Lake with the catamaran. I knew that I had to take things one step at a time, using common sense. Worrying was not the right thing to be doing in that situation!

The children had long since crawled down into the cozy cabin, knowing well that it was better to try to stay out of the way. I don't know if they were scared or just looking for a dry spot. Chäberli sat crumpled up in the corner of the cockpit trying to keep herself warm. I did not want to know what she was thinking, but it looked as if she was praying, wanting to help me get over the mood. I realized that it was a difficult task she had to cope with.

The logbook read 4:52 p.m. when we passed Arnold shoal, moving at about 3.5 knots and approaching the next shoal. At 6:55 p.m. we had passed the first sets of markers and were at the height of Pen Davis Point Shoal, ending up on the left side of the channel. Winds had picked up again and we were slowed down to 1.5 knots. After an hour we were still on the left edge of the channel. We wanted to confirm our position with the only thing we were still able to see close up, the buoys, and, in this part of the canal, they were only on the left side. At least the GPS appeared to be fairly accurate, and our positions did get confirmed once we were right up to the buoys. It was now getting dark, and we needed to make sure to sail on the appropriate side. Ahead of us was the narrow point in the channel, made up by the Joe Flogger Shoal on the right and the Cross Ledge on the left. These were all marked with bright flashing lights, but we could hardly see the tip of our boat and could not rely on a distant light. We were still moving at only about 2 knots.

We decided to radio the ship traffic, announce our position, and make them aware of our situation. It was difficult for us to determine where in the channel we were until we came upon the next marker. At the same time we were trying to fight the wind, waves, tide and rain, keeping a constant lookout, checking the depth sounder, steering the boat and trying to stay warm. It was about 8 p.m. when we called on channel 16 to try and notify other boats about our position. Over the speaker we immediately heard the captain of a commercial boat calling us back. It was a great relief to hear someone's voice. We explained to him our problem of having partially lost the ability to determine our exact position within the channel. He was a very friendly person, and we chatted for a while. He clearly warned us not to try to go out on the Atlantic, where he had just been, but to seek shelter at the Harbor of Refuge in Cape Henlopen. He was curious to know what we were doing out there at that time of day. We explained our journey to him. He immediately called up the other commercial vessels in the area to make them aware of our position. He also mentioned that we should be listening on channel 13 for the commercial radio traffic. We had thought that channel 16 was that one. Most newer radios could monitor two channels but not ours, so we switched at once. When I asked if he could see us on the radar he could not locate us. We were, however, happy to have found someone to talk to. Not much later we suddenly saw the huge front of a ship, passing to our left. We could not read the name but saw only the faint shape and lights passing by. We knew then that someone was watching over us.

We continued to move ahead at about 2.5 knots until 1:30 in the morning when we passed Brandywine Shoal at a speed of about 3.5 knots. Things seemed to improve. The channel then opened up, and no more dangerous shoals were ahead of us. The wind and rain dropped, visibility got better, and we were able to increase speed to 4.5 knots, heading towards the Harbor of Refuge. We could steer the boat with the autopilot then. A look up the mast made me shudder. Our navigation lights were all off. I quickly ran to the panel down below to check the breaker box and found the breaker off. I could not reset it. Somewhere, there must have been a short in the line. Back in Texas, when I installed the new navigation lights in the bowsprit, I had left the old ones on the side intact and wired them to a switch in order to have the use of either one or the other set. Turning this switch brought the lights on again, but then we were using the original lights on the sides, which were partially covered by the dinghy. We reached the harbor safely at 4.00 in the morning, dropped the hook and went to bed. When I woke up towards noon, the sun was out. I felt as if I just returned from hell; at least, that is how I imagined it to be. I woke up with a bad headache and felt quite grumpy, not in a mood to do anything. I was, however, curious enough to test the navigation lights. They all worked as usual, and I never did find out the cause of the sudden failure on the trip. Maybe water had shorted out the socket in the normally watertight light on the bowsprit? Or was I just hallucinating at the time I checked it? I was not too concerned about it any longer but kept it in mind to be checked from time to time along the way. We also noticed that our radar reflector, which once had been mounted on the mizzenmast, was gone, blown off the boat. We obviously must have had some strong winds and rain coming our way during the night. Now I understood why our boat had not shown on the radar of the ship we were talking to. Interestingly enough, on the positive side, the fishnet which had attached itself to us was gone. This saved me the job of diving under the boat. Listening to the news later on during the day revealed the circumstances that had made our trip feel as if we were travelling through hell. Over the speaker the modest voice of the local newscaster reported record-breaking rainfalls, 30.5cm (12 inches) in 3 hours!!

Well, the sun was out and we started to put all our clothing on deck in order to get it dried. The boat needed a good cleaning job, particularly the cockpit, in order to remove any smell that would have reminded me of the previous night. We needed a couple of days rest, just to dry out and recuperate, before taking off again. Overnight winds picked up to around 20 knots, and we enjoyed the protection of the harbor.

Early in the morning, a couple of days later, we were ready to take on the next leg of our journey. The sky seemed to be clear and the water fairly choppy. The wind during the night must have caused the sea to be a bit rough. Once out on the Atlantic a nice wind carried us along, and we sailed at 6 knots on course. It was still cold, and we had to wear socks until the sun warmed up the air. At last, sailing was once again something to be enjoyed. I soaked in the nice sunny warmth of the day and tried to forget the past few miles in the Delaware. The children, when on deck, were wearing life jackets and tied to the safety lines running on each side of the deck, front to back. The sea was still rough, and we did not want to take any chances. Later on, during the same day, the waves subsided and, when in the cockpit, we allowed the children to take off their life jackets.

Marcel installed the fishing gear in the back of the boat. It consisted of a 45kg (100-pound) line with a pink-red coloured plastic piece camouflaging the hook. Shortly before supper the fishing line got tight. Marcel rushed to the winch on the mizzenmast and started to control the outgoing line, trying to stop it before the bobbin became empty. He was successful and proceeded to slowly bring the line in again. The fish did not stop fighting, trying hard to get rid of the hook. Marcel had to be careful in his task. How surprised we were when he pulled a very big fish aboard, a full-grown Spanish mackerel! It made a tasty meal and 3 more full family servings were stowed away in the fridge for the next dinners. It was time to prepare the boat for the night journey under sail. The watches were arranged, just as we had done when travelling across the Gulf of Mexico. There was no change in barometric pressure and the night passed uneventfully.

We sailed in open water along the coast and then towards Long Island, New York state. We planned to enter Johns Inlet. As the morning light provided more visibility, in the far distance to the left, we could soon make out the tall buildings of New York, under a clear sky. The sun reflected the light off the large glass towers, like big mirrors. We reached the inlet at ten in the morning. The tide was still in the outgoing phase, and we had to use the full strength of our motor to get up the inlet to quieter waters. We found a spot on the chart that was marked as a designated area to anchor. It was next to the coast guard building. Approaching the spot, however, we found depths of only 2.3m (7.5 feet) and started to worry if we would be able to make it out again, once the tide was all the way out. We called up the coast guard, to find out the depth of the bay that was next to their building, a bay that looked to us like a shallow pool. They confirmed depths of 1.83m (6 feet) at low tide (just enough for our boat) and offered to show us how to approach the entrance. What an excellent service we received here. They came out with their powerboat and showed us the way into the middle of the pool, all at depths of about 2.1m (7 feet). When we explained our visit to this place, they offered us the use of their portable phone to call our relatives. The answering machine was all we got, so we put our visit off for a later time. There were no other boats around, and we felt a bit isolated.

The West End Boat Basin, as it was called, belonged to a big park on Long Island called Johns Beach State Park. It was Sunday morning and the day was just starting to get warm, with a beautiful breeze keeping the temperature in check. We set our anchor and started to get the boat ready for a longer stay. We wanted to see Chäberli's relatives in the nearby town and spend some time visiting New York. First we set out our dinghy to explore the land. We explored the narrow strip separating the inlet from the ocean and enjoyed a short walk along the ocean shore before returning to the boat. In the meantime, a couple of motorboats had come to anchor in the area. I guess they must have wondered about how we could have got there from Vancouver. We enjoyed a great breakfast and set up for a lazy day on the boat. It was amazing to see that slowly more and more motorboats filled the space we were in and, by noon, the whole place was packed with boats anchored all around in the small bay. Many onlookers asked questions, and we felt like an attraction in the middle of a boat show. The park was now filled with city dwellers who had come out for a picnic or to otherwise enjoy the sunny day. We realized that this park was a great weekend attraction.

The first few days out on the water weren't too hard. The weather was not quite as nice anymore. When we anchored the first night, it looked like we were on the moon; the place was practically deserted. We used the washrooms on the beach, cautiously rowing our dinghy in through the rippling water. There was no one to be seen.

When I woke up in the morning the next day, we had already started on our way again. I could tell from the noise of the motor which made sleeping somewhat tricky. I enjoyed lying awake in bed while moving along. I noticed the hatch to the V-berth was covered with little rain drops that had found their way underneath the dinghy. It probably wouldn't be sunny today. I was disappointed, I wasn't a fan of moist bedding. The best thing for me to do was to stay put and daydream. Along the way Mami prepared us some sandwiches and noodle soup. That's when I got up. When I looked out a small porthole, I saw that we were passing through a channel. The rain was getting a bit stronger. I didn't think much of it. At one point the motor stopped, and the boat was put under sail. It was a bit bumpy, and I could now hear the eerie sound of the wind in the rigging. At the side of the boat I could watch the water go by through my porthole, which was just above the water if the boat didn't lean. They could not be opened but gave a good view to the outside. Now one side was immersed in the water, and it looked more like the door of a wash machine.

Soon the motor started up again. The vibration and noise of the boat didn't let me think straight; my thoughts just wandered randomly like leaves in the wind. During this part of the trip, I never had the least idea where we were going. I didn't notice that the passage we were about to do was a difficult one. At one time I approached the cockpit and noticed that Mom and Dad were completely and thoroughly soaked from the rain. There were drops coming down through the dodger covering the wheel. I just turned around and stayed in my little place out in the front of the boat. It moved gently up and down, a little rough at times and then more softly. I must have fallen asleep soon afterwards. Little more of that trip through the Delaware was left in my memory due to the amount of sleeping and vomiting I did. The letter I sent to my brother gave some more details about what was happening during that passage:

"Dear Fabian: We are at the mouth of the Delaware Bay. We left Annapolis three days ago. The second day we went through a very big storm. There was heavy wind against us all the time and the channel was not very wide. Also there were lots of big freighters coming from the front and back. We were not very fast because there was very strong wind and current and our engine was not strong enough. The next day we heard on the radio that it was a record breaking rain fall. Mommy and Daddy found an anchorage in port Cape Henlopen at 4 o'clock in the morning. The storm lasted a whole day. We were very seasick and tired. We actually wanted to go to Cape May. Are you having fun in Switzerland? I am very homesick and I miss you and Thomas very much. Write back soon. P.S. I for surely do not like the boat a bit. Love, Carina"

The stopover in port Cape Henlopen was a welcome one. Our cushions were all moist and smelled rather interesting; we were all glad to set them out in the welcome sun to air and dry. After the boat had dried up, we all took our bedding and spread it all over the deck for a similar air-dry treatment. The next morning we set out to sail on the Atlantic ocean again. At one point I had the urge to relieve myself and decided to try the newly installed toilet hole cut out of the seat at the back of the boat. I'd not given it a try as yet and was unaware of the risks involved when you are out on the open seas. I placed myself over the round cut out and things were going pretty alright, until a large wave from the side splashed up on the boat's starboard side and covered me with a good load of salty water. It came right out of the blue and I was quite startled. I hurriedly, and quite suddenly, finished my business, glad not to have been washed over the side of the boat. From that time forth I did not use the outdoor head any more.

Annapolis had been a real highlight of this trip. The most enjoyable thing was to have a sailing dinghy. I was eager to get that together, and Daddy was lucky to find the missing parts. I helped as much as I could, going back and forth with the rubber dinghy to get parts and tools. It was funny to see Dad drill holes into the bottom of the dinghy with the old hand driven drill he had brought. Once the holes were big enough, he cut a large slot out of the bottom. I wondered if this was ever going to be closed up. Working in the hot sun slowed us down. The walls for the well to fit the centre-board had to be fibre glassed in. That stuff sure smelled terrible. Just like in the boat yards, but, I felt, much stronger. It did, however, look good once it had all been put together. The next day the rudder was mounted and the mast and sail cut and fit. I could hardly wait to try this thing out although it looked a bit weird to me. It wasn't the same as I remembered the little sailboat we had at the farm. Because it had only one sail, the mast was mounted almost all the way to the bow. I had to do a lot of painting. The centre-board and the rudder had to be coated with a clear stain to protect them from the water. Then the whole thing had to sit there for another day to dry. At last the first test-run was under way. Dad and I were sitting on the water, waiting for a slight breeze, but it was dead calm. We could not get any response from the sail. Later in the day some wind blew through the anchorage, and we had the first ride under sail. Some adjustment to the fitting of the sail had to be made, but after that it worked perfectly.

On one of the first trips I took Pascal along and we sailed up and out of the creek. The wind there was a lot stronger and it became quite difficult to keep the boat above the larger waves. We got swamped a few times, and it was a bit scary because it was difficult to turn around and go back into the creek. I was able to manage but we were wet all over. It sure taught me to respect the elements around me a lot more. It was the first time that I had such an experience.

When we left Annapolis I felt sad. We left behind our new friends, and I wanted to stay on longer. Regrettably, however, I was not the one to make the decision. With the weather on the gray side, things were not up-beat for me at all. I was grumpy and did not want to help *in any way. Dad got upset about this when I was below, doing my own thing, when I was supposed to help tie up at the fuel dock. I did not want to help with our departure. Eventually Mom had to get the line across to the dock. The trip continued like that, and the weather turned cloudy and dull. When we reached the Delaware the next day, the weather got worse and the rain started to pour down. It was really bad. I noticed my parents were a bit nervous and Dad was not in a good mood at all. Maybe he still was upset with me? I felt it was better to stay out of the way and climbed below, lying on the port settee, where I eventually fell asleep. I did not know that we were travelling through a very strong rain squall and were in danger of losing our home.*

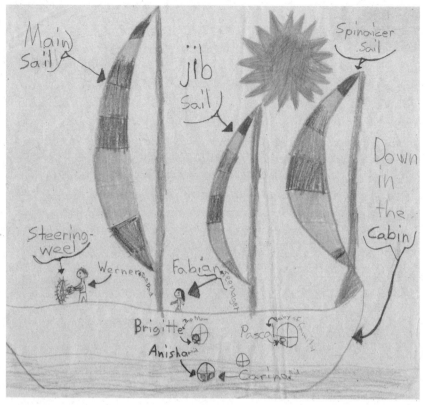

Anisha draws the crew living on a three masted yacht

Long Island

We again tried to get in touch with our relatives, Craig Ash and family, a distant cousin to Chäberli, and were successful. We had not seen each other for a long time. To be exact it was twenty years ago when we had first met them and spent a wonderful time together. We had arrived in New York, from Bremer Haven, on board a freight ship, the Kalinovsky. Chäberli and I had started out on our first long journey together, planning to do a one-year trip through North and South America. Our friendship grew instantly, and we were helped in looking for an affordable car and to get set up for the journey across the USA. It was a great feeling to renew this friendship. Of course the children had all grown to be adults but, in my memories, I could still hear Lois' voice quite well, one of Craig's daughters. She was about age four, when she occasionally hung onto my legs and said "I wove you". With her baby talk she used to bend the "l" to a soft "w". It was great to share our thoughts with them and they again helped us a great deal in getting organized. Craig's son, Hugh, spent considerable time driving us to places. We enjoyed our stay with them tremendously.

There were a few things on my mind that needed to be done on the boat. One battery bank did not seem to hold its charge very well and one of the motor mounts was broken. The vibration of the motor, most probably during the excessive motoring at full speed through the Delaware, must have put too much stress on it and sheared the bolt right off. The nut and part of the bolt were, most likely, in the bilge. All that was left was the bolt, flush with the motor mount.

Because of the sandy surroundings of our anchorage, we had uninvited gnats inside the boat. We would have to organize some more netting. First, however, we were happy to follow up on the invitation to enjoy a great dinner at our relatives' home and only returned to the park late that night. I had not noticed on the way out that there were people at the gate, and they refused to let us enter with the car on our return journey. The park usually closed at sun-set. After some explanations about our unique situation, they agreed to have us dropped off at the boat. At that time of day there were no

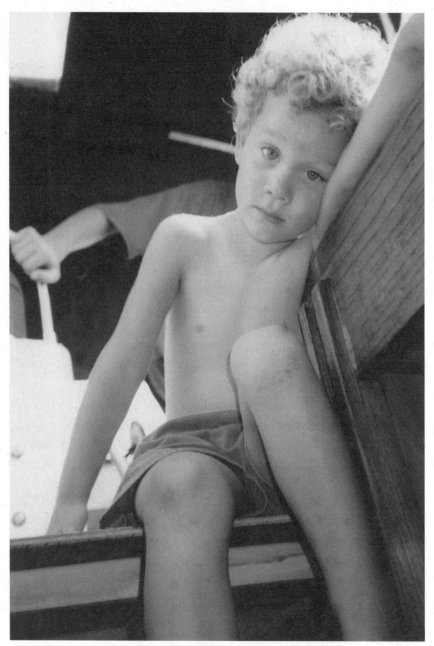

Pascal's legs, covered with gnat bites

problems with gnats or mosquitoes. They seemed to come out only around sunset and sunrise.

We wanted to make a trip to see New York City the next day. This was something the kids were excited about and Hugh had offered to pick us up at 10 a.m. Until then our children had only read stories of the Empire State Building by picking up books at the library. Of course they had seen pictures in journals and brochures too, but it was high time for them to see the real thing.

When going ashore in the morning, we noticed quite a few jellyfish on the wooden pier. They had got washed onto it during the high tide at night. We were picked up at the gate on time and had a quick lift to the nearest train station. From there it took 40 minutes to reach downtown New York. We were quite happy to visit the busy city in this manner, rather than docking at one of the expensive marinas along the Hudson River. There was no cheap alternative such as an area designated for sailboats to anchor. We felt that this was a bit of a drawback and a lack of a necessary service for such a unique and big city. The sight-seeing, however, was fun, and the kids got a good look at the size of the buildings, the traffic and the many busy people in the streets, the latter moving past us in a great hurry. I think the children were a bit disappointed to see that the Empire State building was not the tallest of them all. In spite of that, they enjoyed looking down from the platform of the 442 metre building. Including the TV-tower, it was 787 metres (1449 feet). The time passed quickly and we soon had to catch the train back in order to be picked up again. After shopping for some ready-made food, we all got together at Craig's home and had another great dinner together.

The next day was spent on the boat. We invited Hugh and he stayed for supper. When he wanted to leave, his car would not start, so he slept with us on the boat. In the morning the car seemed to work fine, and we set out to search for a motor mount. I was surprised to find a marine store which had exactly what I was looking for. I thought it was a good time to buy an extra one, as we still had a long way to go. Netting to keep the bugs out was also available there, and brake pads for Marcel's roller blades, which we had brought from Canada, could be bought nearby. We finished all the shopping and went to Craig's home. I promised to repair a few things in their house, after which we had another great supper at a restaurant before being driven back to the boat.

I got up early the next morning to start work on the boat. On a trip ashore, to use the washroom, I came across hundreds of jellyfish which had been washed up on the wooden dock. I remembered having seen a few a couple of days ago but was surprised to see so many again. It did not look inviting at all. I was told that this was normal around this time of the year. Because the park-staff always cleaned the dock early in the morning, I had not noticed it before. The kids put on their roller blades and explored the park. However, this early in the morning, the gnats were still out in full force so they soon returned and decided to plan their activities for later in the day.

Changing the motor mount was not an easy task. The screws holding the mount to the boat's frame were rusted up. I had to undo all of them. Access was very limited. I had to be careful, when using the awkward, hand held propane bottle with its Bunsen burner attached, not to heat nearby wires and pipes. With a lot of patience I managed to undo the two bolts holding the broken mount to the boat. I had to loosen all other mounts in order to lift the motor. Fortunately this required only the loosening of the nuts not the removal of the bolts fastening it to the boat. Our garden tool, the 4-foot iron rod, which had been used to pound out holes for the pole beans back at the farm, came in handy. Wedged under the front of the engine, Marcel levered up the motor to the proper height while I secured it with wooden blocks. Then I could replace the motor mount. Together we lowered the engine onto the new mount. Tightening the nuts was not an easy task at all, working in the confined space and only being able to turn the nut just a bit more than an eighth of a turn each time. A ratchet would not fit into the narrow space between mount and motor, and I just had to learn, one more time, that things had to be done slowly. Once everything was back in place, the mounts had to be adjusted in such a way as to line up the motor shaft with the shaft driving the propeller. Using the filler gauge I could measure the spaces all around the two flanges and make the connection. Once all spaces were equal, I tightened the 4 bolts of the motor mounts, replacing the ordinary nuts with stainless steel 19mm (¾ inch) nuts and using an additional one as a counter lock. By inspecting the old mount I understood why it had broken. The nut had become partially loose, allowing the flange of the motor to cut into the mount's bolt. The vibration of the engine had caused the bolt to become thinner and thinner. Due to the engine's age there must have been a bit more vibration than usual. From then on I checked the nuts holding down the motor after each trip and thus hoped to avoid any further problems.

While I was at it, I checked the oil in the motor as well as the gearbox. The motor had consumed little oil, just like a car, but periodic checking was needed. I also replaced the fuel filters. One of them was the small original one but another, larger and more efficient one, had been installed to make sure that even the dirtiest fuel would be clean enough not to plug up one of the three diesel fuel injectors. These were expensive to buy and not easy to clean. Three small zinc rods had been inserted into the motor's exhaust system to avoid internal corrosion; they were unscrewed and checked. Next came the water filter. It was emptied and particles removed from it. Finally I removed the lid of the water pump to inspect the impeller, a small propeller-like rubber part which pumped the cooling water through the engine block. The heads of the bolts to the lid providing access to the impeller were quite worn. Apparently someone had used the wrong tool to undo them. They were metric ones and I had none in stock. I marked it down to be replaced at a later date. As usual, it was difficult to get at these bolts as the spanner could not be put on all the way. That caused the spanner to slip off and round the corners of the heads of the nuts. The impeller looked fine, so I replaced it and tightened the nuts as much as possible. If the impeller should break, then the pieces of it would become stuck in the cooling channels of the motor and plug them up. That could result in the motor seizing up. I was happy that all the work had gone so well. After replacing all the panels, I turned on the engine to charge the batteries and sat down for a coffee. Having the manual for the engine at hand was a great help and provided vital information for taking proper care of it.

I had to go ashore to make a phone call. I readied the dinghy and started to row toward the shore, taking the usual look back at the boat. I almost screamed when I saw no water coming out the muffler pipe at the back of the boat. Knowing that the engine could quickly overheat, I started to panic, thinking that I must have caused a problem during my work on the engine's cooling system. What could I have overlooked? I turned the dinghy around as quickly as possible. It felt like hours before I was in the cockpit and able to push the shut-off button.

The indicator for the engine heat was at the end of the scale, showing something like 93 degrees Celsius (200 degrees Fahrenheit), certainly not a temperature this engine was used to running at and way more than it should have been. Our lives had depended on this engine while passing through the Delaware and now it was about to overheat. I was quite upset and cursed the engine but at the same moment hoped that the extra heat had not damaged anything. Off came all the panels again and the search for the problem was on. I checked that the zinc rods were still in place, the water pump turning, the belts tight, the hoses and muffler pieces not leaking and that cooling water was in the water filter. It all looked good. I replaced two hoses that looked a bit old but it certainly didn't solve the problem. I started to wonder if I had replaced the impeller inside the water pump the right way round. It had to be checked. Off came the four hard-to-get-at bolts to the lid on the water pump. It wasn't that easy though. Murphy's law was working overtime. During the process of removing the four bolts I had damaged one of them so badly that I could no longer get any purchase on it with the spanner. This was a major impasse. There was nothing in the manual about how to take out such a screw. I had, however, to deal with the problem or the whole boat would be useless. Even when I had the bolt out I was not sure that I would find the problem inside the pump. It was a mechanic's worst nightmare. It was not possible to fit an impound plier or, for that matter, any plier. I had to resort to the last possible means and try the vice grip pliers. Fortunately I managed to fit them onto the rounded head and turned the bolt loose. The bolt was then useless and I had no replacement on board. We called Hugh and, once again, he was very helpful. He gave me a ride so that I could purchase the necessary parts. Back at the boat I pulled out the manual for the motor to confirm that the impeller had been properly installed; it had been.

This had become a real nightmare. I must have cursed the motor several times but that did not help. In all the stories I had read about sailing, the writers had never mentioned the frustration of trying to fix things on board a boat. I felt as if I was the only one with such problems. Once more I had to learn to accept the facts and take it from there. Looking back, it certainly was not the worst thing that had happened on our trip, the engine had always worked well when we really had to depend on it.

I had nothing left to check but the water inlet...again. What I had omitted to check, in the first place, was the "proper" inflow of water. Enough water had flowed in to fill the glass of the water filter. From this I deduced that the water was flowing freely. This was not the case. When I tried to suck on the inlet pipe, only a dribble of water came through. It was obvious that something was blocking up the supply from the outside. I put on my swimsuit and dove down to the intake in order to see what was really causing all the troubles. With all the jellyfish around it was not the most inviting proposal but it had to be done. When I reached the intake I couldn't believe what I saw. There were a lot of jellyfish around and one large one had been sucked right into the screened intake of the water line. Removing it from the outside would have been way too difficult. First of all I did not want to touch the thing and, secondly, it was difficult to keep my body in position under water. Looking at the jellyfish, through the sandy water, I was reasonably sure that it was dead. I climbed aboard and rigged a hose to the pump that had come with the rubber dinghy. I made the other end secure to the pipe from the water inlet. By pumping vigorously I was able to build up enough pressure to "back wash" the obstruction out of the pipe. I was both relieved and exhausted at the same time. Troubleshooting had never seemed to be so intense. The confined work space, poor lightning, marginal access to the parts and the constant moving of the boat had not helped either. Once everything was back in its place the engine started fine. On my next trip to the phone booth I was delighted to see the water coming out of the muffler.

There were no further problems, and I continued to charge the batteries. One of the two battery banks did not hold the charge very well. By constantly topping it up I thought that its performance might improve. I wished that I had installed solar panels. By the time we were finished, it was late afternoon and Hugh stayed for supper before driving back home. He took the two girls, Anisha and Carina along with him. They enjoyed sleeping in a house but, even more so, being able to watch TV and movies, of which there were plenty.

With today's experience still in my mind, I thought of installing a warning system, which would give off an alarm if the motor temperature went higher than usual. The solution was a small and not very expensive gadget found while browsing in a Radio Shack (an electronics store). It was a thermometer that could be set to give off an audible alarm at a given temperature. It came with a 2.5m (8 foot) cable wired to a remote heat-sensor. It looked like the perfect solution and, once installed, worked just fine. I wondered why I had not done this before. Just as with the new anchor, it gave peace of mind and at a reasonable cost.

During the weekdays very few boats came out our way, and we had the place all to ourselves. On Sundays, however, the little pool was packed. I stayed on the boat while the others went for a visit. I needed to look after the batteries, topping them up with distilled water and recharging them. Having the fridge running and one of the battery banks losing its charge, we needed to run the engine every second day for about 2 hours to top up the batteries. Fortunately, this was easily done and the voltages on the banks could be checked with an instrument which had been installed in the breaker panel. We tried not to discharge the batteries to less than 70%. Lead batteries like to be frequently topped up, as in a car. We tried to achieve this, but it was not always easy to do. I often wished that we had installed solar panels. During our stay in Annapolis several boaters had recommended that we buy a wind generator. There was usually more wind than sun. Oddly enough this had never occurred to me, but it certainly made sense. I checked the pricing of wind generators and it looked as if we could set it all up for about US $1000. The only obstacle would be generating these funds.

One more thing had to be checked before we could move on. The autopilot had stopped working on a couple of occasions. It was made by Benmar, and we had not previously had any problems with it. I wondered if salt water had reached the electronics board during the rough passage in the Delaware. This board was located in the back, under our berth and a food storage bin. The space under the berth had been partitioned into two layers, separated with plywood. The top part contained food only, and it was packed full of bags and small items such as pasta, sugar, cans and anything we wanted to keep dry. The lower, smaller space had most of the spare parts such as hoses, cables, stainless steel rods, muffler hoses, parts to the motor, connectors and so on. After some rearranging of things I managed to undo the bolts holding the electronics board and remove it. There was a relay on the board, which had to switch on and off each time a course correction was needed. I suspected it to be the problem and found that the two contact surfaces, due to wear and tear, were barely touching each other. I bent the necessary parts to adjust for more contact pressure and tested it out. It seemed to work fine, and I was certain that I had solved the problem. We were ready to set off.

The whole crew was at the boat pier and, with two dinghy trips, we were able to transport all the stuff, such as freshly washed bedding, last minute shopping and ourselves onto the boat. Everybody seemed rather fidgety, and we were keen to say good-bye more quickly than we really wanted to. It was early in the morning, and the mosquitoes were so bad that we had no other choice. We were very happy to have met our relatives again and very thankful for all their help.

After the disappointment that was caused by leaving Annapolis and enduring a shake-up trip through the Delaware things brightened up when we sailed out on the open ocean. It had been some time since we had last done that. This time was quite different. For the first time I rigged the fishing line we had bought in Annapolis. It was a 45kg (100lb) line with a hook on it almost the size of my hand! We did not have any kind of rod to hold back such a heavy line, so I used the winch on the mizzen mast. It was only needed to set the sail and we did not use the mizzen sail on this stretch. I set up the line so it would go from the 46m (150 feet) bobbin around the winch 2 times and then out the back. Should a fish bite, I would hear the ratchet of the winch. If fast enough, I could hold back the line before it would be all the way out. For some time there was no sign of a fish, and I relaxed on the bench in the back. What excitement when the winch started to turn quickly. I jumped up from my comfortable position and grabbed the bobbin. There was still plenty line on it, and I slowed down the speed at which it was paying out. There was a

good pull on it, and from time to time I let out some more line to give the fish some extra room to tire out in. Then I started to pull the line in slowly. It was not too easy, as suddenly there were some jerky movements that messed up my control and caused the line get stuck on parts of the boat. After some time I got the fish right next to the boat. By then Daddy was next to me and he helped me pull it up. We put the fish on the deck, in the back, and killed it by pouring some very strong rum over its head and mouth. It died immediately. This made me feel better, I was not happy to see the fish jerking around on the deck and stayed well back from it, still holding the line. Daddy then released the hook and asked me to hold the fish to take a picture. I looked at him with a blank face. I should hold the fish? I had never touched a fish and was afraid to do so now. The thought of touching

The first big fish.

the slimy surface was more than I could bear. Eventually Daddy convinced me to show off and a picture with me holding the fish was taken. The meat certainly tasted very good, and I was certain to fish again.

Long Island was a nice place to stay. The most inviting part was the ability to stay in a house and have showers that lasted forever. I was glad to have relatives there. I enjoyed that and also the fact that we could use their TV and watch movies all day long. Outside we sometimes played "Indians", preparing flour with ground up acorns and berries that we had taken from some nearby decorative bushes. Then we pretended to eat it all.

Craig was a collector of things to do with trains, and he had a very beautiful train set. I was so disappointed to know that we could not use it, as it was a very rare item and as such had to be looked after very carefully. The very good food and the pleasant stay, however, more than made up for that. I was also looking forward to going to New York. Other than Vancouver I hadn't really seen a very large city and New York would, for me, be something magical.

We arrived in the big City by underground train. The hustle and bustle in the metro was something I had never seen. Soooooo many people in one and the same spot. It felt crazy. Where were they all going? After some very long escalators we reached the daylight and I watched all the cars going past. I noticed the yellow taxis. They were everywhere, just like there were people all around. What a busy place. The most exciting moment was when we stepped into the lift to go up in the Empire State Building. First of all we had to stay in line for quite some time and this made me get a bit restless. Finally it was our turn. Magically the elevator's door closed. Then I felt how the weight of my body pushed my feet to the ground, my knees taking on extra weight. I had never had that feeling before. Then we came to a halt with a feeling of taking off the ground. We were on top of the building. Everything in the city below looked like toys or even smaller. I could not believe my eyes. All around, the tall buildings looked like stacked up Lego blocks. Mom pointed to some of the very tall ones and told us their names but I forgot them all.

On The Boat

Ref: Six feet on the deck and six feet below
Was all the room there was for each of us to grow (2x)

1. The V-berth where the front waves made the curls
Was shared by the two girls
The aft berth had double beds
For mom and dad, to rest their heads
(ref:)

2. The little guy lie across above their feet
On a cushioned, plywood sheet
The berth in the saloon to port
Was the first mates, little fort
(ref:)

3. The masts were reaching high and dry
For us they almost, touched the sky
The tanbark sails, which curved in the wind
Made the boat move, if all was well trimmed
(ref:)

4. The skipper sitting on the bench in the back
Made sure the sails did not have any slack
Sometimes a smell of fresh bread reached the nose
We all liked the smells, such as those
(ref:)

(Voice and Guitar by Werner M. Gysi)

A CD with colour pictures and songs can be ordered.

New York From The Water, A Turnaround

We wanted to anchor the boat as close to New York as possible so that we would be able to make a trip up the Hudson River the following day. We decided to stop over in Sheep's Head Bay. The weather was not good; visibility was limited by fog. It was with great difficulty that we found our way out of our anchorage, by crawling from marker to marker. We did manage to motor out to sea, and set sail towards New York. The ride was rough and cold. Chäberli felt a bit seasick, but we soon reached the harbor and a place to anchor. In the evening the winds strengthened and we were glad to be in a protected place. The following day was not much better, so the trip was delayed in order to wait out the bad weather.

We left the following morning, at about 8:30 a.m. Two hours later we motored under the huge Verezano Bridge which crosses the Hudson. It was a great feeling to see the tall buildings from this perspective. The sounds of the city were quite muted, except for the occasional sound of a siren. There were no people rushing past us. The city looked as if everything had come to a standstill, glued into position. The tall buildings looked like masts on a huge sailboat. On the other side of us stood the Statue of Liberty and we set our course towards the "old lady". It was a great feeling, to come up to it in our own little sailboat, cruising at our own pace and enjoying the sunny day. Several other boats passed us and some of the crews waved back with friendly gestures. It was great to have the galley a few steps away and be able to come up with a cup of coffee to enjoy the moment.

We had gone as far north as we had planned to go. There was no longer the need to escape from hurricanes, and it was time to think of returning to Annapolis, to escape the cold. It was hard to make such plans while sailing past these huge buildings, representing part of our culture. I wished that we could have explored further up the river. It was definitely a nice tour, for which others would have had to cram onto a tour boat. Our return trip was quite a landmark. Something I still have very vividly in my mind. We pulled up the sails, while still motoring into the wind, turned the boat to pick up the wind, shut down the motor and had a fast sail down the river. Our hair was not getting blown back as is usually the case, and we could hardly feel the following wind. The sun was warming up the deck, and the gentle waves on the river rocked us at a loving pace. We were on our way south again. No motor noise, just the splashes of the boat, gliding through the water. A few more pictures were taken of the monumental City of New York, before we sailed into the open waters of the Atlantic again, leaving all the glamour behind. The wind stayed almost behind us, and we made good way, sailing into a wonderfully clear night. The barometer stayed steady and we had nothing to worry about. Our destination was Cape May Harbor, which we had tried to reach on our way up.

It was already daytime when we approached the entrance of Cape May Inlet. The harbor had a lot of shallow spots, and we were eager to fill up with fuel and water while the tide was still rising. We did not want to run aground during a receding tide. All went well and we found a nice spot to anchor in and chatted with some of the other sailors in the anchorage before retiring. We wanted to make sure to pass through the Delaware quickly on the coming day. We had plenty of respect for this type of passage. This time the weather forecast seemed to be on our side, sunny and warm.

The tide turned at about 6 a.m., and we wanted to take advantage of the incoming tide. Winds came from the side, and we were able to sail quickly up the river. From time to time we used the motor to get some extra speed and also to recharge the batteries. It was amazing to manage our departure from the Delaware by 2 p.m. and enter the C&C canal. We reached Betterton, the same anchorage as on the way up, shortly before 7 p.m. What a successful day this had been. It had confirmed that good weather planning was a must for trips such as these. The anchorage provided a public beach, and we went ashore in order to use the public washrooms.

The next day we started out, under sail, and arrived, still under sail, in Annapolis at 3 p.m. Sailing was just one way to spend such beautiful days. Sun, wind, travelling and at the same time being at home was really all I longed for. We were very happy crewing together, like a top notch team. We respected each other and lived together without difficulty. The kids could always find something to do; homework was the last resort, if at all. The kids knew where we were heading.

They longed to be back in Annapolis and sincerely hoped that their friends would still be there. The spot in the anchorage, which we had used during our last visit, was taken up by a boat from South Africa. While we were looking for a new spot, the children eagerly searched the place to find Cool Change. They were very disappointed not to see the boat in the anchorage, but a lot of new boats had since come to stay here. Suddenly, we spotted some one waving at us from the boat yard and our children brightened up. They saw Cool Change, hanging in the travel lift over at the marina, with the two kids standing close by. They were just in the process of putting the boat back into the water. In no time the dinghy was launched and off went our kids to see their friends. I got the bicycle ready and, later, we joined up with the others at the marina.

For the first time our kids worked for a full morning at their schoolwork. They knew that the other kids were doing the same and that, in the afternoon, they would be free to join them at play. It was a good incentive which I appreciated. The parents of the couple that owned the boat from South Africa, called Aquila, were from Switzerland. The crew could not speak Swiss German but, nonetheless, we became good friends. They had three boys on board and now the kids had plenty of comrades to play with. Once in a while the crew from all 3 boats, 9 children and 6 adults, got together on our boat and everyone had fun over a great spaghetti dinner. Later in the evening, the children would leave with the dinghies to play in the park at the nearby marina. Looking back I realize that it was very kind of the marina owners to be so tolerant towards us boaters, and there was never a complaint from any other boaters in the marina. In general, there was a great affection among sailors, and I found Annapolis a pleasant place to be.

September arrived and we thought of Thomas' upcoming birthday. He had just started the last year of his apprenticeship as a precision mechanic in Switzerland. His aim was to study at HTL (Höhere Technische Lehranstalt), to get a bachelor degree as a software engineer. We often thought about him and looked forward seeing him soon in Switzerland. Our trip across the Atlantic was coming closer. We all understood that we would be out on the water for a longer time than usual but, by then, were able to accept that. A routine pattern had been established on the boat; the children did their homework in the morning in order to be able to play with the others in the afternoon. Most evenings we all got together on one of the boats to have supper. It was a great time.

A boat from California, Stardust, had an owner with a nice sailing dinghy. One evening there was just the right breeze blowing through the anchorage. We came together to have a dinghy race. It was great fun. I lost most of the runs but, when Marcel joined one of the runs with me, he won. It was obvious that our dinghy did not go on the wind so well. I was sailing the faster dinghy to start with but Marcel still won. What a happy kid he was, and it showed that, if he wanted to do something, he would put his heart into it. It was not a disappointment to lose a race, with the four children around. Seeing Marcel cheered up like this made me feel a winner too. What a lovely time to spend with the kids. The weather turned rainy, and we spent a day visiting the Naval Academy located in Annapolis. They had a nice exhibition about their history, and it was a day well spent.

A week passed and our hope of finding some casual work began to bear fruit. For the next few weeks I helped on some projects, renovating houses. Chäberli was helped by getting boats ready for and during the boat show. With extra funds available, we were able to buy another anchor and to set aside the money for either solar panels or a wind generator. I was not yet sure which way to go. We were happy to be able to finally add the equipment we felt necessary. However, with our savings so low, we waited to buy anything, other than the essentials, until such a time as we knew we could afford it. The main additional expense was to get a second heavy anchor, a 23kg (50lb) Delta. We had thought to get a CQR anchor, which was highly recommended, but we could not find one reasonably priced. It later turned out that the Delta anchor had been an excellent buy.

The crew from Cool Change told me that the public libraries had computers which could be used, at no cost, to surf the Web. At that time it was a rather unique service, and I was interested in having an e-mail address. They showed me how it worked and an account was soon set up. I was intrigued and, slowly, started to build a homepage on one of the many free Internet sites. Sometimes the use of the computer was limited to half an hour, if others were waiting. But I had learned one thing: there was no rush, we just had to remember to plan things in small steps.

The weather turned colder, and a visit to the Goodwill store, a second hand clothing store, was more than overdue. We bought much needed, very reasonably priced, warm clothing and shoes. There were no funds available for expensive boat shoes. The ones we had bought in Texas had long since worn out.

October 17th, Anisha's 13th birthday arrived. Everyone was busy getting ready and the kids organized the decorating of the gazebo located in the nearby park. It was an excellent day, even though the weather was on the rainy side. They had a great time playing games together - some suggested by the adults, such as the egg and spoon race, the three-legged race and who could stand on one leg the longest. The birthday cake, of course, had not been forgotten. It was great to celebrate this occasion with all the other kids.

As the end of our stay drew closer, we made a trip to Buddies, an inexpensive restaurant where you can eat as much pizza as you like. The kids enjoyed the chocolate pizza as a dessert. We came out the door stuffed with pizza after we had paid our bill of only $36. Not expensive, if you think of how much we had eaten and drunk. The kids summed it up like this: "It was great, but we like Mr. Mikes (a small restaurant chain in B. C., Canada) better". I didn't want to say anything about how much healthier, and better, it would have tasted if we had been able to raid the garden, as we had done so often when living on the farm.

Friends we made during our first visit, who lived in one of the apartment buildings near

Anisha's birthday party under way

the anchorage, invited us to use the visitor's dock for the last week of our stay, an offer we gladly accepted. We could hook up to the electricity and did not have to run the engine to charge the batteries. Marcel could use his computer as long as he wanted to play games and took that opportunity as often as possible. In the meantime Aquila had been put on dry dock in order to check the bottom. They were busy sanding the whole day and found some spots with osmosis, a problem common to fibreglass boats. The children played with each other a lot outside, enjoying the convenience of being able to step ashore without using a dinghy.

One day, while berthed alongside the dock, I was working in the back of the boat, putting things into the lazarette, the hatch in the back of the boat that was accessible from the outside. There was quite some space available in that locker which also gave access to the rudder post and the ram pushing the rudder. Most of our garden tools had found a place in there, as well as the rudder, centerboard and oars belonging to the sailing dinghy. While rearranging the space, I suddenly heard Carina screaming, as if someone had hit her. I jumped up to see what had happened. She gasped, "Pascal fell into the water!!!!!" I looked at her in disbelief for a second and quickly asked her where. With her hand she pointed between the boat and the pier and I immediately ran to the spot to see if I could see anything. All appeared to be normal. The water's surface always had a gray, murky look and it was impossible to see very much through it. No bubbles were coming up. A few seconds must have passed that felt like an eternity before Pascal's head surfaced. With a quick move I reached down, grabbed his winter jacket and held on to him. I didn't know if he was breathing, but I could not hear any sounds coming from him. Bracing myself so as not to fall into the water myself, I had to use all my strength in order to pull him onto the boat. Water was pouring from his clothes. With his winter boots filled with water and all his wet clothes he weighed a lot more than usual. As he started to realize what had happened he began to cry. I was relieved to hear his voice, a sign that he was OK. He was upset. There was no time to say anything. We had to quickly get him undressed and changed into dry clothes. Below deck we covered him with some extra blankets. The water he had just been in was cold, and he needed to get warmed up again. Carina joined us and explained how it had all happened.

Pascal had wanted to leave the boat to go and play. While stepping ashore he missed the dock and fell between the boat and the pier. I was relieved that the rescue had gone so well! Thanks to the construction of the boat, having the centre part fairly close to the water, I had been able to bend down enough to grab Pascal, otherwise I would have had to jump into the cold water myself. We were all ready to take a longer than usual, relaxing break over some tea and coffee.

I was excited to be back in Annapolis, especially for my birthday. This was an exceptionally special birthday for me. Not only was I going to be a teenager, but it would be my first birthday away from home. In all of our previous travels, we had always made it back home before my birthday came around, or left afterwards. A party was planned, with all of our friends. It was to be in the park with the tall water tower. I was afraid of that tower, I wasn't sure if it would just collapse and spill water all over us. I must have got that notion from a movie that I had watched with the boys in Galveston. No matter where I got it from, it was a real fear. Below the tower, set off to one side and in the forest, there was a little gazebo with a nice blue roof and a rough wooden framework. In the centre there was a heavy masonry table made of marble or some such material. It was barely visible from the boat, as the trees covered up most of the view, and this made it almost secretive and cozy. I soon got over the water tower.

By the time the party came around, Carina and I had gotten somewhat of a crush on one of the boys from Aquila. He was my age, and all of us kids had played many a game together in the marina, playing tag and whatnot. It was one of my most memorable birthdays. I wore a bright yellow sweater, and was very psyched for the games. The weather wasn't as sunny as I'd hoped, with the odd sprinkle of rain, but that didn't really matter. Mom had made a birthday cake for me in the oven aboard our boat. It was not big enough to fit my whole name across it, but had Ani-sha fitted on to it, in two lines. That didn't do anything to the taste, though, and everybody was having fun. We played some games, like the egg and spoon race, a three-legged race, and my favourite one (I won) in which we had to stand on one leg as long as possible, the last one standing being the winner. Dad made that one up.

I can't remember all of the presents I got, but I do remember the one from the skipper on the boat, St. Meloris. She gave me a really nice little "hippy pouch" which I could hang around my neck. I proceeded to wear it almost all the time. In it I carried any bit of change I had, and the femo dolphin I had made with her on board St. Meloris (femo is a material with similar characteristics to clay). I still have it hung up in my room. The boy I had a crush on gave me $10, which was a lot of money for me. We didn't get a lot of pop on the boat so most of the $10 went to cans of coke, bought from the pop machine, by the pool in the marina.

I was a very sad girl when we left Annapolis. I had made many good friends there among the kids from the other boats. I was especially sad to leave the kids from Aquila, they'd been tons of fun to hang out with and play with. We did a lot of different things together: playing on the computer, games of tag, and once we even got to watch a movie called Batman, which was pretty scary. Their boat was bigger than ours so we usually went over there.

They had sailed all the way from South Africa to this region. I didn't really know where that was so I checked my atlas, which I'd received from my grandparents, to find out. I thought we'd come from a long ways away, but South Africa was even farther. They told stories about their travels, showing us pictures of where they'd been and of their home too, it looked pretty dry to me. I remembered our place and shared my experiences on the farm with them, and particularly about my dog. I still missed his company a lot. The stuffed animals, no matter how many I had, did not make up for the friendship I had with Jeffro. I was glad to share my memories with the other children, who had become our very good friends. Before we left, my parents and the Aquila boat parents exchanged plans with each other to meet up again around Thanksgiving, in Vandemere, North Carolina. I had no clue where that was or how long it would take to get there. I wasn't even interested in the details. It was good enough for me to know that we would, eventually, see them again.

Washington

When looking at the map I found out that we actually had to sail a fair bit south in order to reach the entrance to the Potomac River leading to Washington D.C. in the northwest. We could have driven there from Annapolis in less than two hours, but we had good reasons to visit Washington for more than just a day or two. There were plenty of museums to visit, all offering free admission. Big cities are notorious for finding a spot to park a car and not cheap to stay in, overnight, with a family of six. Reason enough to bring along our own house!

Leaving the pier took little effort, as there was no anchor chain to pull up and clean. Saying goodbye to our friends was, however, more difficult. The crews of Aquila and Cool Change promised to line up a get-together further south, in Vandemere, North Carolina. It is a small village, north of Oriental. We had to be helped to find it on our chart and saw that we had no detailed chart for the approaches to that area. With some additional information from the crew of Aquila, who had been there before to visit friends, we were better prepared. We promised that, if everything went well, we would be there before the 27th of November, to celebrate Thanksgiving.

It was convenient, but an odd feeling to step just onto the boat and leave. We were so used to pulling up the anchor first! At 9:30 all the lines were taken off, except the one in the back. Our friends waved goodbye, wished us a hand's width of water under the keel and threw the last line to send us off. We covered the 40 nautical miles to Solomons Island in about 9 hours. It was already starting to get dark when we arrived. We were getting very hungry but were soon enjoying a good supper. While we were eating I noticed that the neighbour's boat was fairly close to ours. I watched this for a while, and it seemed that he had a lot more anchor line out than we had. Because of this his boat swung in a wide arc. We had to pull up the hook and anchor further away. The night brought some strong winds and rain, which continued into the morning.

We stayed put for the day and left to enter the Potomac River the next morning. We followed it, about a third of the way up, to arrive at Breton Bay before nightfall. Rising at 7 a.m. the next morning, we continued upstream, under sunny skies. Soon the wind picked up and, suddenly, we were in very choppy water, with gusts of 30 knots from the North-Northwest against us. Our engine was pushing as hard as it could but we could make little headway. Down below the crew was trying to bake some bread. Carina was hard at it, trying to get the dough kneaded. It was no easy task but she did manage. Four hours later, having covered only about 25km (13 nautical miles), we decided to enter the Wicomico River to get some shelter near Rock Point. It was a good place to wait it out, with only small waves and a light wind. The land protected us nicely. Chäberli was reading "Maiden Voyage", the story of a young girl sailing around the world. I played some games with the kids, one of them called "Eile mit Weile". It comes from the German and means "Hurrying with patience" or "More haste, less speed", a skill we had often required on our trip. The next leg brought us to Mattawoman creek, a nice and quiet anchorage and only about 23 nautical miles away from Washington.

It had taken us 6 days to travel from Annapolis to Washington by boat, certainly not what could be called "moving in the fast lane." One obstacle for most boaters was the bridge, just before Washington, which has a height of a bit more than 15 metres (50 feet). Because our boat was a ketch, the masts were not very tall. At 14.9 metres (49 feet) we fitted under this bridge quite nicely. Others had to wait till 10 p.m., when the bridge would open. In Washington we topped up our fuel tank and then chose a nice spot near the Gang Plank Marina. In the near distance we could see the downtown area of Washington. We were right in the centre of the activity. A fee of $25.00 gave us access to the marina's utilities for a week. We were all looking forward to enjoying a shower. Fall had taken us by surprise and now, with colder temperatures and more rain, none of us felt like taking a shower on deck. We then did some grocery shopping, to replenish our supply of fresh fruits and vegetables.

It was the last day of October before we made our first visit to a museum in Washington. It was the Air and Space museum, which attracted Marcel and me the most. The girls enjoyed the I-MAX movie and the Star Wars section. It was Halloween and in the evening the kids wanted to get ready to do a tour for "trick and treat". It meant that we had to leave the museum a bit earlier. As soon as it got dark, the children put on their home made masks and checked out all the boaters in the marina. When they came back it looked and sounded as if they'd had a great time. In spite of the continuous rain the next day, we took a 30-minute walk to the National Museum of Natural History. This was one of the highlights for all of us. We all found something of interest, but we could not see all of it in one day. From insects to rhinos to gems, it was all there and very illustrative. We decided to continue our visit the following day.

We next went to the National Museum of American History. The museum fills 3 large floors and tells everything about the history of America, such as agriculture, transport, science, energy, music, etc., and of course about the Revolution and later development in the 17th and 18th centuries. The girls found it a bit boring, but there was a section about American Maritime Enterprise that generated some interest. There were also some hands-on sections which were a bit more appealing.

We were lucky to get a nice sunny day to visit the zoo. We had to use the subway to get there. It was overwhelming for me to see such a great zoo. Monkeys were the main attraction and they had a large area set aside for them to play around in. There were a couple of cables, spaced slightly apart and hanging over the walkway leading to another section of their run. With apprehension we could enjoy watching one of the orangutans hang on to these cables while pulling itself across. He looked as if he would fall at any moment but managed to hold on with his tail or hands while, at the same time, making a lot of funny faces and swift movements. What a wonderful experience and a great exercise for our face muscles as they were being used to their full extent!

There were more museums to be seen, such as the African Art Museum, the Arts and Industry Museum, Saeckler Museum, Hirschhorn Museum, etc. There was not much enthusiasm shown by the kids to look at art so the visits were brief. I, however, spent quite some time looking at the marble sculptures, some of them just stunning in quality and craftsmanship. Having done some sculpting myself, using marble, I was overwhelmed by the beauty of these figures. One in particular caught my interest, showing a veil covering a face. It looked so real but was all carved out of rock.

The whole family spent some time inside the Capitol Building and, for a short while, listened to a debate in session. I visited the Holocaust museum. I did not think it would have been right to have visited it with the children. Another day, Marcel and I took the metro to visit the News Museum, while the rest of the family went to see the White House, then the mint. At the mint they print about $440 million in new dollar bills every day, to keep up with the ones taken out of circulation. From there they visited the Washington Monument, an obelisk-like structure finished in 1888, and took the elevator up to the top. They enjoyed an excellent view over the city before returning to the boat.

The weather turned really ugly, making life on a boat somewhat uncomfortable. We did not have a heater, so it was fairly difficult to keep things dry. In the morning Anisha served us breakfast in the bed. We decided to wait another day before continuing our trip southward. We had seen enough museums and were then more interested in staying dry. In the evening the last purchases were made to stock-up on, and the boat was made ship-shape and ready to leave. The dinghy was, once more, securely stowed on deck.

Still a gray sky and cold was my report, when Chäberli asked me how it looked outside. We decided to leave anyway and motored out of the anchorage. To our relief the wind was blowing from the back and was strong enough to allow us to turn the engine off. The motorbike rain gear I had used the previous day was still wet. When I put on the yellow pants, designed for such weather, I found them rather uncomfortable, and they were a bit clumsy to move around in.

The hatches constantly fogged up with condensation and so did the wooden ceilings, as well as spots along the walls that had no insulation. They all had to be dried off once in a while with a towel. We covered about 86km (45 nautical miles) before anchoring. During the night the winds were strong, but our boat stayed nicely in its spot. Pascal had caught a cold and then developed a fever. The next day continued at the same pace, with the wind still nicely from the back. With the current of the river with us, the GPS revealed speeds of up to 8.4 knots. We had never sailed that fast and it came as

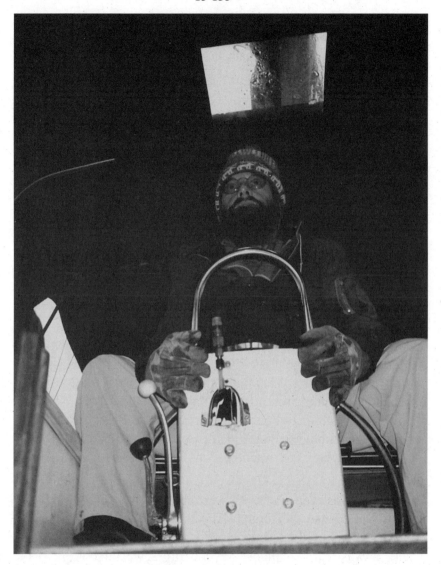

Cold weather rain gear

a bit of a surprise. The inside of the boat continued to stay damp and cleaning off the condensation became a major occupation.

Four days after leaving Washington we arrived in Hampton, on Nov. 11th. This was the place where we had sold our van a few months earlier. Pascal had recovered. With the lousy weather our aim was to hurry south. I visited the library to check our e-mails. Propane for the cook stove had to be filled up and our clothes washed and dried!! I unloaded the bicycle, in order to take a trip to a store to buy a new starter battery for the boat. The old one no longer held a charge and, when banked in parallel, caused the others to drain.

In the morning the temperature inside the boat was just below 12 degrees Celsius (53 degrees Fahrenheit). We switched on the baking oven in order to warm up the inside of the boat. Pizza was on the menu for lunch and that warmed the boat up a bit. We reached a high of about 16 degrees Celsius. During the night the wind was strong again. Finally the day to do our last shopping arrived. We took the bus to town and, on our way back, got on the one heading in the wrong direction, out of town. It took us quite a bit longer to get to where we wanted but we were all together and did not mind sitting in the warm bus for an hour, knowing quite well that the boat was not heated at all.

We set off at daybreak, keen to hurry south. We passed all the now-familiar places such as Norfolk, with its military base of submarines and very large carriers. We also encountered many opening bridges and a lock. It all felt quite routine. By then we were used to all that and the crew knew exactly what to do. No signs of nervousness anymore. What made the trip most pleasurable was the fact that the sun shone for the whole day. We could leave the hatches open and dry out most of our things, as well as the boat itself. In the evening we anchored at Pungo Ferry. Another boat had followed us for the whole day and anchored in the same area as we were anchored.

The next leg was even better. We were able to set sail in the canal and seldom had to use the motor. At about mile 60, counting from Norfolk, we diverted from the canal into a small bay, called Broad Creek. It was a tricky place. Several times we hit bottom while looking for a place to drop the anchor but always managed to motor through the mud or whatever had held us back and, eventually, dropped the anchor. The sun was out for the whole day again and made for another very pleasant trip. Below deck, however, it never warmed up above 14 degrees Celsius (57 degrees Fahrenheit).

Wearing all the clothes we had was the only way to fight the cold weather. Ice had formed on the deck of the boat. We left Broad Creek and were under sail for most of the time, while crossing Albemarle

Sound. Only at the Alligator River Bridge did we have to use the motor to make sure that we did not wander off course. Even worse would have been colliding with the pillars of the bridge. The wind shade of the bridge would have caused the boat to slow down and steering it would have become difficult. The sun was out for the full day again but it was cold. We stopped at mile 104. The same 4 boats were anchored with us as the night before. It looked as if we were a team, all with the one aim, trying to escape the cold.

Once again ice formed on deck over night. There was fog ahead, as well as along the landmass which the channel was leading to. In spite of this we set off again, the desire for warmer regions quite compelling. I carefully measured the markers ahead, from the chart, and programmed them into the GPS. When we hit the fog we would have to completely rely on the accuracy of the chart and the GPS. The water was absolutely flat. The chart indicated that most of the right outside edge of the dredged channel had a depth of 6' so there was nothing to worry about if we left the channel by mistake. Quickly the other boats at anchor followed behind us. Once in the fog we could hardly see them. However, as soon as we came closer to the shore, the fog lifted and the channel could then be seen perfectly well. Winds were mostly from the front, and we had to motor the whole stretch to mile 155. Moonglow, one of the other boats, stayed with us until we reached there.

Over land we were only about 7 miles away from Vandemere. In the evening we tried to call Aquila over the radio, hoping that they had already arrived. There was no response, so we just left the radio set to channel 16, in case they should try to call us. A bit later the voice of one of the kids from Aquila could be clearly heard, blasting from the radio. Suddenly our kids were all over the station, like a swarm of bees, each eager to call back. Excitement was clearly written on their faces.

The following day we were eager to leave the anchorage and join up with the others. It took us about 2 hours to do the last leg. We were met by some of the crew of Aquila, in a motorboat. They pulled alongside and our kids jumped into the boat. We followed in the path of the motorboat, which slowly put-putted ahead of us, towards Vandemere and its marina. The town had been hit by hurricane Fran the previous year and all the piers were a bit twisted and out of shape. Nonetheless, it was great to park the boat in a slip, or what was left of it, and step ashore. The bowsprit of the boat reached the pier where the planks were still attached to the rest of the structure. That was where we could climb on and off the boat. There was even a power hook-up and we were received with a very warm welcome.

It was really nice to meet my cousins Yvonne and Al again in Annapolis. Yvonne is my mother's sister's daughter. I hadn't seen them for a long time. When I was 17 I spent a year with them in Manhattan, New York. Then they had a 3 year old girl, Viviane and a little boy, David, who was born when I was there. That's where I had learned my first English. They came out to see us in Annapolis, in the little park by the water where we were anchored. They brought a car for our use. When it was time for us to leave after our first stay, David came along with his wife, Monica. The children had a very good time with her, she went out with them to buy some games and then played with them.

With the car we were able to drive to Rockville for an excellent meal, and there we met Viviane who I had not seen since I was 17. We got a super present from them, a World atlas. Then we could do some world geography and see all the places we had been and still wanted to go to. On our second stay in Annapolis, they came out again to visit, and we had a good picnic together in the park. Viviane and her friend were brave enough to come out to the boat with the dinghy. Later, when we were anchored in Washington D. C., Yvonne and Al came out again to say good bye. They invited us to go eat in a first-class Restaurant, to enjoy seafood by the water. It was a buffet and we had never seen so many different foods. For the children and us it was a wonderful meal.

Because we did not have too much money to spend we tried to find some jobs. Werner was able to work with someone as a carpenter. Early every morning I took him ashore so that we would still have the use of the dinghy. I even tried to use the sails on the dinghy and was surprised at how well I could manage them. I'm not really a sailor, and I never handled the sails on the boat. For me it was a bit harder to find a job because I did not want to leave the kids alone all day.

Some of the other parents from the boats Cool Change and Aquila got together to clean boats for the boat show and asked me if I wanted to join them. We had to leave very early in the morning to get the boats all cleaned before the show opened. It was hard work but it paid well, so it was really worth it.

It is strange, but I don't remember being so scared during the trip through the Delaware. I do remember getting all wet, and it was then that I remembered that we had some yellow pants on board. We did not buy them; they had come with the boat. After we changed into the foul whether gear, we were at least nice and warm. To get behind the seawall at 4 in the morning, we had to find our way by shining the halogen light ahead of us. I stood on the bowsprit with it.

In the morning we saw that there was another wall a bit closer to shore, and so we went there to be in even calmer water. The captain was very grumpy and ordered everybody around to get everything outside to dry. The crew was not too happy with him and told him to go to sleep. The sunshine brightened us all up, and it was good to have all our belongings dry again. It is easy to dry something that is wet with rainwater, but things that are wet from seawater do not dry very well.

Cleaning the fish, on the back of the rocking boat, that Marcel had caught on our way up to New York was a new challenge for me. Nobody else wanted to do it. Later on I learned that I need not have been so meticulous. I could have just cut away the filets and then thrown the rest overboard. But we all enjoyed the meals of fresh fish we had after that. First we got fried fish, then baked fish and last we had fish soup. We did have a refrigerator, but fish can't be stored too long.

When we got to Long Island we met up with the family Ash, and we were sad to hear that Jane had died a couple years ago. We had not received their last letter and so did not know. Jane's father was a cousin of my grandmother from Switzerland. Her grandfather had come to the US a long time ago and none of them spoke German any more. Craig and Jane had taken me out a few times when I was in Manhattan with Yvonne and Al. One time I remember we went to the famous New York Opera House to see the "Magic Flute," by Mozart. That was very special for me.

Werner had to make many repairs on the boat, and I didn't like to stay on board when he was at it. There was not enough room for everybody once he had taken the side panels off the motor. I could not cook, and there was nowhere to sit when the bench tops were opened up to get at the tools. Sometimes even the bed was dismantled so that he could get underneath it. In addition to all that, Werner could get a bit unpleasant when something did not go too well. Craig invited the children and me to spend some time with him at his house, and I was happy to accept the invitation.

Waking up to fog in the air and ice on the deck

Vandemere

The children played games in the large, park-like setting, renewing their "old time" friendship. It gave us adults time to sit together over coffee and talk about our latest adventures. They too had to fight with the problem of condensation inside their boat. There was not much that could be done about it other than clean it up once in a while. Constant heating did not make it any better. The moist air had no place to go but settle on the ceiling and walls where it quickly cooled off to leave behind a trace of condensation. Open hatches did help to control it to a certain extent but not enough.

For the past few mornings, before getting up, we had heated the boat by switching on one of the burners to the propane stove. We then placed a flowerpot, upside down, on it to radiate the heat. That itself was a great idea and worked well. Unfortunately the hole on the top of the pot channelled the heat to one point and released it as a fairly hot stream of air. One morning I heard a loud zapping noise. After investigating I found the window, located right above the pot sitting on the hot plate, cracked. The lexan, an acrylic kind of material that covered the opening, could not take the concentrated heat coming from the pot's hole and a thin crack appeared from the edge to the middle. The window was double glazed so the outer layer was still OK. To avoid any further damage we stopped using the flowerpot as a radiator. We did think about replacing the broken window, but to find one the same would have been rather difficult. The idea of crossing the Atlantic like this made me a bit uneasy. I hoped to find a suitable replacement before the arrival of our departure date.

Having access to shore power offered another solution to heating the boat. We rigged the heat gun to warm up the cabin. It worked very well and made changing into your cold clothes in the morning a lot more bearable. In addition to the comfort we also had less condensation to deal with.

Our budget had worked quite well. By staying in places such as we had been we expected to stay within our limits. I had thought of raising some funds by issuing a monthly newsletter, in German as well as English, to all our relatives and friends. So far, once a year, we had sent out notes called "Rundbrief" or "Round Robin". This time we included an invitation to subscribe to 12 issues about our travels and sent out more than 125 letters. The response was very disappointing as only 5 subscriptions were received, fortunately all for the English language. We wondered if anyone even read our notes. We certainly could not expect additional funds to be raised in that way, so we abandoned the idea of buying any more equipment with which to publish the newsletter.

Adjacent to the boat's pier lay a beautiful park with lots of trees. On one side it had a lush bamboo grove. Anisha was keen to cut some of them and make a pan flute. She expertly cut the pipes to the perfect length to achieve the right notes. Tied together, the 12 pipes produced nice tones. After some practice I was able to play some simple tunes.

When the sun came up, it rose behind our boat, penetrating the park with its rays and revealing the different greens of the trees, bamboos and shrubs. Early in the morning the pier was usually covered with a thin film of ice. We had to pour a pail or two of salt water over it before we could step onto it, or risked sliding into the water. None of the piers had a level surface, and we did not want to take a chance. We had another incident of Pascal falling into the water. He had been playing on the pier which at that time was just wet. He must have slipped on it and slid off the decking. Fortunately he was able to hold on to the last of the boards. There he hung, half of his body submerged in the ice cold water. He was screaming by then, and I ran to the spot to rescue him. He wasn't too upset but was glad to be released from the dangerous situation.

The little marina belonged to the Yacht Club of Vandemere, and we were introduced to some of the members. There were shower facilities at the fire department, and we were shown how to get the key. It was pleasant to take a hot shower once in a while, especially since the weather was then on the cool side. Thanks to the friendly people there, we had a great stay. A boat builder and sail maker gave us a hand in repairing our jib. The seams had started to rip. We had, temporarily, patched them up with a special tape but that was not a permanent solution. We opened up the seams along the edges, where it had started to tear. After cutting off some of the damaged material, a new fold was put in and the seams restitched with a sewing machine. It was just like a new sail, and I was glad to know that we would be able to use it in stronger winds. We were very happy to have met such kind and helpful people. The sail was, later, well tested on the Atlantic, and it held up to our expectations.

Fabian's birthday was coming up soon. He enjoyed his work as an apprentice cook and was actively involved with sports such as skiing and stunting in the half pipe, with his roller blades. Zermatt was the right place to be for such activities. We longed to be able to visit him. He was then in his second year of training. We definitely had something to look forward to, once we got to Europe. Besides our two older sons there were, of course, Chäberli's parents and many other friends we were keen to meet up with. The plan was to first land in Falmouth and visit my sister and family in Cornwall. After that we would sail as close to Switzerland as possible. The urge to set out was strong, but it would be another four months before we could attempt to cross the pond.

One warm evening our grill, mounted on the back railing, was put to good use and we shared a barbecue with the crew of Aquila. Thanksgiving was a couple of days away, and we made plans for the festivity. The day before Thanksgiving we heard Cool Change on the radio talking to another boat. Quickly we cut in at the end of their broadcast to find out where they were. Before dark they arrived safely and joined us for supper. It gave everybody a good feeling to see the crews of the three boats together again. The children, of course, enjoyed the company tremendously.

Thanksgiving day was celebrated at the home of a friend of the Aquila's crew. Altogether there were 26 of us (half of them kids) and plenty of food to share. It was the first time I had participated in a true American Thanksgiving. There was the traditional stuffed turkey, but also seafood and other goodies and plenty of everything. Two tables were covered up with plates filled to the rims to present all the food. It looked and tasted absolutely great. We were so well looked after. In the afternoon, the sun came out and gave us the incentive to get out and play some basketball with the kids. As it got colder everyone came together inside again, and I picked up the guitar to play and sing some songs. That was the only contribution I could make and I was more than willing to do so. We first sang some Swiss folk tunes. Everyone joined in when we started with the traditional American songs such as My Bonnie, O Susanna, O My Darling and many more. It was late at night when we got back to the boat. Fortunately there was no ice on the dock. Everybody went aboard feeling happy and it quickly became quiet.

The last day together with the crew of Cool Change approached. For the last time the crews of all 3 boats gathered together for a great meal and parting thoughts were exchanged. The following day they left early. It was not yet time for us to leave. We planned to attend a dinghy race that the sail maker in the village had invited us to go to. We brought along our dinghy and Marcel was the skipper. We drove to Oriental and set up the boat. The two older boys from Aquila borrowed dinghies so that they could race as well. It soon became obvious that our dinghy was outclassed, and Marcel came in last. Everyone enjoyed participating, and the food provided was excellent.

Before heading back to the boat, we took a quick tour through Oriental, a small but very charming town. Some of the Christmas decorations were already up. It felt strange to see all this. We had celebrated Christmas away from home before, but this time it would be on our sailboat, and we did not yet know where we would be. We spent a few more days in Vandemere, getting the boat ready and, for the last couple of days, waiting for the weather to improve.

Eventually we set out in the early morning, just as the sun rose. We had to wash off the frost-covered pier before saying farewell to our friends. It was at these moments that I understood that it is important to live life to its fullest. We meet people only for short times, and it is important to share and care for each other as much as possible during that time. We know that the experience will soon be just a memory. I felt the same way about my life. There was never enough time to enjoy all the things you would like to be involved with so I had learned to enjoy the present to its fullest.

I looked forward to being on a pier again. When we landed, however, I missed all the other boats that were usually present on such occasions. Here I just saw a rickety rackety pier, sticking out from a forest. What were we going to do here? Of course I noticed the boat,

Aquila. Soon we were docked by one of the boardwalks, twisting out from the shore. It looked a bit weird and spooky. Our boat could not go alongside the dock, as the water did not give enough depth for our keel. The dock had, at one time, reached further out. The posts further out were still there, so we just poked the boats bow to the end of the left-over pier. Climbing on and off the bow was helped with a little ladder we had on the boat. It felt great to walk off the boat again. Dad told us that it would be quite some time before we would be able to just step of the boat onto a dock again.

We were happy to join up with the kids from the other boat. I was so happy to find someone else to talk with again and to share my thoughts with. The park I found behind the trees turned out to be the perfect playground. There was a lot to be discovered. One attraction for me was those big bamboo shoots, coming out of the ground like water pipes. Anisha and I got to work and we built a small fort. It brought back memories of Galveston. There were no dumpsters there in which to find any canvas, but it was not really needed. We got busy cutting pieces of bamboo, and Anisha started to build a pan flute. I copied her. I always carried my pocket knife with me and it had a saw on it. I wanted to make some cuts with the blade but it was rather difficult. I felt that the knife was to big for this task. Suddenly the blade slipped, and I cut myself badly, between pointing finger and thumb. Did it ever hurt. Mom came to the rescue, and after most of the bleeding stopped, a large band aid was placed on the wound. This of course made me unable to do any more work with the knife and bamboo. I wasn't keen to try, even if I could have .

There was a dog in the park. I found out later that his name was Sonnet, and that he was the watch dog of a lady living nearby. It was very friendly and I became attached to it. Somehow it felt like home again. By then I did not have that longing for home anymore, but was happy to be able to play with a dog. I made him chase pine cones that were lying around everywhere. Suddenly I was hit by one of these cones on my back. It didn't hurt, but I was surprised and turned around. I noticed one of the other kids just hiding behind a tree. I sneaked up to it and soon we were chasing each other and throwing cones at each other. The others noticed and, after some time, we all played tag, using the cones. I enjoyed this the most. Even the football game at Thanksgiving was as much fun as this game.

Because we had shore power on the boat, Marcel's computer came in handy to play games on. We often just sat around the screen, watching each other, and trying to get the highest score. It was mostly the game Worms or one of the Smurf games. I preferred the worms game, as two could play against each other. Each had to control a moving cursor that left a line behind it. Eventually the lines would limit space so much that you could not move any further without running into one. Whoever ran into a line first lost the game. With the smurf game you just had to reach higher levels and pass through dangerous territories, like fire, water, enemies, dirt, cliffs, etc. It was fun too but not, I felt, as challenging. Pascal, at his age, just loved to watch us. Everyone wanted to make use of the opportunity of shore power and use the computer, something we had not been able to do since leaving the dock in Annapolis. Just before we left, we visited some towns and attended a dinghy race which Marcel was part of. I was not so much interested in that but found a playground with swings. I love swings, and that is where Pascal and I spent most of that day.

Anisha's pan flute

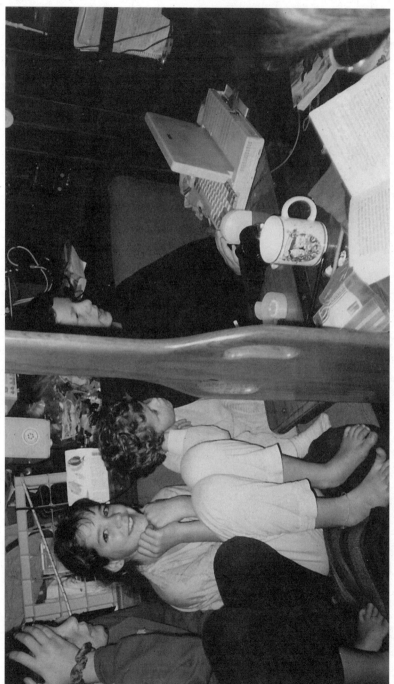

Children take advantage of shore power and enjoy some computer games

Heading South, Looking For Warmer Weather

Most of the days of our stay in Vandemere had been nice and sunny, but there was still a need to find warmer regions. Life on the boat without a heater was becoming very difficult, especially with so many of us. We reached Beaufort in the early afternoon, motoring most of the way. Benefiting from the experience gained on our first visit there, we quickly made arrangements with the museum to borrow the car to go shopping. During our visit at the post office we, unfortunately, left the book "Waterway Cruising Guide" behind. This was an excellent book, detailing places to anchor and other important information. We checked again later but someone had obviously taken advantage of it. From then on we had to do without. We had to manage the waterways down to Florida by exchanging information with other sailors, or just take chances. At least we still had the charts and, with that, knew where to go. To buy another book, just for the few days travel left, was not in our budget.

While we were busy doing the laundry, a parade was being held along the main street of Beaufort, and we could see a few of the vehicles, some carrying the latest model motorboats and other presentations relating to Beaufort's culture.

Our plan was to sail south, possibly taking an outside passage on the Atlantic to Charleston. The boat was made ready. The weather, however, was rainy and the forecast for the day out on the Atlantic was more than disturbing. We decided to wait a day and then make a decision. I spent most of the day reading a book I had just bought, at a reasonable price, in a local bookstore, about the French Canals. It sounded as if a boat our size could go from Le Havre to Marseille without too much trouble. The main canals were supposed to have a minimum depth of 2.15m (7 feet). It did not, however, mention if there were spots, along the sides of the canals, where we could anchor. The scenery along the canals looked beautiful, and the descriptions of how to navigate them were clear and inviting. I became very enthusiastic about planning such a route.

Before we went to bed I listened to the latest weather forecast. It did not sound good at all. Plenty of rain and strong winds were in store, with waves on the Atlantic of up to 4m (14 feet). It certainly did not sound inviting for us to take an outer route. We decided to get up early and stay in the ICW so as to, at least, get somewhere. On our way up, we had bypassed the part of the ICW we were now about to enter. Several sailors had told us that it had some shallow spots.

We did encounter some problems. We got stuck during a wait at the bridge to Onslow Beach but not because the channel was not deep enough. Our boat was not easily controlled when standing in one place and aligned with the channel. For that reason we would usually circle up and down the channel, in front of the bridge. We were making such a turn when the bow of the boat ran up on a sandbank. I had, obviously, been steering too close to the shore. I had no success getting off by reversing the motor. The screw just churned up the water but there was no movement of the boat. In the meantime the bridge had opened for the other boats. We tried to get an anchor out to pull us off the mud. Chäberli timed this operation. It took us 7 minutes to ready the dinghy, put it in the water, bring out the anchor and winch the boat off the bank. The last boat passed under the bridge, just as we were ready to approach, but the bridge had started to close again. We had to wait 30 minutes for the next opening. In spite of all that, we still reached our planned anchorage for the night. The chart indicated that there would be 3.4m (11 feet) of water there. On our approach to that anchorage we touched bottom lightly but did make it through the opening leading to the 11 foot basin. No depth had been marked on the chart for the short entry to this anchorage. We did not know if the tide was high or low but decided to trust to our luck. Four more boats came to anchor in the same spot.

Early the next day we were the first to leave, eager to make the most of the day. We were prepared to touch bottom, as we had on our arrival, and revved the engine to its maximum output in order to ride over the rough spots. It did not work. Our boat slowed down, sucked into the soft bottom. It seemed as if someone had put a whole lot more sand on that spot! We sat on sand, right in the middle of the marked opening, the shores a good distance away. Of course it was the tide that had affected the level of water enough to get us into trouble. In the meantime the other boats in the anchorage approached the narrow spot but had no problem in getting through. The second last one came in such a hurry that its wake rocked us off the bank,

Stuck in the mud, while leaving early in the morning

while we were still trying to motor forward. We were smiling when our boat came free but then a second bank, dead ahead, brought us to another abrupt halt. We were stuck again and the wake of the last boat did not make any difference. They helped us set an anchor to the right and forward of our boat. But that was not enough. We launched the dinghy and secured a rope to the Marker on the port side, about 30m (100 feet) ahead. Both ropes were put over the winches, one to port one to starboard. Marcel turned one of the winches, while Carina was tailing and Chäberli was on the other with Anisha. I was at the helm using the engine to help along. Inch by inch the boat moved over the sandbank. What felt like an eternity took only about 20 minutes and we were free. I wondered if the water guide would have mentioned the shallow entrance to this anchorage. There was nothing on the chart, except the marking of 3.3m (11 feet).

The following day continued to bring cold and wet weather. We were getting closer to the entrance to Cape Fear. With dark setting in, we looked for a spot to anchor but could find nothing suitable. Finally we decided to anchor, with two anchors, just outside and alongside the channel. Our first attempt failed. As soon as we approached the edge of the channel we touched ground and decided not to risk another attempt. Edging as close as we dared to a marker, we dropped our front anchor, just on the inside of it. The current nicely turned our boat around and we let enough line out to drop the back anchor. Then the front line was pulled in again while more line was given to the back one. Soon we were parked between the anchors, just like a car along the curb. It didn't take long before a motorboat stopped and mentioned that big barges would run through this channel at night and that we would be better off further ahead, to avoid being "at risk". There was, however, a lot of space between our boat and the marker on the other side of the channel. Night had already closed in, so I decided to stay put. During the night I heard a couple of barges going by without any problem. The rain, which was still coming down steadily, put me back to sleep.

We had had enough of travelling in the ICW without a guidebook to confirm our route. Leaving the ICW at Cape Fear (North Carolina), I guessed that we could make the one-day outside passage to Charleston (South Carolina). The barometer was forecast to stay steady for the duration of our trip, so we decided to leave the next day. It was just before noon, when we sailed into the rough waters of the Atlantic and with that the crew soon got seasick. It did not affect me this time, but Pascal was in poor shape. At his age he was not able to control his body very well, and the cockpit was soon in a big mess. Chäberli and I split the time for the watches between us for the coming night, and we reached Charleston just 24 hours later. It was quite some time since we had last fuelled up, and we required 60 gallons of diesel. We washed the deck to clean it of all the salt spray from the previous night and then anchored in the 3.5 knots tidal current of the Ashley River. The movement of the boat did not bother us but I was a bit worried that the anchor might get loosened up with the opposing forces acting on it twice a day. There was about a 1.8 metre (6 foot) difference between the high and low tide, the largest we had encountered so far on this trip.

We first took showers and then started to do the laundry. I had never been fond of driers but now they seemed to be the perfect invention! How else could we ever have got dry clothes again? It was time to visit the library and check our e-mails. There were so many computers installed here that it was possible to finish the setting-up of my homepage in one long session. Then we took the bus to do our grocery shopping and some sight-seeing.

Charleston is a nice town with some old buildings. It was tedious, waiting for better weather, but finally, a nice sunny day arrived. We were able to dry the boat out. The mattresses in the V-berth had started to mould on the underside and needed some extra care. I checked the weather forecast again, and it looked as if the next two days could work out all right. It was December 11th and storms out on the Atlantic were common. I decided to leave in the evening in order to arrive in St. Augustine (Florida) early on the morning of the 13th, sailing along the coast of Georgia. Everything had to be made ready for a rough run. We all took pills against seasickness. In the evening we left the anchorage, navigating the long, marked channel towards the ocean while Charleston faded behind us, into the darkness.

I noticed that there were no gnats around at that time of the year. I hated those little pests. Their flesh-eating habit had caused me much pain. There were no longer even any mosquitoes around. All we had to fight with was the dampness. The cushions and bedding all felt a bit moist. It was not as cold anymore; it just felt cold. I felt uncomfortable because there was nothing I could do about it.

I got into trouble with Dad. One day we took the cruising guide ashore to read while doing the laundry. It gave very valuable information about where to anchor and what to visit. We had planned most of our trip with this guide. It was a rather expensive book and Daddy gave it to me to look after, while he was busy carrying the laundry. We were headed for the post office to drop off letters. I still today can't remember what I did with the book, but when we walked back to the boat Dad noticed that I was not carrying it. He asked me to whom I had given it. I had not given it to anybody but must have put it down somewhere while we were in the post office. We went back there but could not find the book. Someone else must have had a need for that valuable book. I felt quite sad and that made the situation even more uncomfortable. It was Mom who made my life a bit more bearable again. For supper she prepared pasta that we covered with apple sauce and bread crumbs. This was one dish that I just loved to eat. The day was not so bad after all.

Once we had arrived in Charleston, we were able to use the Internet at the library. I was glad to check my mail and to browse for things. I was looking up the sites for the proposed NASA space shuttle launch. We were planning to be near Cape Canaveral around the time of the launching. We did not know exactly when that would be. I did not manage to find out but did read up on a lot of space related stuff.

On one occasion, we all wanted to go ashore. The current passing our anchored boat was quite strong. Daddy had to decide when to leave, and he thought we should give it a try. I was not so sure and wondered what we would get into next. We did not take the motor in order to avoid the extra weight of the motor and battery. Daddy was at the oars in the peak of the dinghy. There were oar-locks in two positions. A set to be used when sitting in the centre of the dinghy and an additional set to be used when sitting in the peak. Of course, with so many people in the boat, there would have been no space to use the centre oars. On the right, Mom and Carina took their seats, then Pascal, Anisha and myself followed by sitting on the left (see picture on back cover). The dinghy was full to the brim. There were no waves but, as soon as we cast off, the dinghy gently glided down the river, away from the boat and out towards the opening of the protected area. Daddy started to paddle like crazy while we were clutched on to the rocking boat. The oars splashed into the water and I could feel how the dinghy would make a move forward, before gliding to the side again. With steady strokes Daddy moved the oars through the water. That way he could make some headway. From time to time Mom told him which way to steer. This was useless because the boat would not go where we wanted it to go. I was really scared that we were in big trouble. We did, however, make it safely to the shore, a few hundred feet down stream and on the other side of the river. There the current was not at all so bad, and it was much easier to paddle upstream again. When we reached the dinghy dock, we tied up and I enjoyed a long visit in town. The tide turned and the current was minimal when we returned to the boat.

Approaching St. Augustine

We met an Atlantic ocean with fairly rough seas and gusty winds from the side. With the latter we made good way. It didn't rain at all during the whole night. When daylight broke the boat was gliding nicely through the waves. The wind turned to the north, pushing us along at a good pace. With the wind from the back, it was hard to tell how strong it was. Towards evening the waves got bigger. In the far distance, lightning was visible. The storm slowly moved closer, and it started to rain. I had to reduce sails with a reef in the mainsail. As the wind picked up a second reef was put into the mainsail. Soon I had to take down the jib and use the staysail. It was amazing to see how quickly the boat moved downwind. The waves were about 3.5m (12 feet) high. We were moving faster than I had thought and were forced to lower the mainsail altogether. We sailed with only the staysail, on a downwind course, and the GPS still showed a speed of about 5 knots. The logbook showed 7:20 a.m., as the time we arrived at the outmost marker of the entrance to St. Augustine (Florida).

Poor weather in sight

Due to constant movements of the shoals, the markers for that inlet were not shown all the way out on the chart, except for one tower bell way out in the water. We had heard that the channel had been dug out and the spoil deposited to the sides of it, so it was important to stay in the channel. The tide was about to rise again, so at least we didn't have to worry about fighting an outflowing current. We took down the staysail in order to enter the channel under motor power. The boat slowly edged in, almost sideways, the nose pointed towards the wind so as not to be blown down and out of the channel. The speed slowed to a snail's pace of about 2 knots over ground. I asked Chäberli to take the helm while I kept a lookout for the next marker. We passed the first green one, a couple of boat lengths to our left. We were level with the next one, when we lost sight of the marker after it. Neither a red nor a green one was visible. We had to turn around. With the wind from the side it made a lot of spray come over the deck and visibility was terrible. It reminded me of the trip in the Delaware, but at least it was daylight this time. We returned to the outermost marker, using the GPS.

Once well past the bell tower we hove-to, a manoeuver I had practised a few times with my small sailboat on the lake back home and now put to the test on a greater scale. It worked surprisingly well. We sat down and started to rethink our situation. First of all I wanted to make sure that we didn't drift south and frequently checked the GPS to verify our position. The boat was moving slightly forward, giving it stability, while swooping over mountainous waves. When sitting at the table it was just possible to hold ourselves in place.

First of all we had to find out the location of the markers. With that information we would be able to enter their positions into the GPS and then follow its bearings, using the depth sounder to confirm the boat's position in the channel. I radioed the coast guard to get that information. A voice came on the air and asked us to switch to another channel. The person on the other end was very concerned about the situation, and we talked for maybe half an hour. There were many questions to be answered such as our position, the boat's name, look and size, how many crew members there were, if we wore life jackets and so on. For them, I guess, this was important information. They did not, however, want to tell us anything in relation to the channel entrance. They strongly recommended that we should not attempt to take the entrance in the present conditions. They advised us to head further south, to use the entrance there, or go back. The latter was impossible, as we could never have sailed back into the wind in such conditions. To go south would have meant another day at sea. With the barometer dropping we knew it would have been a terribly long day. They offered to dispatch a tugboat to tow us in, something that flashed big dollar signs in front of my eyes. With our boat weighing in at 18 tons, it would have needed a fairly powerful tug, especially in these weather conditions.

During the conversation we were able, at least, to find out how many markers there were. They would not tell us how they were arranged, straight or in a curve, nor the position of any of them. In case of an accident, they did not want to be held responsible. They asked us to stay in contact every half hour or so in order to confirm our position.

In the meantime daylight seemed to have become brighter, due, perhaps, to the rain having stopped. It did not look bad. I thought it was worth another try. This time I asked Marcel to take the wheel. He was more than happy to do so and, once we were past the outer tower bell, slowly steered towards where we assumed the next marker would appear. It was difficult to know how much to compensate for the wind. We thought the channel to be fairly straight and with that expected the markers to be due west of us. Marcel was first to see it, forward but more to the south than expected. I asked him to steer quite a bit higher in order to compensate for the wind, which was now blowing from the side, at about 30 knots. The constant spray was obscuring our view and we both lost sight of the marker, which had been straight ahead just a minute or so ago. Marcel tried to hold course. I could not see any fear in his face, and I knew he was not aware of the dangers we faced. With the boat moving so slowly, it was difficult to steer a straight course. The first marker reappeared, still in about the same direction. As we passed it, the next marker became visible for a little while. A few seconds later, both of us lost sight of the forward marker, as well as the one in the back. We desperately hoped for its re-appearance. I quickly left the cockpit cover and stood outside, to avoid looking through the dodger's window. I hoped, that way, to obtain better visibility. It was a constant fight to try and keep my glasses from getting sprayed on. Taking cover behind the cockpit's dodger to avoid the worst helped some. I noticed that it was drizzling again. For a moment I watched the white tips of the waves around us and noticed how the boat moved up and down, tipping sideways and then up and down again. The wind blew right over the starboard beam, and there was no way of telling if we were moving straight ahead or not. We frantically looked out for any markers ahead. For me it soon became evident that I couldn't see any better outside the cockpit, so I took refuge under the dodger's cover again. It was time to have a look at the depth sounder. Through my sprayed up glasses I had to look at it twice. I usually first wiped my glasses clean, using my spare hanky, but there was no time for such niceties. We were in 4.5m (15 feet) of water! I knew from the first approach that the channel had a minimum reading of about 7.5m (25 feet). I could not believe the reading and told Marcel to turn back in order to find the channel, hoping that we would still be far enough out and in deep enough water to do so. Slowly the boat turned into the wind and we were outward bound again. While turning southward, heading towards where we judged the channel to be, the reading of the depth sounder changed and my heart was about to stop pounding. Then the depth sounder's digital display rapidly dropped to 2.1m (7 feet) but rose up to 4.9m (16 feet) a few seconds later. There had been only one foot of water left under the keel. Obviously we had encountered about 3m (9 feet) high waves over very shallow water. I guessed that we must have been right over the edge of the channel, where the soil had been deposited. In the meantime the new readings from the depth sounder indicated that we were back in the channel, a great relief.

We must have just passed over the spoil bank, but the question now was, which way did we have to go? Just at that moment Marcel saw a green marker over his right shoulder and kept it in sight, steering the boat ever so slowly towards its location. And what a relief it was when we were able to make out the next one. Soon there were red ones visible too to mark the other side. Visibility improved rapidly as we came closer to the coast and the spray diminished. More markers could be seen, and it became clear that the channel was a straight cut. Breaking waves could be seen on our side of the channel; a sign of very shallow water, but by then it had become easy to follow the markers. The height of the waves dropped, and we heaved a sigh of relief, knowing well that we had come very close to disaster. In the distance we noticed a tugboat coming our way. We wondered what they were doing out there. When they got level with us they waved, turned around, and zoomed back in again. Were they about to come and check on us? If so, I felt good to know that someone cared for us. It had been a close call, and I promised myself never again to attempt an approach in an "unmarked" channel, except in absolutely good weather conditions.

The channel became wider, as it joined the ICW, and it was still difficult to make out the sides. I almost misinterpreted a red marker for the entrance to a bay located to the south and therefore wanted to pass the marker on its right. It was, in fact, the marker for the right edge of the ICW, as Marcel quickly pointed out to me. We argued for a few seconds, re-checked the chart and found out that Marcel was, indeed, reading it correctly. Once close enough to the marker the number confirmed his thoughts and a swift turn on the wheel brought us past the correct side of the marker. Anchoring in the rather large area along the shore of St. Augustine was easy, and we dropped our anchor not too far away from the dinghy dock.

 *Getting in to St. Augustine was one of the experiences I remember very well. I think it was one of the times I was really scared. Being out in the open water in a storm did not bother me as much as being in a storm, close to shore. Out in the water you could not hit anything but just go up and down with the waves. In this case we did not have such freedom. It was early in the morning, and the children were still asleep. It was up to Werner and me to navigate the entrance. Werner asked me to take the helm so that he could look out for the markers. He could not see much and I had a very hard time to keep a straight course. The wind was so hard that it constantly pushed us sideways. We had to steer northwest to be able to go west. I got so nervous that I asked Werner to stop and go back out. We had never hove-to before, and I was a bit uneasy but it seemed to be all right.*

We were exasperated with the coast guard. They asked us so many trivial questions. All we wanted to know was where the markers

were, but that they would not tell us. We had no choice but to try again on our own. In the meantime Marcel had arisen, so he took over the helm. He was much more calm than I. I don't think he had any fear. I was standing down in the galley and praying hard the whole way in, asking God to guide us. I was relieved when we made it and thanked God for his help. I was sure he had helped us. Many times I felt we had some help; our guardian angels did not have an easy job with us. We were always getting ourselves into difficult situations.

Anchoring in St. Augustine

St. Augustine

Shortly after our arrival, the winds picked up again, and the rain came down in buckets. We could not leave the boat under such conditions. Even in the anchorage, the water became so rough that the dinghy would, probably, have been swamped. Without a strong motor, it was just not possible to go anywhere. We had no choice but to stay put. In the evening the town of St. Augustine could be seen, with the Christmas lights decorating the buildings along the shore. It appeared as if we had arrived in a totally different world.

In the morning, Chäberli woke me up. She thought that our boat had moved backwards, towards the bridge. After what we had experienced the previous day, I thought that she was a bit over-anxious. We had already been at anchor for a whole windy night and the boat had not moved at all; why should it move now? She insisted, so I got up, in a grumpy mood, to check out the situation. I woke up fast and my hesitancy changed to high alert when I noticed the neighbour's boat appear to be slowly moving forward! There was someone on the boat shouting something and pointing towards the bridge, but I could not hear what he was saying. The wind carried his voice away just as it was carrying our boat. I quickly understood, we were dragging our anchor and heading towards the bridge which was definitely not as far from us as it had been. I started the engine immediately and put it in gear to push the boat forward. To our great relief the boat slowed its backwards movement, and then stopped moving back altogether. The motor kept it in place, balancing the force of the wind. I got myself dressed and together we set our other anchor. Everything was under control, the motor off, the boat holding.

Pulling up the fouled-up anchor went along well, until I got it to the water's surface. It became extremely heavy. I secured the chain in order to peek over the bow to see why. There I could make out a great amount of chain wrapped around the anchor, just like a Christmas wrapper. All this chain added weight and it was extremely difficult to pull the whole thing out of the water. I had to use the winch. There it finally hung in front of our boat, like an iron sculpture. I was unable to get at the chain and undo it from the boat. With the whole weight hanging on the chain it was constantly pulling itself tight and with that made it impossible to clear the mess. The only way to solve the problem was to lower the whole mess into the dinghy, unhook the chain from the anchor and then unwrap the chain.

Our first priority was to have breakfast. We were just about to sit down when we heard someone calling us. We climbed on deck again and were surprised to see Cool Change, circling near our boat. They pulled up alongside, and we had a short chat. We could not convince them to come aboard. They wanted to keep on heading south. On the two occasions when we had sailed the outside passage, they had stayed in the ICW. They said that they had heard our conversation with the coast guard on the previous day. They were glad to see that we had arrived, unharmed. They were curious about our tangled up anchor and we had another event to talk about. The time soon came to say goodbye and to wish each other safe travels. I wondered what they thought about us as sailors, getting into one scrape after another.

After breakfast I readied the dinghy so that Marcel would be able to lower the anchor into it. After a struggle with the rusted-up shackle holding the chain to the anchor, I managed to get the chain detached. A long process of unwinding the jumbled up chain followed before the shackle was reconnected to the anchor. We were anchored very close to the bridge and decided to move the boat further away. This time we set two anchors, spread apart and in line with the tide. The boat just moved between the two anchors, selecting the anchor which suited the tide. The chain was no longer able to tangle with the anchor. The pull on each anchor was always from the same direction. Another small problem had, however, been created. When the boat swung around in a circle, which it did occasionally, the two chains would wind around each other at the point where they left the bow. Sooner or later this mare's nest would have to be untangled.

I soon worked out a technique to deal with the tangled anchor chains. One of the anchors had a shackle connecting the 30m (100 feet) of chain to the extra 75m (250 feet) of anchor line stored under deck. We set the anchor so that the shackle still came to rest on deck, which meant that about 30m (100 feet) of chain was out. That was enough to set the anchor safely in the 6m (20 feet) deep water. To temporarily hold the anchor, a heavy rope was secured to it, outboard of the twists, with a snap-on shackle. The shackle was attached to the anchor chain as far out over the bowsprit as I could reach. This held the anchor chain firmly to the boat and the twisted-up part of the chain could then be slackened. Next, the shackle connecting the chain and the anchor line was undone and the one chain unwound from the other, the latter holding the boat. I did this, of course, only under normal weather conditions. The system worked very well and our boat was securely anchored.

We had not yet been able to go ashore. Because we had moved our boat north, the dinghy dock was now a fair bit further away. The strong tidal current, gusty wind and occasional heavy rain all made it difficult to row a dinghy such as ours, and we did not feel like using it. The boaters next to us, on Dream Catcher, must have noticed this and it didn't take long before they zoomed over with their motor powered rubber dinghy. They said that they were on their way to do some shopping and asked if we needed anything. We felt very thankful for their kindness. Chäberli put on her heavy rain gear and went along with them. She later came back with a whole bunch of goodies. The crew was happy to see fresh food again.

It was great to know that the children could keep themselves busy while we waited out the weather. In the small space below deck we all managed to get along well. The forecast for the night was for heavy winds and rain. I made sure that the anchor lines were free and that chafing guards were securely placed over the rollers on the bowsprit. It got dark and the wind became stronger. The noise generated on the rigging was quite noticeable.

We turned on the radio to listen in for any boater's calls on channel 16. There were several calls but one came from the bridge operator. He had worked on the bridge for many years and was excited to announce that his wind speed indicator had just recorded 50 knots of wind. We sat in the saloon looking at each other and tried to imagine what the weather would have been like out on the Atlantic. We were glad that we were not out there, looking for an entrance. I went up to the cockpit, curious to know how it felt with 50 knots of wind blowing through the anchorage. It was my first experience with exact known wind speeds of that scale. The wind came from the north and all the force was on the one anchor. The boat moved sideways in a slow pace, following the pattern of a pendulum. It was difficult to make out the other boats at anchor, and I soon returned to the warmer cabin. We appreciated the fact that our anchors were holding so well.

Day broke and the sun came out. A large steel boat, named Daystar, was anchored a fair bit away from us. I rowed over to it, curious to know more about their travels. We started to exchange our experiences. They had been frightened during the night. Their boat stuck out of the water much more then ours did so it created a lot more wind resistance, and they feared that their anchors would drag. They were relieved to have it over and done with. They were happy to talk about their belief in Christ. They were in the process of gathering old clothes, toys and other goods from this area. They intended to ship them to parts of the Caribbean. We were invited to come over for tea. I remember their boat as having boxes everywhere, full of books and other items, stacked on shelves. One cabin was completely filled with clothes. Due to the boat's large size you felt just as if you were in a regular living room. They had done this kind of trip several times before and were about to carry on southward. The owner had recently undergone a heart operation and asked if we could get the hooks up together. I was more than willing to help. Early next day I was over at Daystar pulling the first of 3 anchors. It was hard work to bring it up. The look of the second anchor puzzled us both. The shank of the Danforth anchor was bent back 180 degrees. We could only guess about the force this anchor had been put under when the storm had gone through the anchorage a couple of nights before. An hour later, with the last anchor up, we waved goodbye to them. It was a sunny day, and we decided to go ashore, for the first time at this anchorage.

We were back in Florida where everything had its price. In order to go ashore a minimum fee of $7.00 per day was charged to dock the dinghy. We decided to use the showers and laundry facilities and paid a $37.00 fee, allowing us to tie up the dinghy as well as use the nearby facilities for one week. The coming few days were a great change. The sun was out every morning and we could, finally, dry out the boat and walk around in t-shirts again. Taking showers and doing the laundry was high on our list of priorities. We used a lot of quarters (25 cent coins) to get all our stuff washed and, more important, dried. St. Augustine is a tourist-oriented town and has many old buildings and churches. Right along the water is a wide walkway leading to the oldest stone fort in the USA, the Castillo De San Marcos.

A street-train-like shuttle drove through town during the Christmas festivities and offered free rides to everyone. Its main purpose was to link up the parking lots surrounding the town. We took the ride a couple of times and listened to a tape explaining all the points of interests along the one-hour tour. There were many old houses and points of interest in St. Augustine giving it a historical ambience. The Spanish people, under the admiral Don Pedro Menendez, arrived in 1565. They took over the village of Seloy, then belonging to the Timucuan Indians, and renamed it St. Augustine. The Spanish then fought the French settlers on the St. John's River and gained power over the coast of Florida. That made St. Augustine the oldest permanent European settlement on the North American continent. Our boat was anchored right in front of the fort. I tried to envision how it would have looked to the Spanish sailors and how difficult it must have been to navigate their large wooden ships along this unknown coast. The fort was built to protect the town from the English, who had settled in Georgia and the Carolinas. Major attacks had been made by the English in the years of 1702 and 1740 but they were defeated. The fort was never captured. After a few more quarrels with the English over the territory and after the American Revolution, Spain sold Florida to the USA in 1821.

We all enjoyed staying in St. Augustine. One day we found out that the local toy store "Charlotte Street Toy Shop" had a contest. Children could enter home-made toys that had been built entirely of scrap material. I told Marcel to enter his sailboat. He was not keen at all, but I did convince Anisha to enter her pan flute. A bit later during the day Marcel felt challenged and agreed to give it a try. We then had to do some brainstorming in order to find another toy that Carina could enter. We came up with an idea and she built a contraption with which you could test your manual skills. The openings of two one litre plastic coke bottles were secured to each other at the neck. We cut the top out of one of the bottle caps and formed a coupling. This allowed the two bottles to be screwed together, one from each side.

Placed inside the bottles were equal numbers of small shells and large shells. Tipping and shaking the bottles carefully made it possible to separate the two sizes of shells. We had fun playing with it ourselves. A trip to town was made and the projects entered in the contest, a couple of days before the judgement date. All the toys were displayed in the store and it was great to see the many interesting projects. Our kids could hardly wait for the day to come to attend the prize giving ceremony. First prize was a $100 gift certificate for the toy store, second prize was $50 and 3rd was $25. We all assumed that our chances of winning were small so, with that in mind, everyone felt relaxed. The day approached, and we all lined up at the store.

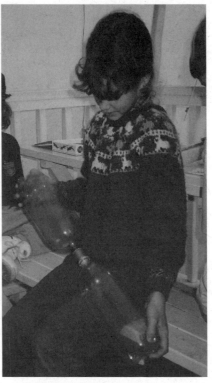

Demonstrating the newly designed toy

One after the other, the builders described the function of their toy and, if possible, gave a demonstration. This took almost the whole morning and towards lunch the great moment came. We could not believe it. After the 3rd and 2nd prizes were handed out, Marcel, with his sailboat, was announced the winner of the first prize. We were a group of happy people. Pictures were taken for the local paper. At first Marcel could hardly believe it, but then it sank in, and he started to search out the store to find the things he wanted the most. The choices were many. In the coming days we made many more trips to the store. Eventually the boat was loaded with gift-wrapped parcels of every shape and size and hidden all over the boat.

It was three days before Christmas and the Baptist church had a service which included a concert with a symphony orchestra and two choirs. We all went to the concert. Chäberli and I felt it was a great evening. December 24th arrived, but there were no Christmas cookies, something which Chäberli had always prepared for such days. It was high time to start baking, and after I had shopped for some additional ingredients, the small oven in our boat got loaded with goods to turn out 4 different varieties of cookies and the cabin was filled with a wonderful smell. The children helped with the tasks at hand, mostly with cutting the shapes out of the dough.

Marcel wins 1ˢᵗ prize

Earlier on we had met new friends, from the boat Drifter, which was berthed in the marina. We had talked to the couple on several occasions while ashore. They joined us for the visit to the Presbyterian church's Christmas service. It was a candlelight service and everyone received a candle. It was quite a nice atmosphere and we enjoyed some musical presentations by local artists. On our way out of church we were greeted with the sound of heavy rain. We waited out the worst and then headed for the boat. Our new friends from Drifter agreed to come over and celebrate Christmas on our boat. We quickly had to clean up the worst of the clutter before the visitors arrived. Soon we all sat cozily around the table. On it our friends placed a 60cm (2 foot) tall, perfectly proportioned, Santa boot, made up of sail canvas and filled to the edge with nuts, chocolates, fruits and many other goodies. It was a very agreeable evening, singing Christmas songs and telling each other about our experiences of past Christmases. It was late before everybody settled down for a good night's sleep.

Over the next few rainy days the children played with all the new toys which they had received. Our permit to dock the dinghy ran out, and we were no longer able to leave the dinghy unattended at the dock. We had to alternate visits to the town, leaving some crew on the boat.

One sunny day, I tried to take Chäberli to the dock, under sail. The current and wind were against us. We had great difficulty making way under sail. As we passed under the bridge, where there was a strong current, I had to lean into the oars heavily, or else we would have been pushed back again and again.

Some nice sunny days followed, but the air stayed cold because of a steady wind blowing over the water. The back part of our cockpit had been covered up with blankets to make the cockpit become a closed in area. With the sun shining, and the wind kept out, it made for a warm and perfectly nice place. Most of our activities were now done in the cockpit. Below deck it stayed cold, just bearable to the point where one could do the essentials such as cook or sleep.

On one of the return trips with the dinghy the top aluminum bar, which was holding the sail, broke into two pieces. We had to fall back on the oars, again. From then on the electric motor was always mounted in the back to give extra power when fighting wind or current. This particular trip had been to buy the ingredients for a special supper. Sylvester night (New Year's Eve) would soon be upon us. Chäberli started preparations for this event by grating and mixing some cheeses together, to prepare a Fondue. The portable propane stove, which we had used in our van, was set up in the centre of the table. The lid from one of our storage bins secured the propane bottle and the bottom of the pan came to rest just a few inches above the table top. Everyone enjoyed the smell of cheese in the boat and we had a great meal. Pascal went to bed early. The rest of us waited for the New Year to arrive.

I still had a few more pictures to add to the homepage so few more trips to town were needed. There was an Internet café that could scan our pictures and I used their services to quickly upload them. To save money I did the rest of the work at the public library. It took some time to get the pages looking nice. I added a logbook to describe our latest adventures. To my surprise some people had sent us e-mails saying that they had enjoyed reading about our travels. For me it was a good exercise to keep up-to-date with the latest computer technology and to learn how to use the HTML programming language. Over the past few months I had also checked the NASA Internet site to find out the date for a launching of a space shuttle at Cape Canaveral. We were on our way there and I had noticed a launch date posted on their site for the 18th of January. If we encountered no more problems, it was possible that we would arrive in Titusville before that date. From there we should have a good view of the launch.

Some days the wind in the anchorage was so strong that we had to stay on the boat. During one of Chäberli's dinghy trips to pick me up, she had to use all her strength to reach the dock. On the radio they were forecasting winds of 28 knots for the day. She must have been fighting winds of about 10 knots when she came to get me. She had Pascal along with her and he kept control of the electric motor while she worked the oars. When they arrived at the dock, they were both wet. Chäberli was exhausted and not in the best of moods. From then on we paid to leave the dinghy at the dock in order to avoid unnecessary trips. We did not know how much longer we would stay, so we paid on a daily basis. Thanks to one of the staff at the marina it did not cause much harm to our budget. It seemed that the person in charge of collecting the fees had pity on us. He always issued a permit for two days for the cost of one. I didn't mind at all and was happy to see someone trying to help!

Double Crow, a boat flying the Canadian flag, anchored close to us. They had noticed our children and, because they had two daughters, aged 8 and 10, decided to visit with us. They would be heading south the next day, so we spent the few hours left together, chatting about our travels and sharing supper. We mentioned to them that we had been in Nova Scotia in the summer of 1996 and had gone on a whale watching tour in Cape Breton. It turned out that the person who had given us a free tour to see the whales was a neighbour of the crew on Double Crow. What a small world we live in!

Washington was on my mind for a lot of the trip back south. I had such a great time visiting the Smithsonian Museums, although some of them were pretty boring. The one I found the most interesting was the Museum of Natural History. There were all sorts of really awesome and interesting things in there, including stories of the evolution of man, and a huge mammoth standing right in the entrance. There were also a lot of incredible crystals, one of which especially caught my attention because it was massive (or so I remember), and a beautiful shade of purple. I don't remember how many times we visited that museum, but I do know that it was more than once, and I also remember that once we rented a headphone set that told us all about the displays.

One of the most bothersome trips we did in Washington, according to me, was visiting the White House. Apparently, we got to see a "senate in session", which really meant nothing to me, and definitely did not make it worth the trouble it was to get in. Before they let us in, they checked all of the items we had on ourselves. The officer even insisted on taking my pocket knife. It was securely fastened to the pouch I had been given for my birthday in St. Augustine, so that it could not fall into the water. He wanted me to give up my whole pouch, but there was no way that would happen. There was nothing left to do but to undo all of the tight knots I had made to secure it.

Mom was getting restless about waiting, but I did not want to give up my pouch, so she helped me, and we finally got the knife off. The officer promised to make sure I would get it back on the way out. Once inside the building, we had to climb up a whole bunch of stairs and walk through a lot of corridors. Then we had to be absolutely quiet, and as we entered a big room, we could see a whole bunch of people talking below us. It was hard to understand what they were saying, and it didn't sound like anything interesting anyway. It was incredibly boring, and, in my opinion, definitely not worth the trouble of undoing those 20 or so incredibly tight knots. Not to mention having to tie them all up again.

One more thing about Washington that I remember well, was when Mom told us that we were going to see a mint factory. I was looking forward to this prospect, because I liked mints, and I was sure they'd give us samples; after all, chocolate factories always did. However, it was somewhat of a disappointment when I figured out that this was in fact not the case. It wasn't a mint candy factory, but a place where they made money. But I got over that quite quickly, because it was pretty interesting to watch the machines printing all that money.

On December 6th, it was a tradition for us to make "Gritibänz" with Mom. Or bread men, for those who aren't familiar with that Swiss word. This year, however, we were a bit delayed. The rather bumpy ride out on the Atlantic had to be completed first, a ride I was not looking forward to, because I knew I'd get seasick again. Listening into the conversation while still in bed about entering the channel to St. Augustine with the coast guard was a bit scary, because it didn't sound too positive. Dad seemed alright, though, so that calmed me down a bit. They were asking a lot of questions. What scared me, though, was when once we were in and anchored, Marcel called Mom to tell her that we were dragging. Once we got the anchor to hold well in the ground, everything seemed to be OK, except for the occasional wind that made us have to stay on the boat. I sure was glad that Marcel had noticed our boat dragging in time, because according to the adults, we could have hit the bridge. After that I always checked around us whenever I went out on deck.

We definitely had enough things to do to keep us busy, and one of those things was to make those bread men. We all gathered around the wooden table in the saloon, and started to use the dough that Mom had prepared to form it into different shapes looking like people. I loved doing this, making faces, and adding clothes and hair and things. It was also fun to compare each other's art work. And there was always that exciting moment when they came out of the oven all fat, and we could see who had made the nose too long on theirs so that the tip got a bit black, or who hadn't pushed the raisin eyes in far enough so that they had been burnt. They had to be in the oven for about 40 minutes, during which time the boat finally got a bit warmer. They always tasted great.

The town of St. Augustine was very inviting. I loved riding on the little street train. There were also horse carriages offering rides, and I liked to go up and pet the horses. The fort there was fun to explore. I also liked the library in St. Augustine, because they let me use the computers as long as I wanted to, and didn't charge me for the paper I used to print out the e-mails I received from my friends. I kept all of them and put them in my binder as souvenirs.

On Christmas eve, the park's walks were lined with thousands of candles, and there was a stand which sold candied apples. Mm, they were so good! I'd never had one before, and it was just so yummy. I'd never seen so many candles before in my life. It looked so beautiful under the large trees. The candles made so much light that just the trunks and the lower leaves were visible, with the tops kind of disappearing into the dark.

With all of the toys that Marcel had bought with his first prize money from the toy store, everyone got a present from him. It was nice, because he was sharing it with everybody, and that Christmas was very memorable. I got a tambourine, which, of course, drove everyone crazy after a while, and we all got some more beanie babies. We always had fun playing with them. Carina's favourite was the flying dragon, a pink one. I wasn't really sure which one was my favourite, but Stinky the skunk was the one I would hold in my hand when I went to sleep every night. He was the first one I ever got, while we were still living on the farm. I was also collecting all of the cats and birds that I could get my hands on.

Finally! Warmer Weather

Life on the boat was becoming very difficult as the weather turned wet and cold. Not that we couldn't live close together anymore, but we were forced to use every opportunity of sunshine to dry out the bedding, boat's cushions and clothes. Anisha called our home Mould City. A heating system would have made life a lot easier. We decided that the time had come to move further south.

In preparation for our departure, we took the boat to the dock, at the marina on the other side of the opening bridge. There we were able to give the anchor chains a good wash with the dock hose. While Marcel was busy washing the chains, Anisha helped me to get our water tank and fuel tank filled. Chäberli arrived at the dock with bags full of shopping. It was handy to be able to load them directly onto the boat. Carina helped her to put the groceries away.

We seized the opportunity to take a shower and had our last shopping spree in town. The girls still really liked to collect beanie babies, these stuffed, small animal figures. The whole boat was filled with those little creatures. Walking through the boat felt like being part of a mini-zoo which all these stuffed animals had slowly taken over. I stayed back at the marina to finish the laundry. Later the moon was out, reflecting on the water, as all six of us took a quiet dinghy ride, back to our boat. There was a slight feeling of sadness at the thought of leaving this place. We had anchored on the south side of the bridge, so as to avoid having to wait for the bridge to open and were ready for an early start the following day.

At first light we had a clear sky, inviting us on, towards Daytona. Following the chart became a routine matter and the water depth seemed to be adequate. We were becoming quite adept at this type of sailing, and steering the boat through these waterways was enjoyable and easy. Water depths were good and there was no further danger of running aground. The water was totally calm and, with our engine purring away happily, we made about 5 to 6 knots.

On one of my routine glances over the instrument panel, mounted on the console behind the wheel, I noticed that the oil pressure gauge showed no pressure. I knocked on the glass with my fingers, thinking the instrument was stuck. Nothing happened. Could there really be no oil pressure with the engine running so smoothly? What if there was indeed no pressure? I could not bear the thought of our engine being ruined. Immediately I switched the engine off, the boat gliding through the water with only its momentum left. I called Marcel for an emergency stop, something we had never actually practised. He had to steer the boat, close to the edge of the channel, while I prepared to drop the anchor. Things had to be done quickly in order to use the little speed we had left, otherwise we would risk running aground, controlled by the slight current of the channel. Marcel steered the boat neatly along the side of the channel, and I dropped the anchor. The boat swung around and came in line with the channel's current. Another anchor was dropped in the back, just in case. The crew of a passing boat asked if they could help but, at this stage, we did not know what our problem was. We only knew that our engine seemed to have failed, but could not tell why. The other boat moved on.

It was again time for me to remove all the panels covering up the engine and to start troubleshooting. It didn't look good. On top of the bilge water was a heavy film of thick motor oil, still warm. How could the oil have got there? I looked for cracks in the motor block, blown caps, leaking lines but nothing seemed to be at fault. In the meantime I decided to pump out the water from underneath the oil and then salvage what oil I could. Marcel turned on the bilge pump while I leaned over the rail, checking the water being discharged. As soon as I spotted some oil on the surface of the water I called to Marcel to stop the pump. What a mess. I could clearly see the rainbow colours on top of the water. I was ashamed. At just that moment a coast guard boat came passing by. "Any problems?" they shouted. I did not know what to say, nor do I remember what I said. Whatever it was, they did not bother and left. Had they seen the oil on the water? I was very tense. I knew things were not going the way I wanted, but there was no time to think about that then.

I took a flashlight and inspected all the parts of the motor. Finally I uncovered the mystery. The bracket holding the alternator had broken off the engine mount. The alternator had come to rest on top of the oil filter. When I removed the alternator, I found that a small hole had been punched into the outer casing of the filter. The oil had slowly leaked out through that hole and into the bilge. It was a great relief to know the problem was a simple one to remedy, namely to change the filter. However, what had happened to the engine? Had it been damaged during the process of losing oil? Answers to these questions had to wait. The first thing to be done was to clean out the bilge completely. Fortunately we had 3 empty one-gallon milk jugs with us. The yucky stuff was sucked out of the bilge into these jugs. The little oil left in the engine was removed too, a new filter mounted and new oil put back in. I was relieved that we had brought enough oil along with us. The alternator had to be removed until a new bracket could be found to hold it in place. Our batteries were fully charged so we had a couple of days before the alternator would have to be replaced. The engine started without any problems. No smoke and no unusual sounds.

I took a couple of minutes to review our situation. It was absolutely essential for our survival to have a fully-functional engine. We could not have entered St. Augustine harbor without one. Since then the engine had only run a few hours to recharge the batteries and now had to cover the 38km (20 nautical miles) along the ICW. It dawned on me that we had had a close call when approaching St. Augustine. A failing engine, at that point, could have caused an end to our travels. Who was taking care of us?

We had not planned to stop over in Daytona. However, with no way to charge the boat's batteries, the fridge would soon have drained the remaining charge. It was important to get the boat ship-shape again as soon as possible. We anchored across from what looked like a marina. I took the dinghy across the ICW towards the docks and looked around for some sign of human presence. There was a boat in a slip with someone busy putting things away. I asked the man if there was a dinghy dock close by. He asked if we had any problems. I wondered why someone would jump to that conclusion. Was it my shoulder length hair or the beard covering my neck at the front, or just the thought that boaters always seem to have troubles? On the other hand boaters do like to help each other. It is mostly that which brings them together and makes things work. I admitted that we had problems and was invited aboard so that we could talk about it. After introducing ourselves I pointed out our boat, at anchor across the waterway. I explained that I would need to have a bracket made and showed him the two pieces. Putting them together himself he nodded and mentioned that it would be difficult to find someone there to bend and drill a new piece but that a welder was close by. He offered me a ride in order to find the place. Off we went American style, with the car to cover a few blocks to the marina. An American seldom would walk somewhere if there was a car to be used. It was a small shop along the side of the street. After a thorough inspection of my two pieces the owner of the shop agreed, "We will get those two pieces together again for tomorrow morning." Because one of the holes in the bracket was close to where it had broken, he decided to solder rather than weld it. Otherwise the hole would have been filled in and the whole thing become dysfunctional. He felt that the soldered joint would be strong enough. I did not have much choice and agreed.

While waiting we two boaters got into talking about our travels and, in the early evening, we all sat together on their boat telling of our latest adventures. We were able to leave our 3 jugs of mixed oil and water and dirty rags at the marina, for safe disposal. Back at the boat more troubles awaited me. The propane system was on strike. I traced the problem down to the solenoid, an electrically controlled safety valve, which shut off the propane at the bottle. The solenoid was controlled from a switch below deck. This allowed us to shut off the propane supply at deck level so that no pipes inside the boat would be under pressure. An important feature to have when the boat was under way. The solenoid was completely useless, it had been rusted-up when we bought the boat so I had purchased a spare one. I installed the spare and, with a bit of a delay, supper was ready for us to enjoy. "Every day, something else to fix," became our latest motto.

On the next day we took a walk through the centre of town. It was not very exiting. What triggered our attention were a few restaurants catering to motor bikers. Every year they had a get-together of bikers from all over the U.S. It reminded us of our helmets and leather gear which had travelled on the boat with us for over a year. So far we had found no need of it. I once read that a sailor used a helmet to protect him from getting knocked on the head while doing some work on his boat during a storm. He also felt that it cut down on the weird and scary noises as the winds piped through the rigging. We were prepared for the worst, should the need arise. In the meantime we enjoyed the sunshine and a stroll through the streets of Daytona, looking for a boat store. West Marine, one of the larger boat chain stores was located in downtown, and we picked up a new winch handle and a boat hook. We also needed to buy charts of the Atlantic, the approach to the English Channel, and a detailed chart for Falmouth, England. A boat hook was on sale, and it looked to me as if its handle could very well be used to replace the broken aluminum pipe from our dinghy sail. I bought it and it indeed proved to be the right piece to do the job. Our second stainless steel winch handle had fallen overboard on one of our trips, and we replaced it with a cheaper, plastic one.

We made a trip to the welding shop but the bracket was not ready. The welder got to work on it right away, and an hour later, we had the repaired bracket. The piece came right from the welder and had been painted black but the paint was not quite dry. A newspaper wrapping kept the paint from getting on my hands. When we returned to the boat, I got to work right away. It was fairly easy to put it all back together again, but the black paint ended up on my hands and on everything I had touched. The engine seemed to run just fine, the batteries were charged, and no excess oil consumption could be detected. One more new thing had to be remembered before commencing each journey: to check this bracket. I also made a note to have a new, more reliable piece, bent as a spare. Before remounting the soldered piece I measured it out and made a drawing of it, including the holes. If I could get a piece bent the same way I would be able to drill the holes myself. I definitely did not relish the idea of going across the Atlantic while relying on only the soldered bracket.

Anyone who has never worked with my Dad should consider himself lucky. I can just try to describe what it is like. The day broke quite nicely and I slept in for a few hours before climbing out of the V-berth, to have breakfast. For a while all was normal and the hollow mumbling sound of the motor covered up all other sounds. This kind of peace, however, did not last for long. Suddenly I *heard Daddy shout something across the deck to Marcel who came running to the cockpit and took over the wheel. Before he got there Dad had switched off the engine and everything was quiet, for a short moment. Dad was all excited about something and instructed Marcel harshly about what to do next. The quiet was filled with a kind of tension. I could follow the conversation up to the point where he said something about an emergency stop. I had no clue what that could have referred to and I am sure neither had Marcel. It turned out that all he had to do was to steer the boat so it would glide along the edge of the channel. Next I heard the clatter of the anchor chain falling onto the deck. I got up from the table to have a look. We were going at a slow pace, quietly gliding along the edge of the channel. A splash from the water out front and the noise of the chain rolling over and out the front roller told me that we were anchoring. I was familiar with that noise but could not understand why we wanted to anchor here, in the middle of the day. The boat turned around and Dad put down another anchor in the back before returning to the cockpit. He was not very happy and in a grumpy, loud voice told me to get out of the way. Then he hurried away down below to open up the motor panels, talking to the different parts in an unpleasant way. I noticed that it would be best to move back to my V-berth. Everyone else left the scene. Mom in the aft cabin and Pascal with Anisha and me. In no time the whole saloon was cluttered up with spanners, pliers, rags, papers, and other undefined objects while Dad himself was deep inside the motor compartment. He was still talking with some of the parts in there, mentioning tight space, no room, filthy place and so on. His mood did improve when he found the source of the problem. He announced it with a happier voice. There was something about a filter. I could not make out what he was saying but of course I pretty well knew that we were stuck in this place. I did not dare ask for how long. From time to time I watched what was going on, just out of pure curiosity. Dad was now even further inside the structure around the motor. The next thing I saw was his one arm, totally black. To me it looked as if it were burned. I was relieved to hear that the ***** (he called it a very impolite word) filter had got a hole and spread the oil into the "bloody" bilge. The latter swear word he used once things had started to settle down. I had been hoping for that for some time. Mom made some coffee and things got* *back to normal. There was of course still a big mess all around. Milk jugs, rags, plastic bags, motor covers, wood boards, a bilge pump or whatever it was which showed some white through its oily surface and some smaller parts that looked like nuts and bolts. We were happy to know that things could soon be put together again. That meant we would be under way again. I was happy to know that my Dad could fix anything to get us moving along and that compensated for his sometimes unusual behaviour.*

As soon as we were under way, Anisha and I spent the rest of the day with the newly-purchased beanie babies. I also started to read a new book, called "Lassie And The Secret Of The Summer".

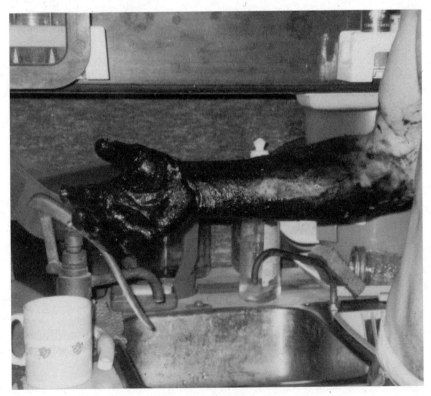

After cleaning the bilge

Pascal rides his imaginary dinosaur

Titusville

The weather was both rainy and windy when we left Daytona, early in the morning. With the wind on our nose, we were forced to motor south, along the ICW. Our time was filled with routine events such as watching out for markers, passing under bridges, writing in the log book and doing other chores that made up a routine journey.

When we arrived at Smyrna Beach, we noticed the boat Bon Bon anchored nearby. Their catamaran had a four foot-draft, which enabled them to anchor inside a channel with less than 1.8m (6 feet) of water. We had to anchor away from them, along the ICW, in deeper water. Our first encounter with them had been about seven months earlier, in Beaufort, on our way up. Our paths had crossed again in Annapolis. It was great fun to get together again, even though the rain kept pouring down. Our rain gear really paid for itself. The following day was worse, and we decided to wait out the strong winds and rain.

With the tide running against the wind, our boat was pushed against the current in the channel, tipping it slightly to the side. Using a hand held gadget, which I had bought on our last visit to the boat store, I measured steady winds of about 22 knots. Our large anchors held securely. In the evening things returned to normal. Over the VHF we invited the crew from Bon Bon to have supper with us.

The next morning the sun was out again. Around eight in the morning we left on our way to Titusville, one day before the planned shuttle departure. In some spots the channel was not very deep. We had to make sure to stay in the marked channel, which soon opened up into a large lake. We set sail and made good headway. Shortly before our next anchorage Bon Bon, who had left a couple of hours after us, overtook us. They were already at anchor when we arrived, and it was there, in Titusville, that the crew of Bon Bon made the only picture of our boat with the sails up. Once anchored, most of us got a ride in the motorized rubber dinghy from Bon Bon. They went to visit a nearby playground. Marcel and I stayed on board. It was almost dark before the others returned.

Kristy Nicole, under sail and towing her dinghy

We were eager to visit the post office and hoped to find that some of our mail had been forwarded to it. Nothing, however, had arrived so we would just have to be patient. The space shuttle launch had been postponed to the 22nd, due to poor weather. This gave me the opportunity to take care of some long overdue tasks. On my last visit to the boat store in Daytona, I had looked at a wind generator. I had designed a mounting device for it and wanted to get that made. After some inquiries I found a boat yard with plenty of junk lying around. There I found some aluminum plates for the mast and a pipe that could be welded between them to hold the shaft of the generator. The owner was willing to weld it all together, according to my drawing. I also showed him a drawing of the bracket to hold the alternator and asked him to make up two pieces. He offered me an excellent price, the work was done very accurately, and I was extremely happy to find such a skilled person. These pieces were important to me for the continuation of our trip, especially when thinking about the proposed crossing of the Atlantic.

The 22nd arrived and together with Bon Bon's crew, we watched the launch of the space shuttle. Everyone was prepared for the moment, camera at hand. It was already dark when all of a sudden a very bright light, just like the sun, slowly made its way up the dark sky. The boat and surroundings were well lit up. Because of the distance between us and the launching site at Cape Canaveral, we could not hear any noise. The light soon became smaller, moving faster and faster. At one time we could see two glowing pieces separating from the rest. They must have been the empty booster rockets, which carried the fuel for the launching system. Then the spot of light got smaller and smaller and soon there was nothing to see anymore; a short but impressive display.

While reflecting on the technological achievement we had just witnessed, I was struck by the big gap our society has created. On the one side we have this marvel of high tech equipment, put together by very intelligent people, in search of new insight into the workings of our universe. On the other hand we still kill each other over religious differences and material possessions. Iraq, Ireland, Israel and Kosovo were instances which sprang readily to mind. Obviously some knowledge has not been passed on correctly to encourage us to live together in peace. Even worse was the fact that millions of people on this world are starving to death, in a world which supplies more than we need. It was a privilege to be on the boat and be able to watch and contemplate it all from a distance. I had no solutions for these problems but was sad to know that our highly-developed society could not deal with them either. Technology certainly has made an impact on how we live in our western society. Without the advanced equipment, we could not have used a GPS to navigate with such ease. We were also able to travel freely, for a limited time, through other countries such as the USA and Europe. In some ways this has brought the western world closer together, but what about the rest, and larger part of the world's population? I had often thought on these matters but, lacking any solutions, simply had to accept things as they were.

The next day we were very surprised by the arrival of Aquila in the anchorage. The kids immediately launched the dinghy to go and join their friends. The crews of all 3 boats spent the evening together, with a big celebration. The crews of Aquila and Bon Bon decided to continue south the next day. It was the last time that we would see Aquila on that trip. I did run into the skipper of Bon Bon the next year while we were in Falmouth. He had just sailed the boat back to Europe. The rest of his crew had flown back to Germany.

We would have liked to sail south with Bon Bon and Aquila, but we were still waiting for our mail to arrive. On the 30th of January I telephoned the post office to ask them to forward our mail to Palm Beach. To my surprise I was told that our long-awaited mail had arrived. I borrowed a bicycle from the owner of Moonglow. We had met him at Mile 155, near Vandemere. He was a single-handed sailor, enjoying life on the water. We had talked to him several times in the marina. With his bike I made a quick trip to pick up the mail. At the same time, I visited a copy centre to make copies of the most important charts for crossing the Atlantic. I did not want to use the originals, just in case the two most abundant elements, wind and water, might get hold of them.

When I returned to the boat, we got things ready to get under way. We planned to arrive in Melbourne the following day. It had been decided to buy our wind generator and new batteries, to replace one of the existing banks, there. It was time to replace the 3 old parallel wired 12-volt batteries with two in-series wired 6-volt batteries. This way, if one of the batteries got weak, it could be detected by measuring each battery's voltage. This was not the case with the present setup. The batteries were connected in parallel so, if one of the batteries got weak, it would drain the others. The batteries making up the 2nd bank were still working well, so I decided to leave them as they were.

Finally it became warmer again and the condensation problem disappeared. My bedding was a bit drier. From all the rain during the past days the inside had become moist anyway, but not as bad as when the walls were dripping wet. This time our anchorage was quite a way from the dock. I could not see it, as it was behind a wall which protected the marina. The water in this area was not calm. In the evenings it usually got fairly rough but our boat did not move much. I could watch other boats' masts sway sideways a lot more than ours as the waves passed by. We hoped that we would be able to see the shuttle launch from our berth. I had been reading up on the Internet about the launch for quite some time. There was a museum

at the site, which I really wanted to go and see. Daddy told me that we might be able to do so, along with the children from another boat.

On the night of the launch, I was so excited about what would happen. It had been on everyone's mind for the past month or so. We had planned our journey to arrive here in time. The sky was clear. We had some sunshine during the day. Not that it got extremely warm, but at least during the day it was pleasant. We spent the day exploring a nearby island together with the kids from Bon Bon. I was allowed to go along in their rubber dinghy. Wow, was I ever happy. I was allowed to steer the dinghy. It had a 15 horsepower motor and when I opened up the throttle that thing just zoomed away, its nose poking up and the water splashing to both sides. This was a real thrill for me. Never before had I travelled through the water so quickly. Actually we were on top of the water most the time. It was an exhilarating experience with me controlling the action. The island was about a 10 minute ride away, going as fast as we did. I cannot remember what speed we went but, for me, it was definitely fast enough. On the beach of the island we found some nice shells and driftwood. There were bushes on it but the island was quite small and, most likely, got covered with water once in a while; I assume that it would not have been a good spot for a house. There were a few birds flying to and fro. We played tag, running up and down in the sand, and spent most of our time just fooling around.

By evening the crew from Bon Bon had joined us on our boat. Darkness covered the scenery and all we could see were a few lights, far off in the distance, where the action would take place. I stood there with my eyes glued to a spot in the darkness which Dad had told us to look at. It seemed to take forever but, finally, a big fire ball was visible. The light was very intense but I could not hear a thing. Then, slowly at first, the light lifted off the ground, which was clearly visible as a dark horizon. Minutes later all that was left was a tiny little glow way up in the sky and eventually that disappeared from view as well. That was it. I was a bit disappointed. I had expected a lot of noise and smoke. We were, obviously, too far way for anything to be seen or heard, nor did I feel anything.

Our visit to the space centre was a great compensation for the lack of excitement during the launch. There we really had some action.

What interested me the most were the heat resistant tiles (reinforced carbon-carbon tiles RCC) on the nose of the shuttle. I had not thought that it would get so hot on the surface of the space shuttle, when it returned and entered our atmosphere. As a demonstration, one of these ceramic tiles was heated up to 2200 degrees Celsius. The back of the tile stayed nice and cold. A space shuttle has more than 24000 tiles on its outside and they have to withstand temperatures of about 3000 degrees Fahrenheit (about 1650 degrees Celsius). I was allowed to wear one of the space suits, or at least the helmet of one. That sure felt weird. The person demonstrating it talked to me via the helmet radio. It sounded as if he were talking through a pipe. I felt rather clumsy. Of course I was only the size of a kid and the helmet was for an adult. We also saw a real space ship, set up outside. It looked so big! I felt like a dwarf. I was tired and happy to go back to the boat for a good night's rest. That had been one memorable day.

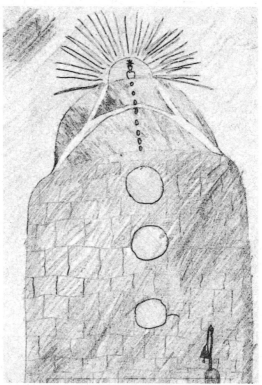

Lighthouse, as seen by Pascal

Chapter 20
Melbourne

We arrived in Melbourne in the early afternoon. The water was almost flat, and we anchored close to the spot which had been recommended to us by other boaters. This put us as close to the store as we wanted to be.

I enquired at the store about getting new batteries and was told that I would have to go to Sam's. His place was a fair bit away, but we had to replace the faulty batteries. The next day I loaded one battery on the bicycle's back carrier and put the other in the packsack on my back. When sitting on the bike I could rest the packsack on the first battery and it was securely fastened to the carrier. I could not go very fast like that, but it worked. It took me over an hour to get to Sam's place. They had the batteries I was looking for, so I traded my old ones in for a rebate on the new ones. The new batteries were even heavier than the ones I had just got rid of. I made sure to secure them on the carrier with extra care. It was too valuable a cargo to be dropped. Recalling the time in Annapolis, when I had carried the heavy fire hose, I knew that the bike could carry the load. In due course the batteries, and a tired biker, got back safely to the boat.

In the afternoon the water became a bit rough. With the anchorage in the wide open, we were more than anxious to have good weather. We could not leave the boat unattended in a strong wind lest the anchors drag. While the rest of the family visited the library, just next to the anchorage, I went a couple of blocks further up to purchase all of the hardware necessary to mount the new batteries. The boat store had wind generators on sale. There were none in stock, so it looked as if it was a popular item and I had to order one. I purchased the required cables and wires, including an A-meter which was to be hooked up "in-line". Once installed, this meter would indicate if all was working properly, as well as giving an accurate reading of the current produced by the generator.

By the time we were ready to go back to the boat the wind had picked up considerably and the water was very choppy. I decided to make two trips. I set off with Marcel, Anisha and Pascal. Marcel and I each used an oar and we got along quite well. Water often blew in over the bow. Because we were sitting on the front bench of the dinghy our backs got soaked. Anisha was kept busy bailing the water out again while Pascal kept the motor handle in position to steer us towards the boat. It was hard work, rowing into the wind. At the boat I unloaded everyone and turned back to get Chäberli and Carina. That trip was easy, with the wind at my back. I had to row the second load on my own, Carina dumped the incoming water while Chäberli steered the boat. It worked, but by the time we reached the boat, everyone was soaked to the bone. For once, Carina had actually enjoyed the challenge and had a big smile on her face.

The wind had, fortunately, abated by the next day and we were able to row the dinghy ashore in the hope of getting the ordered parts. A couple was standing on the dock and asked if we knew the crew on Rhiannon. The name instantly reminded us of Beaufort, where we had met the crew (see Chapter 7). We remembered that they had mentioned that they knew a couple with their boat Lindsey Christine staying at the marina in Melbourne, behind a monumental sculpture called The Dragon. We had seen The Dragon from a distance when we arrived and it was now visible, just a mile or so across the water and to our left. It was such a great feeling to meet people and make friends like this along the way.

The couple suggested that we should anchor behind The Dragon and enjoy a much more protected mooring. This would also bring us much closer to their boat. We agreed but first went to the store to pick up the wind generator. It was still on backorder. There were now inverters on sale. These would convert the 12 Volt current from the batteries to 110 Volts. I would then be able to use the electric drill on board the boat. I had to weigh the usefulness of this gadget against the unexpected drain on our meagre finances but decided to buy it. It was much easier to mount the support bracket for the wind generator and to drill the holes needed to fit the bolts and cables.

Towards the evening we moved our boat behind The Dragon. As soon as we passed behind it, entering Banana River, the water became smooth. What a difference. There were several boats already at anchor along the river, and we found a nice spot, about 500m (500 yards) up from the marina. We could see the fuel dock and a few boats along the river. Mathers Bridge, a swing bridge, was about 100m (100 yards) further north. It was a great spot. To the west were houses along the shore and the other side was lined with expensive housing, developed in the latest style, which was mainly characterized by large windows and spacious yards.

While we were dropping our anchor, a police patrol boat passed. The officer had a short chat with us, and we asked him if we needed to display an anchor light. He felt that it was not needed here, as the channel was well lit and the place a no-wake area. We thanked him for his information, knowing that with the light on we would have had to use the engine, to re-charge the batteries, more often. We looked forward to installing the wind generator and with it to become independent of the engine, at least as long as the wind was blowing.

The next day we visited our new friends in the marina. It gave us an opportunity to take a shower and do our laundry at the marina. Of course we had a lot to share with each other about our life on the boat, and we met their two children. It was great to see the kids playing in the trees along the pier while we sat in the cockpit of their boat, secured to the gangplank. This also gave us a place to go ashore, leaving our dinghy at their boat.

Our new friends were both self-employed. He was working independently, doing office repairs and a paper route. She had some success writing articles for magazines. Their boat was smaller than ours but a small dog still had his place in the cockpit. They intended to stay in this area for a while. They were very kind people indeed. On several occasions we got together for outings, barbeques and of course shopping. Their children were also home schooled, and we hoped that ours would pick up on the habit of working in the mornings, just as they had done in Annapolis. That was too much to ask for. Carina was not at all in a mood to sit down and work on her maths. She could be very stubborn about that and did not want to be told when, or what, to do. It sometimes was a real struggle and was the reason that work was delayed or not done at all.

I started work on a small table to fit around the compass in the cockpit. It would hold the GPS, a mug and the VHF. This would make it more comfortable to steer and the 12V cables would be out of the way.

The weather forecast was for another cold front to pass bringing with it very strong winds. This situation continued for several weeks to come. We had to plan our trips ashore between the blows but, sometimes, we did get wet, even though we were in a fairly well protected location.

The wind generator finally arrived, and we then had all the parts required to install it on the mizzenmast. Marcel was a great help. Together we mounted the bracket where we thought it to be far enough up on the mast so that it would not interfere with the topping lift of the mainsail. Next, the wires needed to be placed, secured and connected, making sure to select the correct polarity on both ends. At the first moment I was absolutely overwhelmed with joy. Once switched on, the three blades gently started to turn pointing into the now just light wind and the newly installed meter showed a steady current of 2 Amps. We had got our own power plant! This was a day to celebrate. Finally we had a device that could put a balance on our consumption of energy, and from now on, it was a free service. No engine noise, pollution or worry about fuel consumption. It was obviously the right choice. As weather fronts passed, our batteries were soon charged up to full capacity, one by one. We were then able to use the cabin lights as much as we pleased.

We installed a rain catcher on the front deck. It had, originally, been designed as a sun cover between the two masts (see picture on page 301). As a rain catcher the canvas covered the whole area from the bowsprit to the mast . A hose was mounted to a funnel-like insert that lead to the deck-mounted lid of the water tank. With the rainy weather during the coming days we caught plenty of water and filled our 700 litre (200 gallon) water tank with ease.

During the odd days when the sun did come out,we got together with the crew from Lindsey Christine and arranged for a barbeque or walks in the nearby park. On one such occasion, we noticed a manatee and its baby swimming in the canal which flowed below the bridge we were crossing. This was an animal we were not familiar with, so we spent some time watching them slowly moving along in the shallow water. They are a protected species and usually live in the calm waters of the ICW. Many more outings were made to the nearby park. Here is a short extract from Anisha's diary about one such outing.

Drilling holes for the wind generator mount

"Yesterday we went to the park to roller blade. When we got to the shore, the other kids were on their roller blades and said they would go to the park soon. Well, we did not have our roller blades with us, and a pretty hard wind was blowing where the boat was. So I rowed out again, Carina and our friend with me in the dinghy to

make my load heavier. The way to Kristy Nicole was all upwind, so I had a pretty hard time. When we got there, Mommy came out to take the painter (the line to tie the dinghy to the boat). I told her that we came to get our roller blades and were going to go to the park. So she came too. We went back to the marina and then to the park."

The next sunny day I helped sand down the deck of Lindsey Christine to prepare it for a new coat of paint. It was a dusty job but enjoyable, talking and sharing thoughts. I was very happy to be able to contribute ideas and to share in their way of life. I was dusty from top to bottom and ready for a shower. Earlier on, the manager of the marina had hinted that I should stop using the showers because we were not berthed in the marina. He would have liked to see our boat pay the fee for a berth. It was an edgy issue, because guests of boaters did have the permission to use the showers. He obviously did not like something about me or felt that I took advantage of the situation, and promptly caught me again leaving the showers. During the short conversation that followed, he muttered a few insulting words threatening to call the police should I use them again. It was clear, that we were not welcome.

February 22nd, 3 weeks since we arrived in Melbourne. The winds had changed, not only from the management of the marina but also with the weather. They were blowing from the south, making it warm and pleasant. They stayed strong for the whole day, separating the clouds and letting the sun peek through. I was on the deck of Kristy Nicole, watching the clouds to the east, when something unusual happened. I saw a funnel shaped cloud forming. As it came closer to the ground it changed its whitish colour to a gray and then got wider. I had just witnessed the touchdown of a Tornado. I called the children and ran for my camera. The thing moved north and was about 8km (5 miles) away. A huge, mushroom-shaped plume of cloud formed. The whole scene may have lasted a few minutes and all that was left was this huge cloud. I had never seen such a thing, and it clearly demonstrated that great force was involved in creating these clouds. We were glad to be far enough away from it. In the news there was a report that several houses had been damaged but, fortunately, no one had been killed.

That was just the beginning of some very nasty weather passing through the east coast of Florida. Tornado warnings were issued several times during the following days. Early the next morning, a sudden gust of wind shook us out of bed. After the main blow had hit the boat, we measured the wind with our hand-held device, and it recorded about 40 knots. The boat tipped a fair bit to the side. When I had a chance to look through the porthole of our cabin, I saw the boat moving wildly over the surface of the water. I ran up on deck to find out what was going on. By then our boat sat a fair bit further out in the channel and both anchor chains were stretched tight. Gradually the wind lessened and the boat moved back towards its normal position. The wind was coming from the northwest and with it strong rain followed. Listening to the news in the morning, we heard about several terrible tornados, killing 40 people and leaving hundreds injured. Once more we were lucky to have been missed. A nearby heavy pier on the oceanfront had been completely washed away overnight, a scene that had been shown on international TV news casts. Because the news had been broadcast worldwide, Chäberli phoned her parents in Switzerland. They would have been worried for our safety.

A boat which was anchored south of the river, stopped by to chat with Chäberli and invited her for lunch. They had a car available and planned to go to the laundry the next day. Since my last encounter with the manager at the marina, we had avoided using the marina's facilities as much as possible. I am sure they would have liked our money in the washing machine, but we thought that we should be consistent.

Later that week we met up with our new friends and shared a great supper with them. During our discussion, I was offered a spinnaker pole, suggesting that I return the one I had just bought at West Marine. That was a great gift. The pole I got was much stronger, the kind you dream about having. With some extra hardware I was able to mount it and provide a storage position for it along the stay. It seemed to look as if our trip across the Atlantic was coming together bit by bit.

The days were still short, and we usually retired at around 8 p.m. One night, when we had just gone to bed, someone called from the outside. I was unable to understand what they said, but it sounded strange. I got half way dressed again and went on deck to find two officers, in their speedboat, clinging onto our boat. They complained about our boat not displaying an anchor light! We had been there for close to a month and had seen many patrol boats go by. Why, I wondered, had they taken so long to notice the lack of our light? I tried to explain that I had talked to one of their colleagues when we had arrived and that he had given us permission to leave the light off. Unfortunately I had not asked that officer his name but that was what the two on patrol wanted to know! There was no mercy and the officer handed me a ticket for US $55.00. I was very upset to see how they were more interested in making money than in giving a warning. In the back of my mind I was thinking that, with the excess of power from the wind generator, we could have easily run the anchor light day and night but had not seen any need to do so. By then the whole family was on deck. When I refused to sign the ticket the officer pointed out that I should appear in court, as stated on the ticket, or else they would have no option but to arrest me. The appearance date in court was set for March 25th. This date gave me no chance to defend myself either, as our sailing visa was good only till March 23rd. When I pointed this out to the officers they showed no interest and left us in the dark. The next day I phoned the court to find out if I could have a court appearance earlier and was asked to appear on March 4th. For a moment it looked as if we would be given a chance.

I took a long bike ride to arrive at the court before 2 p.m. on the date of my appearance. I was directed to a door. The room I entered had no windows and benches were arranged like pews in a church. Before I got accustomed to the light and the new surroundings I was asked, by one of the many officers in the room, to take off my hat. Not a good start at all I thought! My mother had taught me to take off my hat when entering a church but then I was not even aware that I was in a courtroom nor that I still had my hat on. Some men were chained together and standing in the very front row. What were they doing here? There I sat, together with other "accused", some of them handcuffed, on trial for things I would not have dreamed of being part of, nor keen on being associated with. The next couple of hours were sickening for me. I had to listen to all these trials. On the other hand, in retrospect, I appreciated the glimpse I had of the kind of society these officers had to deal with and live in. After all the cases were heard the judge asked if anyone else was appearing. Obviously, they did not know of my presence so I asked to be heard. The judge, however, didn't want a hearing but just asked if I was pleading guilty or not. I said, "Not Guilty" so he gave me a new date for appearance, the 24th of March. Great help, I thought. Another form had then to be signed. The heading read: County Court, Brevard County, Florida, and below: Criminal Division. I refused to sign a form with such a heading and told them that I was not a criminal. They were not sure how to handle the situation, but let me go anyway. As I prepared to leave one of the police officers pulled me to the side and told me, in a snooty voice, that the court could not set dates to please any dude who happened to walk in. He then pointed to the exit. In the hallway I went to a lady sitting in a glass booth, hoping that she could advise me if I had any other options. As I was talking with her, an officer nearby asked me to leave the building. So much for a free country, I thought. When I asked him to wait till I had finished my conversation, he got very angry. It was obvious that I was getting nowhere and felt that I was being stereotyped as just another long haired, bearded criminal. It was time to leave. Back at the boat I was not in the best of moods. I sat down and compiled an article to be distributed to a couple of newspapers; one of them was published.

Because the new court date was one day after the expiration date of our sailing visa, I decided that it would be better to pay the fine and not risk being denied reentry into the US. I asked our friends from Lindsey Christine to give me a ride to the office, in order to pay the ticket. It was way out in the countryside and hard to get to by public transport. At least we had friends to help us get over the whole situation, something we valued highly. They certainly helped me overcome the frustration that had built up during the whole process. It had brought back memories of encounters with police I had experienced during our travels in Florida. The fences and security officers appeared in my mind again and again. I remembered the comment someone had once made to me, saying that Florida was called the waiting room to heaven, a place where the older people came to stay, mostly for the warmer climate, until their time was up. I could not understand why they would enjoy living in these fenced in and, probably, fairly expensive places. Did they need to be protected from the rest of society? I assume they would not have had to wait to purchase a wind generator for their boat nor bother about paying a ticket for not displaying an anchor light.

As my mind wandered over such thoughts it became apparent that, to a large extent, we could choose where we wanted to live. It was a great and liberating feeling to be able to go back to the boat, mind my own business and pull the hook to leave when, or if, I wanted to. Not belonging to any particular place or society brought a great sense of freedom.

We were again preparing the boat to head south, to Lake Worth. It was to be our last stop in the USA before heading across the Gulf Stream to the Bahamas and then across the Atlantic. It gave us a strange feeling even thinking about it. Previously, we had spoken with the crew of a nearby boat. They knew that we intended to do a crossing and asked if we had a radio. This was something for which we did not have the money. The next day these same people appeared with two fairly large boxes. They explained that they would be throwing that radio away because its transmitter would no longer work. We could have it for free, if we were interested. Of course we were, and, at the same time, thankful for their thoughtfulness.

We installed the radio immediately to determine if we could receive weather information from Herb, a retired sailor living in Canada. He broadcast weather information to boaters on the Atlantic. And so it was, we received his signal fairly well and could listen in on weather forecasts for different boats across the Atlantic. It created a good feeling, to be able to access this information. That was the last piece of equipment we required to enable us to set out on our adventure. It was the people we met that made this country a great place to remember.

We pulled up to the fuel dock to top-up our tanks so as to be ready to leave in the morning. Trying to take off from the fuel dock caused a small problem. We had to do a sharp turn, using the opening between the dock and a wall. Every time we were about half way around, the wind blew us back. The barnacles growing on the underside of the boat did not help to improve the situation. Kristy Nicole just did not want to swing around. After a few more trials our newly-made friends came zooming along with their rubber dinghy. They had been watching us from their boat and had seen that we were having difficulties. On the next try they used their dinghy to push the bow of Kristy Nicole, and the extra help turned her nicely.

It was difficult to part from all the new friends we had made here, but it was time to move on. One final evening was spent with our friends. I was very glad to have met these people. The mixed feelings about Melbourne stay to this day. The slogan imprinted on their public buses, "Tourism works for Brevard," did not appear to hold true for us.

 *I liked St. Augustine a lot, the old town with its old houses and the fort. I loved walking through the little alleyways and looking into all the little stores. It was especially nice with the Christmas decorations. I very much enjoyed the concert in the old church. To me a concert is like a church service, glorifying God in song. The only problem to me in St. Augustine, was that we were anchored so far out. It always was a big effort to get into the dinghy with all the wet gear and winter clothes, because it was not too warm even though we were farther south. Rowing against the current and sometimes against the wind was a big job. That day when I had to go pick up the others in the blowing rain and choppy water is still in my mind. I complained to Werner why were we not closer to the dinghy dock? He wanted to be well away from the bridge after the first night there and being pushed almost into it. At night when the wind blew hard I could not sleep very well. I always checked out the little porthole beside the bed to see if we were still in the same spot.*

On our way to Titusville we were sailing with two sails up when we saw BonBon approaching. We quickly pulled up the third sail and shouted over to them to take a picture of us. We did the same for them and later when we had the pictures developed we were able to exchange them. I also had taken pictures of some boats sailing on the way here in the ICW and found one of them, Moonglow, here in Titusville in the marina. I went there to bring the pictures and the owner of the boat was very happy. He invited us for tea and we had a nice chat.

I did not like the open anchorage in Melbourne at all. It was too wild and the trip back to the boat in the bad weather was not great at all. I found it funny that Carina would actually enjoy bailing water. It was a struggle to row and to steer and getting all wet and almost drowning. Who would find that fun? Things like this were very stressful to me.

Finishing the installation of the new wind generator

Chapter 21
Lake Worth

On the day we left Melbourne, Chäberli's diary already read the 10th of March, 14 days before we would have to leave the USA. No matter what, our permit was about to run out. As we came closer to the south, we noticed more houses and roads. Some of these houses were built like mansions, some in strange colours, some shaped like castles, reflecting the owner's individual tastes!

The day started out windy, but we could motor through the ICW most of the way to the anchorage at Ft. Pierce. Our boat did not move as quickly through the water as it used to. The many barnacles that had settled on its hull caused it to move about a knot slower. Most of the growth had gathered while we were staying in St. Augustine and Melbourne. There was nothing we could do about it. The water there was way too cold and not clear enough to see well while working under water. Cleaning the bottom under such conditions was out of the question. A haul out would have cost money that we could not afford to spend. Looking forward to the Bahamas, we postponed the job, hoping for cleaner and warmer water which would allow us to do the job with ease. Our life raft also needed attention. Each year it should be inspected in order to ensure that it still functioned properly and to check that the contents, such as the flashlight, food supply, thermal blankets and other items packed inside, were in satisfactory condition. A call to the company from which we had bought the raft brought unwelcome information. Just to inspect the raft, a cost of over US $250.00, plus pickup and delivery charges, had been quoted. We had not budgeted for this and there was no way we could afford such an expense. We assumed the raft was still functioning satisfactorily as it was only a year since we had purchased it.

Sailors anchored at Ft. Pierce mentioned to us that they would take the one-day outside passage and use the safe entrance at Lake Worth. The weather seemed to be holding up, and we decided to do the same. We were eager to get on, and this would cut out the drag of waiting for 9 bridges to open while we were on the ever-busier ICW.

The spot we had anchored in was quite shallow, some parts reading only 2.1m (7 feet) deep. At 6:45 in the morning we left the anchorage and did not encounter any serious problems. While motoring towards the main channel, however, all eyes were glued on the depth sounder. We motored at about 4 knots. Every time we read 2.4 m (8 feet) we became nervous, wondering if we should follow the boat straight ahead of us, which belonged to the people from whom we had received the radio. Should we turn to line up with one of the other boats to either side of us, or just stay in the middle, between the right hand shore and some islands on the left? The options were many, but it appeared to make no difference which way one went. An hour later we had reached the ocean, relieved to be in deeper water. We had often wished for a boat with less draft, in order to sail in shallower water. On the other hand, however, we knew that the deep keel gave the boat more stability once it was out in the open water. In our case it would have made perfect sense to have a boat where you could adjust the keel's depth. As an afterthought, it may also have meant having something more that could have broken down or gone wrong!

The open water offered slightly larger waves, maybe 1.5m (5 feet) at the time that we reached it. Anisha and Pascal had taken medication for motion sickness ahead of the trip. Chäberli and I took the new homeopathic drops, which helped a bit, and Carina and Marcel tried to do without. While Carina slept the whole morning in the back of the boat, all others were on deck, busy doing something. Marcel felt a bit uneasy and this time Pascal was the most active. The drugs did help him not to get seasick. At the same time his energy level was abnormally high.

The wind died down and was not strong enough to keep the needed speed, so we motored all the way to Lake Worth, arriving at the inlet around 4:30 p.m. We planned to cross over to the Bahamas as soon as possible and tried to anchor in an area close to the entrance. There were a lot of boats anchored there but, with the strong tidal current, our first try to anchor failed. We changed our plan and agreed to motor another hour to reach a quieter anchorage further north. With the wind on the nose we had to run the engine at full speed in order to make some way.

Lake Worth is a large anchorage. On arrival we noticed several boats that we had seen on our travels up north. Unfortunately our toilet got plugged up again. We had run out of toilet paper and a paper towel had plugged up the system. By then I knew where the critical spot was along the pipe and the next day I had the pleasant work of unplugging it one more time. At least we were at anchor so I was not thrown back and forth all the time while at work.

It was amazing how many things we had learned about the boat's ins and outs. To have such a long trial trip, before undertaking a long journey, had definitely turned out to be a good idea. I knew where the weak points of the boat were, such as the motor mounts, the alternator mount, the steering mechanism, which needed some steady replenishing of oil, and the many more other little things, just like the toilet. We had become accustomed to Murphy's Law which we changed a touch to say, "Anything which could go wrong - would go wrong and at the most inconvenient time." With that in mind, we tried to prepare for such pitfalls.

We had noticed that the small, automatic bilge pump stayed on if the boat leaned to the side in such a way that its side rails would just glide above the water. There were two automatic pumps with control switches and lights to show their functioning, and in such circumstances, we usually switched the smaller pump off. Besides the two pumps we also had a manual bilge pump. I had replaced it after it had broken down when we were emptying our wastewater tank. This was the tank the toilet wastes could be directed to, using a Y-valve. The valve was mostly set to empty overboard but, in Florida, a law was put out recently stating that boaters were no longer allowed to pump these waters overboard while close to the shore. It certainly was a good way to prevent pollution. Boaters, however, felt that the present pollution of the water had come from sources other than the few boaters living aboard their boats. It was just something more boaters could be checked for. We had one such visit to our boat by the Florida Coast Guard while we were anchored at Lake Worth. They were checking our boat for safety installations, including the proper installation and use of a wastewater tank. They were happy to see everything was in place; the toilet switched to the holding tank and secured with a lock, the fire extinguishers charged, the life jackets ready, the emergency rockets up to date plus a few other details. They were certainly happy to see our children being able to experience the world at sea and wished us good luck on our crossing. Thank God that we made this very upbeat experience with officials before leaving the States. This time we had adhered to each paragraph, as spelled out in the law. I could vividly remember the episode with the anchor light. After all this I wonder if these officers really chase the ones who need to get caught in order to protect society?

On one of our shopping sprees, I found a new model coffee machine, where you push a handle, mounted to a round shaped screen, down into a round glass cylinder, in order to separate the grounds from the liquid, just like a filter would. Some called this a French press. So far I had used a filter setup. On the farm this system worked quite well, but on the boat it did not always work that way, especially when the boat was under way and moving in all directions. The top filter part usually fell off and, because the one I used was made of ceramics, it became severely chipped and, on one occasion, the handle went missing. The time was right to replace it. I was one happy sailor making coffee the next morning. Another gadget I had to part with, which had served us well during the stay at our farm, was the little hand-driven coffee grinder. With it I could grind my own mix of coffee. We still had some of this mix on the boat. Because of its usefulness, I had brought the little thing along on all our trips. During the journey across the Gulf of Mexico, I had used it for the last time. Standing in the galley I was not prepared for one huge wave rocking the boat so, while I was concentrating on trying to hold on to parts of the boat, the removable handle flew off the mill and vanished. After recovering from my fall, I checked out the floor. I was sure I had seen where it fell, but no trace of it remained. Many times later on during our voyage, I looked for it in all the nooks and crannies but with no success. Maybe it had taken a flight past the companionway, cockpit and rail, and landed in the ocean? I, for certain, knew that it had not fallen into the toilet.

Treatment of boat bites was taken care off by applying the juices of the Aloe Vera plant which was growing on board. We had bought it as a small plant during our stay in L.A. The plant had grown to a good size and had become a permanent fixture on the bridge. We were happy to have this plant aboard. We often had to rely on it to heal bruises, cuts and burns. The plant did not seem to mind travelling about with us, first in the car and then on the boat. Sometime later one of the children added another small-sized flowerpot beside it with a cactus. They both grew well on the boat. When Kristy Nicole was sold we took them off the boat and with us to Switzerland. There the plants were placed outside the living room window. We were not able to see them there and forgot about them. One night the frost killed the Aloe Vera plant. It was sad to lose such a valuable companion. All through our travels it had helped us heal our cuts and bruises. During our stay in Switzerland, we never bought a new one, even though the opportunity existed. The cactus still survived and became part of the science lab I used during my assignment as a teacher in Switzerland. More about this will have to be told in another story. The cactus always brought back memories of our sailing adventures. One particular story I can remember came from Pascal, during the above-mentioned trip from Ft. Pierce to Lake Worth. Even though we had a bit of a rough sea, Pascal was in good spirits, thanks to the medication. He noticed that the cactus placed on the bridge was leaning over the edge of its container just a bit. He pointed it out to me and suggested that the cactus was, most probably, seasick. Maybe he was right, who knows. I did not feel quite up to par myself for the first few hours and didn't want to argue.

Herb garden. Aloe Vera was on the starboard bridge

It certainly lightened my thoughts listening to Pascal's comments. We will definitely never forget how he called certain things around him. At age four for example he called the companion way the canyon way. When it came to mushrooms they were called washrooms. We never did figure out if he didn't like mushrooms because of what he called them. The word washroom was not in use much during the trip on the boat, as we called it the head. And then there were the baberries (strawberries), which we all liked very much.

We were ready to leave Florida, a place that had given us so much but, on the other hand, where we could not feel welcome. It had, of course, been the State where we had found Kristy Nicole and we had made many good friends there. Our trip along the east coast was a great adventure. The many highlights along the route were ingrained in our memories but so were the experiences with the authorities. I came to feel that living in a society based entirely on the written law rather than trust won't develop very well. One thing had become obvious, we had reached a turning point; it was time to leave it all behind and to seek out new horizons.

It was also high time to find out how we should approach the Bahamas and to get some charts and information about the islands. We were looking forward to visiting the northern part of the Bahamas, the Abaco Islands, before taking off across the Atlantic. We had heard a lot about the area and, after a recommendation, bought the "Guide to Abaco," by Steve Dodge. Because it did not show the charts as other publishers presented them, I was, at first, a bit sceptical and looked for some other publication. However, looking back, it was that guide which we relied on the most and which helped us navigate perfectly well through these islands. Some of the most helpful information was the Tide Tables and, of course, the many waypoints given to safely navigate the islands by using different routes and anchorages.

The first question was how we should approach the many islands. We already knew that it would be the easiest to start out as far south as possible. Lake Worth seemed to be a good choice. The above-mentioned guide did explain what to watch out for and gave waypoints to travel to when taking off from the coast of Florida.

Lake Worth, however, was not one of the points shown but could easily be approximated. The only question in my mind was related to passing over the reef: from the very deep water of the Gulf Stream to the suddenly marginal 2.7m (9 feet) of sandy bottom spiked with corals. At least that is what we were told to expect when entering the archipelago just south of Memory Rock. Other approaches such as the Indian Cay Channel would have offered only 1.5m (5 feet) of water. It seemed best to take an almost straight cut across the Gulf Stream to enter just below Memory Rock and then to follow the guide to the Mangrove Cay and anchor at Great Sale Cay.

A few more things needed to be looked after. We had to stock up on books in English, to make sure our time on the boat could be filled with reading. A second-hand bookstore filled some of the needs. The bookstore next door to it supplied some more reading. Marcel was just starting to read a book series called "The Animorphs", a science fiction series by K. A. Applegate. The girls were about to read the series about "Anne of Green Gables". Some craft materials were needed as well and, at a nearby store, the girls found crochet hooks, knitting needles and more designs to do with cross-stitches.

Carina's 11th birthday coming up, March 15th was the great day. Some of us enjoyed a meal at McDonald's, fulfilling one of her wishes. At the same time I got busy working on the upgrade of our homepage. There would, most likely, not be any computers available to access the Internet for some time to come. Unfortunately the computers we had found in the libraries here were all old, text-based systems. It was very awkward to use them for the kind of work I intended, and so I ended up at an Internet café to finish adding some pictures and text to our page. After that, I guessed, I would not be able to access the internet until we were half way across the Atlantic, most likely in Horta, a large city in the Azores. We had heard that at Marsh Harbour, one of the larger cities we planned to visit in the Bahamas, internet service was available but not at a reasonable cost. Before heading back to the boat we stopped at the grocery store and bought a pack of ice cream. Carina felt happy to open a few gifts, one of them a stuffed hand-sized dog from the "beanie baby series", something she really adored. The ice cream was a highlight before everyone snuggled into his or her berth.

The next few days were rather windy and we started to wonder if we would be able to leave before our sailing visa ran out. Waves in the anchorage were about a foot in height, and it became impossible to go ashore in our rowing dinghy. Winds were up to 30 knots and there was plenty rain. Our rain catcher worked very well, and the water tanks were filled to the brim. We still hoped for some better weather with winds, preferably, from the same direction as the Gulf Stream, namely from the south. If not, the waves would become rather choppy. However, there was another weather front coming from the north, which did not provide the perfect scenario. The latest forecast I listened to was on Friday, March 20th, and it called for winds of 15 knots from the NW, turning to West, then South during Saturday, ahead of the next front passing. I felt that winds from the back and then the south seemed to be the best scenario, though not optimal. Waves were predicted to be around 2.1m (7 feet). A trip to the fuel dock was made to top up with diesel and all the gear stowed away safely. These were to be our last few steps on American soil for some time to come.

I wish we could have stayed in Melbourne longer. We made such good friends and played together a lot. They had a computer on board, and we were allowed to use it sometimes. The only thing about that was that Marcel and his friend would budge in and kick us off all the time so that they could play their games. It didn't usually bother us too much, because there were plenty of other things to do. We had some plastic horses to play with, and these kept us amused for hours, as we would pretend they were wild horses out in the plains (on the lawn). We also had beaded lizards, of which we made lots to produce complete families to play with. When it came around time to leave, Carina and I were allowed to keep one of the horses each, which made us very happy. Carina got the chestnut mare with the flaxen mane and tail, which she named Nutmeg. I got to keep a pinto stallion with black mane and tail, whom I dubbed "Fly". They had saddles and bridles and everything.

On another day, us three girls got together and taught our friend how to do cross-stitching. It felt funny to teach something like this. We all enjoyed doing it, and it didn't take long before we were all sitting in the bushes nearby, working on our patterns. In return, our friend was helping out with painting. She was very good at it, and she painted a picture of our dinghy and gave it to us as a present.

One time we were sitting in our "fort" (mainly just a bunch of trees that were climbable with lots of leaves around them so that you couldn't really see in from the outside), and some people from a rowing club were warming up nearby. I guess they heard us, and started throwing little pebbles into the trees. We thought this was pretty silly of them, and left to find something else to do. We also had "cork boat" races in Melbourne. We would make little sail boats out of corks by sticking a coin in the bottom and a toothpick with a piece of paper as a sail on top, and race them against each other between the docks of the marina.

With all of these memories and our outings with the roller blades and the wonderful food and barbecues, it was hard to say goodbye when the time came. Before we left, we went to see the crew on Kristilla, and I gave them a painting I had made of their boat. It was my first real painting, and I was very happy to be able to give it to these wonderful people.

The outside trip to our next destination was not one that I found particularly pleasurable. Right to start with, the wind was blowing and we had waves of at least 1.5m (5 feet). I tried to make some Raman noodle soup, but most of the contents ended up on the floor. It was impossible to clean it up with the boat lurching constantly, so I just braced myself and drank the stuff that was left over in my cup. It didn't make me feel too much better, and I was glad when the wind died down somewhat and the ride became a bit more balanced. Dad, however, was not too impressed. The boat was moving too slowly for us to arrive on time, so he switched on the engine. I didn't really mind at all.

We were in the anchorage of Lake Worth for 2 days when us kids and Dad decided to go ashore to find a birthday present for Carina. I didn't know what to give her, and she didn't ever give reasonable answers when I asked her. The usual gist of it was that she wanted to marry a prince or something. That not being in my power to give her, I was at a loss. We went to the library first. The computers there didn't have the graphic internet layout, but were all text based, and I couldn't figure it out at all. We soon decided it was too bothersome and left. There was a mall nearby up the main street, and we looked around for a present in there. There wasn't really anything that made much sense to buy, so we decided to return to Kristy Nicole. The mall was so big, though; we had a hard time finding the doors that we had come in by, and we finally just left by the next doors we came across. So we returned to the boat without a gift. I decided I'd give her a cross-stitch that I had made of a cow with beads on it that I had put in a little frame.

On Carina's birthday, everybody went ashore but Mom and I. I was, to say the least, not very impressed with this arrangement. I would have liked to go ashore, too, but they decided that they would go without me otherwise Dad, doing the rowing, could not have gone due to lack of space in the dinghy. The wind was blowing pretty strongly, but I didn't see it as a very good reason for me to be left behind. Anyway, Mom promised me that she'd take me ashore tomorrow. When they came back, they were full of stories of how they had visited a McDonald's and got free coke there when they just asked for some water, and how they had gone back there for lunch. Needless to say, I was pretty jealous. At least Mom had made a cake that day, though, and we all celebrated Carina's birthday together over a wonderful dessert.

During some of our time in Lake Worth, I knit a sweater and little slippers for one of my dolls. This one, for some reason, never did get a name. I just referred to her as my doll. It turned out pretty good, and made it look pretty cute. Next I needed two hair elastics to finish off her new look, so I crocheted them. With her cross-stitched nose, eyes, mouth, and pink cheeks, she looked almost like she had a little clown face. Mom and I had made her while we were still on the farm. Her black hair was now braided into pigtails. At one time on our trip, I almost lost her when she fell into the water at an anchorage. It proved to be a scary rescue mission because Dad managed to get her out, with the boat hook, just before she sank. Then we had to leave her hanging on the rails for a few days before she was all dry again (see picture on page 218). After that, I never took her on deck anymore. It was much too scary an ordeal to risk repetition!

The Bahamas

It was March 21st, just two days short of a full year of sailing along the east coast of the USA. The day started with rain, and winds were, as forecast, from the NW. We had already waited 8 days, in the hope of finding a weather window with the lowest risk, to make the short crossing to the Bahamas. We had not had to run the engine during our stay in the anchorage, as the wind generator had constantly topped up the charge of the batteries. I cleaned the dodger's window with some Rainex, a product that made the drops magically disappear and provided a visibility that was astonishingly good. It had been designed for cars with failing windshield wipers but worked wonders on our dodger's windows. The improved weather indicated it was time for our departure, and everyone was getting ready, cleaning up any items which had not been put away or tied up.

An early evening departure would allow us to arrive in the Abaco Islands just before low tide the next morning. Low tide would be half a foot above the chart's indicated depth of 2.9m (9.5 feet). High tide would give us another 0.8m (2.5 feet). That would quickly refloat us if we should run aground. It was obvious that, in order to find deep enough waters for our journeys in the Bahamas, we would have to pay attention to the tide tables.

When we left Lake Worth, I did not take anything for preventing seasickness and once in the open water everybody was ok, except me. Not that it was bad, but I had to check the railings once. The wind had turned to the SW as forecast, and for the first two or so hours the water was rough. When the winds subsided, we had to use the engine in order to make way. Travelling at about 4 to 5 knots in about 2.2m (7 foot) waves, the Gulf Stream pushed our boat a fair bit to the north and my magnetic heading was at about 145 degrees; about 50 degrees higher than needed. But the further out we got, the less our course got altered by the current. We were then able to point the boat on a fairly straight course towards Memory Rock. The waves gradually diminished.

As expected, when we reached the waypoint just below Memory Rock, our depth sounder changed from about 180m to 2.7m (600 feet to 9 feet) within a mile or less. There was no turbulence in the water, and once over the bank, the waves subsided. We passed Mangrove Cay and anchored in the early evening at Great Sale Cay, one of the many islands. What excitement, we had finally made it and arrived in the Bahamas. No noise, only a few more sailboats around at anchor reminded us of the sparse spread of civilization in this remote area. After an excellent night's sleep, it was decided to stay for a day to relax and to wait for better weather.

It's hard to describe how I felt while sailing in the Abaco Islands. It appeared to be the most beautiful spot to go sailing, at least during the off-hurricane season. We believed that we would find clear water and a lot of Islands, but we found so much more. Sailing through the crystal clear water and seeing the bottom of the ocean at any given time, was one aspect. The protected waters and mostly moderate winds were another inviting fact and the gorgeous settings of palm trees, along rocky islands, mangroves and sandy beaches made for spectacular scenery, a perfect environment to be in. The people we met were friendly and inviting. These formed lasting impressions.

It slowly sank in. We had left behind the busy world of commerce, with its people driving to and fro and, instead, were enjoying crystal-clear waters through which we could study the sea-bed. What a feeling. Daydreaming seemed to become part of life again. Only about 100 miles away from the US coast and we had no murky water at all. We were not able to hear weather forecasts from the US anymore, so we listened to Herb's forecasts or the local radio. Chäberli started to put together a new Canadian flag. Our first one had started to fall apart. By doing it herself she could make it the proper size for our boat and build it to last longer.

The following days were sunny and warm. Continuing on our journey, we passed several little islands and Marcel had his fishing line out. Within an hour he caught a lane snapper measuring over 60cm (2 feet). Once more we had the fridge full of tasty food. With the light winds and perfect visibility we arrived at Powell Cay under sail only and dropped the anchor. We had never approached an anchorage like that. Usually there were too many boats, and we had to motor between them, changing course continuously. In that case we were the only boat there and anchored wherever the wind put us. Later, in the afternoon, another boat anchored in the same area.

That was also the first time that we manoeuvred the boat off the anchor while under sail. Marcel took the wheel while I pulled up the mainsail. The boat gained momentum, and once we were just past the anchor, Marcel steered the boat into the wind while I winched up the chain. All that was left to do was to pull up the genoa, our largest sail in the front, and off we went under sail. Everything went like clockwork. Our next destination was Green Turtle Cay, the first place possible to check in with Bahamian customs officials. I was a bit nervous about that, having memories of long-drawn-out proceedings to get our sailing permit in the US, and other encounters with officials.

The place to anchor was fairly shallow, and we had to allow for low tide. I therefore stayed in a bit deeper water, looking forward to a long dinghy ride ashore. Dressed up in my best clothes, a shirt and black pants I started out, safely keeping the travel documents in a sealed plastic bag. The town of New Plymouth was a small colourful-looking village, resting on the Southwest shore of the island. It looked so inviting, with narrow roads, few motorcars and some people walking by with smiles on their faces. I asked my way to the office, which was about to open soon. I had another short stroll around the many lovely-looking well-maintained houses until the time came to see the officer. He was a kind and friendly person. I had to fill in 6 cards, one for each of us, with a stub at the bottom containing a summary of the upper part of the card. I kept the stubs, which I was asked to send back, once outside the Bahamas. Then I filled in several duplicate forms, one for customs, health, vessel registration and for a fishing license which I felt obliged to pay for, in view of the fact that we had caught such a nice fish on our way there. The handling fees came to $10 respectively and $20 for the fishing license. I felt happy with this and after an hour or so I left. We had received a visa for 3 months, more than we needed. Our plan was to leave for the Azores, 2534 nautical miles (about 4815km or 3009 miles) to the Northeast across the Atlantic, in about a month; in other words at the beginning of May.

As I jumped into the dinghy, I remembered that it was March 25th and with it another day to celebrate. This was Pascal's 5th birthday. Five years had gone by quickly, I reflected, recalling the days under palm trees in Mexico when Pascal had been born. This place inspired me even more, having people with the same dark, tanned skin, living in small decent houses. The particular smell of saltwater mixed with the people's activities brought back memories of those Mexican towns. Bobbing along with the dinghy to reach Kristy Nicole, I knew that the family and I had to investigate this place in detail. I arrived at the boat just in time. The birthday cake was already prepared, and we had fish for lunch. It tasted just wonderful and everyone on the boat was upbeat.

Our present anchorage was quite in the open, and after consulting the guide, we decided to move the boat to White Sound, a nearby and protected anchorage belonging to the same island and about 3.8km (2 nautical miles) from New Plymouth. Its approach had a minimal depth of 1.5m (5 feet), in some spots. Our boat however drew 1.8m (6 feet). Being loaded with food and everything else for the long journey ahead, we would, perhaps, draw even more. With the tide still being fairly high, we gave it a try and it worked out just fine. It was just marvellous to see the bottom pass under the boat as it slowly travelled through the water. You could make out each and every plant or animal below the keel. It was all sandy bottom and there would have been no need to worry, even if we had touched it. We soon reached the deeper water at the opening of the Sound, and had to look for a place to anchor. There were many boats there, and the depth of water was more than adequate in most spots. Palm trees were growing all around and in some places, to the north and west, houses were visible. It was quiet, no jet skis, motorboats or other disturbing noises. It took us some time to find a suitable spot to anchor. Some places were a bit too shallow so, to avoid running aground, we found a spot further out from the shoreline and the main pier where a convenience store was located.

March 26th, my birthday, started out with coffee served in bed. I felt content to celebrate my birthday on the boat and in such beautiful surroundings. Last year's birthday had been overshadowed by the fact that someone had stolen the motor for our dinghy. This year we had nothing to worry about. First of all we did not have an outboard motor worth stealing and, secondly, there was not much else to steal from us. The sun quickly warmed things up and we were able to enjoy a swim in the crystal-clear water. It was the perfect place to clean off these mussels which had stuck to the hull of our boat and were now visible through the water. Some were already sticking out half an inch (12mm), especially around the hinges of the rudder. I started to make a list of things I still wanted to do before our departure. In addition to cleaning the boat bottom and mounting new zincs, there were some minor things to do such as sanding and painting the oars and deck rails, cleaning the gunwales, strengthening the dinghy supports with fibreglass, chiselling out some cracks on the sides of the boat and sealing them off so the steel bars inside would not be exposed to the salt water and, finally, touching up the hull's side to remove the dinghy marks which had been made where we tied up. First of all, however, we wanted to relax and the extra month or so we now had to prepare for the crossing came as a welcome opportunity to do just that: to sit back and explore the Abaco Islands.

Days passed with mixed weather at first, but it soon warmed up and we had mostly sunny days. We visited the beaches. One, the ocean beach, was the most captivating. Miles of sandy beach mixed with some rock mounds were stretched out before us. Shells of all kinds

Enjoying the wonderful scenery

were trapped in the holes formed by rock mounds along the shore. The kids gathered many interestingly shaped rocks, shells and other small items while I watched the ocean reflecting the sunlight in different shades of green. Depending on the depth of water, it was dark blue or, further ashore, it changed to a turquoise green. Not too far out I could see a reef, breaking the bigger waves, and the white foam was glistening in the sun's light. It was a dreamlike picture of harmony, and I could imagine myself looking down from outer space and contemplating a world free from strife and pollution where mankind and the planet could live in symbiotic harmony. I feel that, if a person is going to dream, then they might as well dream in colour.

We made several more visits to different beaches, all inviting places to spend a day.

The water in the small bay we had anchored in seemed to be warm enough to do some work on the boat, so we prepared for a swim. I got the 5cm (2 inch) wide spatulas ready. Marcel helped, and together we dived around the boat in order to scrape the barnacles off. We tried not to damage the protective anti-fouling paint. Marcel cleaned the propellor and I started on the front starboard side. We measured the temperature of the water to be about 24 degrees Celsius (about 76 degrees Fahrenheit). Even though it sounded warm, after about 30 minutes of diving we were shivering and had to take a break. I also measured the salinity of the water to be 1025. According to the table I carried along, this transferred to about 36.8g of salt for every litre, I believe. These measurements would be vital in reporting whale sightings. So far we had not seen any, but I thought we should at least try the equipment out. Salinity affects the quality of the feeding grounds for whales, who feed on a host of zooplankton species. Temperature and light are also factors which make feeding grounds for whales more attractive.

With all the other activities in train, scraping the bottom took several days. We unplugged the wheel feeding the knot-speed-log and inspected the hull. When I checked the rudder I found a small piece cut out, next to the space for the screw. I had patched that spot already when we were in dry dock in Galveston, but it seemed to have been damaged again. It did not look serious and gave no reason for concern. The hull looked fine once cleaned, but it was sure a slow process. The payoff was the increased speed of about a knot (one nautical mile per hour) and the boat could be manoeuvred more easily. Marcel had started to write a diary a while back and wrote:

April 1st. "Yesterday we started to clean the bottom of our boat. I didn't finish much. After that I pushed Anisha with the dinghy over to the neighbours boat Celebrian, using the flippers. The crew gave us some very pretty shells and sand dollars. One of the shells had a hermit crab in it and we were trying to get it out. We are now getting ready to leave for Switzerland today (ha, ha April fools day)".

The radio channel used in the Abaco Islands was usually 68, the one where boaters exchange their messages during certain hours of the day. We had our radio set to that channel and turned it on once in a while, depending on how well we could charge the batteries with the wind generator. On one such instance, we heard the name Cool Change during an announcement by the host. The last time we had talked to them was in St. Augustine. We tried to contact them over the radio but did not receive a response. With the help of the host on channel 68, our position was relayed to them and sometime later we got confirmation that they were on their way to see us. In the afternoon they arrived with their small but very roomy catamaran in the anchorage. We had another great get-together before they took off to return to the US. This was the last time we had contact with them. Many times we remembered the good times we had together. We could not find out if they had safely reached the US coast and where they went. Their e-mail address did not yield any response either. All that is left are our memories and some pictures that we have. We would sure have liked to know how they were doing.

My birthday at Lake Worth was not as much fun as I'd expected. We couldn't really have a great party like we had in Annapolis on Anisha's Birthday. However it was fun enough and I got a wicker basket which I still have to this day. It was made to be used as a laundry basket but for me it was immediately clear to accommodate all my beanie babies. I was so happy with it and many of my stuffed creatures now found a place to go. I placed the basket at the end of

my bed in the V-berth. It made me very happy to have the basket, and I imagined how well it eventually would fit a real cat, one thing I wished for all along the trip. But I understood that this was not possible on our boat, already crammed tight with all of us. I also started to read in the book about Lassie and I enjoyed it immensely.

I was happy to be back in warmer climates. The constant dripping from the walls was so unpleasant. I always had to make sure that my "stuffies" didn't touch the sides and of course my blanket felt wet most of the time. That alone would not have mattered so much if it wasn't so moist underneath the mattresses too. Every morning we had to lift them up and keep them on an angle so it could air out, otherwise it would have started to mould and smell. It forced me to stay in the saloon or on the deck, the latter not always an option due to weather or boat movement. Since I got washed up once while in the back of the boat, I was not at all interested to stay on deck, except while on anchor and here in the Bahamas this was mostly the case. Of course I could now stay in my cosy, dry cabin again. The water was just awesome, not too cold and sparkling clean. By then I had got used to swimming in the salty water, so I had the odd jump overboard for a swim, and there were other kids around for us to play with.

On one occasion we had to socialize, the kids from Scud came ashore, and we went to one of the hotel's pools. The manager there was very friendly and let us use the pool. We had a great time playing Marco Polo, the game we played many times with our friends in Annapolis. Of course we were all swimming in and around the pool which made the game so much more fun and a bit more difficult.

On one occasion our whole family planned to go out for a visit to the nearby town. We had done that before by foot, but this time we decided to rent a golf cart which was available at one of the stores on shore. We were all very excited about that, because Daddy promised that we could drive it for some time. I had never driven anything like that. I knew how to ride my bicycle up at the farm, and I was good at that. I could even make it back up the hill without getting off the bike, something that took a lot of energy to do. This of course was not an issue, but I could remember seeing movie stars driving these things while watching videos and it always looked rather easy to do. So I looked forward to be one of these relaxed actors holding the wheel with one hand and swinging it back and forth while talking to the person beside me. We started out with Daddy steering the cart and explaining all functions and how to use the pedals. There was a brake and a gas pedal as far as I can remember. We took turns driving along a narrow path leading through the forest and along the ocean beach. Marcel was the first to try it out. We all grabbed a tight hold and I closed my eyes tight. We were pretty jammed on that thing, with Mom, Anisha, Pascal and me in the back and Marcel together with Dad in the front. Finally it was my turn and everybody was keen to see how I would do. Of course it did not take long to find out. I managed to keep the cart on the path for a short time, but when I tried to use just one hand to go along I lost control, and we zoomed between the trees into some bushes. I got bumped off my seat and with that lost my foot on the gas pedal which slowed down the ride, and we soon came to a stop in the middle of some of these mangrove-like thick bushes. By now everybody was laughing their heads off and promising me they wouldn't ever let me drive again. No one got hurt, and they decided to change drivers again in order to continue a safe trip back. On the way along the beach, we found some really nice rock pools carved out by the ocean. We had to walk through the bush first to get there, and we were all happy to have our shoes along. The needles and pine cones on the ground were hard on my bare feet. So walking barefoot was no option, something I otherwise always did.

Easter approached and we prepared for an egg hunt. The parents of the boat Scud, anchored next to us, helped prepare the event, cooking and decorating eggs. Then together we went to the nearby beach to set them all out for us to find. It was a lot of fun to look for them under shells, drift wood, rocks and in the sand. Some were hanging in the bushes or were placed into the tree's forks. Then we had a picnic at the beach together with everyone before heading back to the anchorage. One more very fine day to remember.

Anisha's doll, drying out after a "Man Overboard" experience

Exploring The Abaco Islands

There was little work left to do on the boat. I found some time to play my guitar and sometimes put on the fins and snorkel to check out our surroundings. One day I saw a wonderful fish, about 1 foot long, and almost crystal clear, like a window. All I could really see were the eyes, edges and fins. The edges were all purple blue and it looked amazingly beautiful. I followed it and, after circling it 3 times, I gave up and went on exploring. Later on we went to Coco Bay, about a 10-minute walk away, through a forest. It was a small bay with trees along most of its edge, leaving a small strip of sandy beach almost all around the bay. Due probably to erosion, some of the roots of the trees along the shore were exposed to the air, and it was possible to sit on them. We could then rest our feet on the sand and have them washed by the wavelets. The dark branches of the pine trees arched ever so gently down to provide some shade and contrasted with the blue sky and the light turquoise surface of the bay's water. Pascal enjoyed playing with the sand, and the time flew past.

I started to listen to Herb's weather forecast on a daily basis. I wanted to get used to the way he presented the weather. Usually he called up boats that had previously contacted him and gave them a forecast for their position. It was quite interesting to listen to him. The radio did not produce the best sound, and I experienced a lot of static noise. It was, however, great to know that we could get some weather predictions when we were out on the ocean, at least for boats that would be close to our position. Our transmitter did not work, so we could not contact Herb directly.

On one occasion I was busy working on the boat when several motorboats anchored south of us. One huge motor cat with no better name then "Awesome I" anchored so close, that we had no choice but to listen to the generator all day long. Not just that, but with the wind from the south, we also got all the diesel smell as well. It looked as if I was being punished for criticizing peoples' lifestyles, something I had done, from time to time, during our stay in the US. I certainly wondered why these boaters would keep all their tower lights on during the night, while we tried to save as much energy as possible so the little wind left during the days could be enough to charge up our batteries. They left the anchorage the next day, so we did not have to put up with the situation for long.

We had looked at the chart of the Atlantic before, but now was the time to make a decision about which course we should take. The further North we went, the more chance we took of getting hit by a cold front and/or an iceberg. At this time of the year these fronts were still coming south. On the other hand, if we were to take a course too far south, we might not get enough wind to fill our sails. We wanted to pass about 190 to 380km (100 to 200 nautical miles) to the south of the Bermudas, cutting through part of the Bermuda Triangle. Sailors usually try to avoid this area as there are many stories of ships mysteriously disappearing in it. With all this information I had a good idea of what course we should start out with. If the weather forecasts continued to improve we would have been able to depart as early as April 20th. Our children were starting to get ready for it too. Anisha wrote in her diary:

April 5th. Yesterday Cool Change left and we got Super Mario 1 from them for Marcel's game boy. Carina was crying because she could not play it. We have a lot of books now because they gave us lots of them. Well, I am going to clean my nails now and then do my maths. Amazed? Well, I don't have anything else to do, and I do not want to be too far behind when we get to Switzerland. I'm still not very keen on the idea of crossing the Atlantic. Well, I have to go now.

For the first 21 days after our departure from Lake Worth, we did not have to recharge the batteries, the wind generator kept them topped up. The next few days were so calm, however, that we were forced to use the engine. With the weather so nice it was hard to catch any rain. Sometimes I installed the rain catcher in the evening, hoping it would rain. When it eventually did rain, however, I had forgotten to put the rain catcher in place and had to get up and install it in the dark. By daybreak there was hardly any more water in our tank, it had just been a sprinkle. We continued our chores sanding wood and varnishing. Even the flagpole in the back got some new paint. The boat looked ready, and we were able to spend some time socializing with other boaters in the anchorage. We celebrated an Easter egg hunt with the crew from the boat Scud. We once rented a golf cart to ride into Plymouth.

With all the work on the boat finished we were eager to explore the islands around us. Our first trip was a small island, supposedly uninhabited, called Munjack Cay. We had passed it on our way to Plymouth. It took about 1.5 hours, under sail, to reach it. The boat moved through the water much better with its clean bottom, and we sailed at about 6 knots through the small waves. There was a pier sticking out from shore, and we guessed that someone must have lived there once. To our surprise we met a couple from the US who had lived there since 1993. They had started to build a house and did some gardening but at that time still lived in their boat, an Albin 43. The soil was quite sparse, and everything needed a lot of tending. They did a great job considering that their water was all gathered from the rain. They certainly were careful about using it. The island is remote and has some nice beaches and a big mangrove-covered area with channels opening up between them, just begging to be explored. We borrowed a canoe and Marcel joined me for a trip through the beautiful shallow waters. One of the animals we were not familiar with was the sea cucumber, a black slippery animal the size and shape of a cucumber. A stingray followed us gracefully along some of our paths and we could see the odd fish passing by. The ocean beach was covered with driftwood of every size and shape, sometimes the remains of boats, pieces of plastic in any odd shape as well as the remains of commercial fishing gear such as ropes, lines, nets and some floats. The trip was a great success for both of us. Tired but happy, we returned to the island and shared many memories with the couple living there.

Later in the day I took out the guitar and we sat around the fire. Drums and other percussion instruments were already there. Some of our kids roasted marshmallows, and we played music together way into the night. It was great to have met these people and to see how they tried to live, along with nature, on this island. We left the cozy place with some great memories and thanked the hosts for their kind welcome. By then we understood the meaning of a sign along one of the paths from their pier to the building site which read: "Trespassers welcome".

Further on our journey we reached Backers Bay to the south, part of Great Guana Cay, around mid afternoon and dropped the hook as close to shore as we thought possible. There was a large pier in the bay. It was not a very protected anchorage, but the weather seemed to be holding. The Northwest end of Great Guana Cay had once been developed to provide a tourist attraction called Treasure Island. The last big cruise ship had visited the place in 1993, but it was abandoned after that. We went ashore and were amazed to see the infrastructure still in place, with buildings and walkways weathering out the forces of wind, blowing sand and rain. There were many coconut trees with ripe fruits, and we took some along to the boat. Otherwise the whole thing looked a bit spooky. We inspected the empty store and a large theatre, but soon left, using our sailing dinghy to get back to the boat. With the waves a bit bigger than usual, we had to make two trips. The wind was against us on the way to the boat, and it took some time to manage the ride back. On the second run, the sail started to rip at the top. In order to spare the rest of the sail from tearing, I decided to use the oars. The wind was about 20 knots, and I had to give my best to get back to the boat with Chäberli and Pascal in the boat. They got a bit wet but, with the weather being warm, nobody was upset.

The following day we set out, under sail, towards the town of Settlement Harbor to the south, also located on the Great Guana Cay. With the wind from the south, we had to tack once and reached the harbor in about an hour. The place was small but we found a nice spot to anchor in, close to the shore. The houses along the harbor looked inviting and colourful. Too bad that the anchorage was wide open to the winds from the Southwest or we would have planned a longer stay. The Ocean beach to the east had some excellent coral reefs close to the shore. According to the guide, it is supposed to be the world's 3rd largest barrier reef. Marcel, Anisha, Carina and I explored it and were very impressed with its beauty. There were huge brain corals, mosses in green and yellow (changing to red as the angle of light changed) and lots of sea ferns with fish swimming all around us. Parrot fish, one of the larger species, had their own underwater tunnels. The colours were brilliant because the sun was directly over us and the top of the reef was only two or so feet below the surface, at half-tide. What a wonderful experience. The beach

Coral reefs, near Settlement Harbour

was mostly fine sand with some rock formations here and there breaking up the smooth curves of the shoreline. In some spots rocks were poking out of the water, and the waves washed around them. With the tide rising over them, they formed splashes of beautiful white foam. The children enjoyed climbing the rocks and dodging the waves. I enjoyed the sun and excellent weather.

The store in town, where we bought a film and some suntan lotion, was owned by an older chap whose parents had arrived in the Abaco Islands in the 1600s. He told us that his wife had sailed here and had been shipwrecked while anchored in the bay. The store owner must have liked our children and gave them each some pop and lent us fins to go snorkelling the reefs. People in general were very friendly and helpful. We had a great time in this place, but we wanted to move on to more protected waters, our next destination being Marsh Harbour.

I really did enjoy the stay at Munjack Cay. The family there had a small sailboat that I could use to go sailing with. It was not so small at all for me, but had one large sail only. The hull was made of wood and was very slim. It glided through the water with the lightest of winds and that is what I really enjoyed. Then there was a large barge they used to transport things. It was a veteran military thing, which had been used to bring soldiers to the shore. Due to that it could go into very shallow water, and it had a very powerful motor in there making a lot of noise. At one time we took a short ride on it and for me that was great fun. During one of the rides with the canoes into the little paths through the mangroves, I saw a very large stingray and I was really scared. It looked as if it wanted to attack the canoe as it swam at top speed back and forth underneath the canoe. It looked like an air plane but with large wide wings. I had never seen these fish before. After some time it left, and I continued the trip looking for other sea animals. One I had never seen was the sea cucumber. I wanted to pick one up from the shallow bottom I glided over, but its slimy surface made it slip right out of my hand. I did not expect it to be slippery, and so I left it at that. I did not like to give it another try. Continuing the trip was like in one of those movies about nature by David Suzuki. I saw all the different colours around me and saw more different kinds of small fish passing me as I glided among the mangroves. Then I pulled the canoe up onto a sandy beach and took a walk along one of the islands to make it to the other side. There I met the open ocean making large breakers farther out on a reef. The shore was littered with all kinds of wood. In between were pieces of garbage and pieces of fishing gear or what have you. It looked so strange and almost scary. I was here all alone and decided to get back. Later on I explored the place further together with my Dad. We found a nice piece of plywood that my Dad thought would be useful.

It was sad to leave such an inviting place. I had so much fun, but again it was time to go on. The next place was a rather small anchorage and open to one side. There was however a reef that Daddy wanted to go and see. So we got some snorkel masks and fins to do some diving. We had to swim out a bit first, but with the fins that was rather easy and a lot of fun. We looked around for some time to find a reef and then suddenly we almost hit our knees on it. There was a huge reef top right in front of me. I saw plants growing on it and fish passing through some openings. It looked like a big garden, under water. But it was so much more colourful and exotic that the description would not have fit like that. I had never ever seen anything like that except on TV once, and that was just not as impressive as what I experienced then. Some of the fish came so close I thought I could touch them. Others were so fast that you could hardly notice them. Then there was one so colourful that you thought it to be a rainbow. It was unbelievably beautiful. If the mask wouldn't have started to hurt my face, I would have stayed a lot longer. However I did go out one more time later on during the day, and I was not disappointed to see it all again.

I hoped that Marsh Harbour would have been as challenging as the adventures I had before. The anchorage was very large, and there was always a gentle wind going. I set up the kite we had carried along since the toy store in St. Augustine and it was amazing to see it go up without any effort. I played around with it for a while and then just tied it onto the rail of the boat. Seven hours or so later the kite was still up there flying. In the meantime we went swimming at a nearby beach. It was here that Daddy sold one of our bikes. It was already so rusted up that he decided to trade it in for some jewellery for Anisha. I was a bit sad to see it go, because I did sometimes use it and still remember when I used it in that place where the tires all got punched up by cacti stingers. Back home at the farm it was Fabian's first bike. He used it to go to school in Enderby. When he left, I took it over and used it a lot on the farm, riding the tracks through the bush. It had served us well, but the extra room on the back the boat was a welcome change. The other bike, however, we still used.

During our stay in the anchorage we made some friends with the people on a motorboat, and we had some cool outings. One was to the light tower on Elbow Reef, near Hope Town. The tower was built in 1864 and was still in good shape. There was a staircase going up to the top with 101 steps. Of course I had to count them to confirm. It was nice to look down from the top and see all the boats and islands around. In the far distance the open ocean was visible towards an endless sky. I was thinking about us going out there soon. It was a strange feeling. I did not know what was waiting for me out there and felt quite happy to look forward to a challenge.

Bahamas

1. Fine white sand against the blue open sky
Islands to sail between just like a piece of pie
The sun's rays reflecting leaving the white sand dry
This harmony is like a drug it makes you feel high

Ref: What a wonderful place
Where creation shows Gods grace 2 times

2. The boat sits on anchor in a bay so nice
With palms around so lush you can't put a price
In the morning you watch the most beautiful sunrise
This is when perfection unfolds in front of your eyes
Ref:

3. No matter what God you may believe in
The Abaco Islands appeared to me so pristine
I will never forget them but carry them within
No matter what God you may believe in
Ref:

A CD with colour pictures and songs can be ordered.

Marsh Harbour

A route had to be planned for our sail to Marsh Harbour. I toyed with the idea of crossing the Sea of Abaco in a straight line, passing between Foote's Cay to port and, a bit further on, Fish Cay close on our starboard side. With the winds from the south, we would be able to reach Marsh Harbour with only two tacks. The risk was, however, that my charts did not show the depth of water in the areas around the Cays, and we would have to pass fairly close to them. The different routes which were laid out in the chart, for the most part, went along the shore line. I assumed that the depths in the unmarked parts of the chart would be much the same as those in the marked parts. I thought it would be worth a try and marked the waypoints on my chart and entered them into the GPS. The course taken from Settlement harbor was at 221 magnetic, towards the waypoint of N26 degrees 36 minutes, W 77 degrees 9.6 minutes. We set out on a great sunny day with the winds from the south as expected. There were hardly any waves, and we could see the bottom very clearly. Marcel was standing out on the bow to check for any changes in the pattern of the sea floor and to look for any coral reefs or any other obstructions. We sailed at 6 knots and soon passed the first cay with enough water under our keel. As we came closer to Fish Cay, we read a low of 2.3m (7.5 feet) just as we came in line with the islands. The first island was really just a rock, peeking out of the water. We were about a mile away from this rock which was to the north of us. I took over the position in the bow, relieving Marcel of the stressful job of warning the skipper early enough about any shallow water ahead. Marcel then watched the autopilot steer the boat, reading changes of depth on the depth sounder and making sure we kept on course. The water soon regained a depth of about 2.7 to 3.7m (9 to 12 feet). Considering that we had started out at low tide, we had been quite lucky. We soon tacked to port on our new heading of N26 degrees 35.5 minutes, W77 degrees 3.3 minutes. On this course we sailed as much into the wind as possible. With such calm water the boat sailed beautifully and at good speed. Our 2nd tack took us just in front of the opening to Marsh Harbour, to our starboard side.

The entrance to the harbor was straight-forward and we used our engine to enter the anchorage. There were lots of boats spread out over a large area and plenty of space to anchor. We found a spot, not too far from shore, and used only one anchor to keep us in place. The weather forecast was for more sunny and warm weather. One of the propane bottles needed to be refilled, so I unloaded the bikes in order to explore the town. There was also a leak in the hydraulic steering system, just behind the steering wheel, where the copper pipes fit to the pump mounted on the wheel. I was able to find the necessary parts which would enable me to replace the old piece of copper pipe and seal the leak properly. After picking up the propane bottle I headed out to Mermaid Reef to join up with the rest of the family. Chäberli, in the meantime, had got a nail in the back tire of her bike. As soon as I arrived at the beach I had to return to the boat to get the repair kit. Eventually we got it all patched up.

On the way back home, Pascal sat in the front basket of my bike. He managed, by accident, to put his foot into the spokes of the front wheel while we were under way. He was badly hurt. Fortunately it was an open wound, around his big toenail, and it healed quite quickly. The bikes were rusting up at an alarming rate and with the limited space on the boat, we were anxious to sell one of them. Unfortunately we could not find anybody to buy it but did manage to trade it for some jewellery at one of the small gift shops in town, a welcome present for the girls.

The next day I wanted to check my e-mail, for the last time before setting out across the Atlantic. The only place to do so was at the local computer store. I went there first thing in the morning. When I was connected to the phone line, the speed dropped to a trickle. I could not call up my messages and after 10 minutes had to quit. The owner of the store charged me $5.00 and explained that it was a problem with the phone company Batelco not providing the necessary infrastructure to be able to connect to the Internet. As I was about to leave the store an older gentleman walked in and asked if they could repair the hinge of the lid to his laptop. He had a strong German accent. I was enjoying the warm weather, in front of the store, when he came out. I asked him, in German, as to when his laptop would be fixed. He was disappointed, the store keeper had said that it could not be repaired. He cheered up when I offered to give it a try. We talked to each other for a while, introducing ourselves, and I explained to him that I had my tools out in the anchorage, where I lived. He also was in transit with a boat and was anchored at Man-O-War Cay. We agreed to meet on our boat.

Later in the day, he and his wife arrived in their 8.5m (28-foot motorboat), which had been set up for fishing. We tied it alongside and they were introduced to the rest of our crew. He had been a dentist in Germany and they had moved to Marsh Harbour for a sort of semi-retirement. We got to work on the laptop and, with some improvisation and the special glue I carried along with me, fixed the hinge so that it would work properly. Everyone was happy to see it come together like that. Their motorboat was called Molly, and they invited us to take a trip on it to explore Treasure Cay. That Cay was further north, and we had not stopped at it. Our kids were keen to go, anticipating the thrill of zooming over the water at a speed of 17 knots. We thoroughly enjoyed the following day on the beach of Treasure Cay.

Our new friends invited us to move to the anchorage at Man-O-War Cay and visit them in their home. We agreed to do so, before heading out to the Atlantic, but we first had to stock up on food and water. I hoped that they would know where to get good water on this island without having to buy it in one-gallon jugs. We needed to fill the tank to capacity before leaving, and I estimated that would take about 100 gallons. When asked about it they immediately offered to give us the water from their home cistern. For us, this was just like hitting a gold mine. We were very happy to have met such kind people. They took us to Man-O-War Cay and showed us their home. It was a large, beautifully-built house which was topped by a little tower. Everything was designed to make it as hurricane proof as possible. We spent the afternoon on their porch and, when it got dark, they gave us a lift to our anchorage. It was pitch dark by then and difficult to navigate between all the anchored boats in Marsh Harbour. Finally we found our boat between all the other anchored ones. Our green masts were not visible at night, something I had not been aware of until then. As we parted with our hosts, we promised to visit them during the next few days and thanked them for their kind help.

On April 23rd we stocked the pantry with about $200 worth of food. The Solomon's Wholesale Foods had almost all the things we needed, mainly spaghetti, milk powder, cheese, potatoes, onions etc. At the Golden Harvest store we stocked up on apples and butter. I also picked up the 100 grapefruits we had ordered from a small store along the harbor. It was quite a job to get them all onto the dinghy and then store them on the boat. The water was a bit rough, and we had to pack all the groceries into plastic garbage bags in order to bring them to the boat dry. We started to do last-minute preparations, Chäberli finished stitching up of a couple of flags for the Azores (Portugal) and England. During the charging of the batteries the old, soldered, alternator bracket broke, and I had to finish drilling holes in one of the spares I had made in Titusville. It worked quite well, and I was confident that it would hold much better due to the thickness of the material. I had drilled the hole in such a way as to allow the alternator to sit a bit lower. With that the belt-adjusting bracket could be shifted to its full extent.

It was time to fill our fuel tank. I took hold of the anchor chain and Marcel moved the boat forward, as we had done so many times before, to pull up the anchor. Once over the hook the boat stopped abruptly, pulling the bow down, into the water. Wow, I thought, the anchor was really well set. Even with a second, more vigorous try, we were not able to get the hook to come loose. I put on my swimsuit in order to investigate. Following the chain I found it wound around the fluke of a big, buried anchor that had only one fluke sticking out of the mud. Thanks to the clear water it was easy to locate the problem. That would have been a perfectly secure set-up, even in a hurricane. Once the anchor chain had been untangled it was routine work to get under way. I was happy that the water had been clear and not too cold.

While we were docking at the fuel pump, the port rail of Kristy Nicole hit hard against one of the posts. I was certain that another hairline crack had formed due to the impact and knew that something more would have to be taken care of. After we had anchored out in the harbor, I inspected the side and found it had indeed been cracked again. This was the last time we would have to secure the boat to a pier before our crossing. If it had not been, I would have considered mounting a rub line at the place where the boat usually touched the landing.

The following day we hauled anchor in order to move to Man-O-War Cay. This time it got hooked on the dolphin striker, loosening the mounts to the boat's hull. The mount was quite rusty, and I decided to replace it with another one I had in stock. Murphy's law seemed to have become attached to us. Soon we were under sail again for the one hour sail to Man-O-War Cay. We already knew that the entrance to the new anchorage was a narrow one and to be approached with due care. Passing it went without a glitch, and we found a nice spot to anchor. We took the short dinghy ride to the pier and a quick walk through bushes and trees brought us to the house of our new friends. They had planned to go to Hope Town and invited us to go along with them.

I was a bit worried when the 8.5m (28 foot) motor boat came alongside. We had never had a boat tied up alongside ours before, and it felt a bit strange. I was concerned that the anchor might not hold. While the men worked on the computer I visited with the lady and showed her our boat. It took a bit longer to fix the computer than we expected because the glue had to dry. It became time for lunch, and we were all hungry. Marcel sailed the lady and me, in our dinghy, to a nearby restaurant to get some food. She had never been in a small sailing dinghy like ours and was not so sure about it. The two men had to assure her that it was quite all right. We got Conch Fritters and French Fries. I don't understand why Conch Fritters are considered to be so special, I thought that they were a bit too tough. Never-the-less we did enjoy the food as we ate together on our boats. They were so happy to have the computer working again. They invited us to go along on a motorboat outing to Treasure Cay. The sand on the beach was fine and all white and the sea light blue, very beautiful. Everyone went swimming except me. I am not very fond of the water, and it has to be very hot for me to want to get in. We all enjoyed the ride; it was almost a bit too fast and loud after being on the sailboat. I think I liked it better on our boat. They also showed us their island and the house. I wrote in my diary: The view is magnificent over the trees. And the house is equally grand. There is

nothing in the area to compare with it. It is made entirely from wood. The people around say it is the house of the crazy German Doctor. It was placed on a small hill top, giving a great view all around. This also meant that it was more exposed to the hurricane winds that regularly pass over the Bahamas during the seasons. There were no cars on that island; people only used golf carts. On our way back to our boat, in the dark, we had a hard time to find it among all the other boats, dodging through them, guessing where they may be, as most displayed no anchor light! We had to use the search light to locate ours.

While reading my diary I came across this little episode which might be worth mentioning. On one of our dinghy trips back to the boat the water was a bit rough, so I took my pants off in order to keep them dry. About half way over a ferry passed us and left a big wake. Werner, who was rowing in the front of the boat, stood up so that he would not get too wet but that made the dinghy dip. Lots of water poured into the back, I was glad that only my underwear got soaked.

At Settlement Harbour we went to the ocean beach to go snorkelling. Werner and Marcel had been out before and asked me to join them. They promised it would be beautiful. So I tried just with a mask on. When I finally made it out into the water, I had a hard time breathing and got all panicky. I did get back to the beach all tired out and with a bad ear ache. I tried it again later on in Marsh Harbour; that time I put on a swimming vest and enjoyed looking at all the beautiful fish and coral.

It was good to have a last shower before we set off across the Atlantic. I knew that there would not be another for a long time. It is just not the same standing under a shower as pouring water over yourself with a bucket while in the back of the boat, especially when the boat is leaning sideways or going up and down. I just had to accept to stay a bit dirtier for some time. At least we all had the same problem and could not complain about each other. We were, literally, all in the same boat.

We had brought along a bag of spelt and a bag of rye to make bread. Every so often I would grind some on the back bench. Before we left for the crossing I got some flour ready. For that I used the little hand flour mill we had carried along with us since leaving the farm. It was a tedious job. A lot of force was needed to keep the grinder going, and I was glad to get some of it done. Most of the time I used flour that we bought from the store. The bread, of course, did not taste quite as good with the store-bought flour as it did with the freshly hand-ground flour.

Grinding Flour

Some of the grapefruits we stocked up with

Peeking out of the hatch, while standing on the bed in the aft cabin

First Days On The Atlantic

The following day kept me busy repairing the damaged mount for the dolphin striker as well as filling in the hairline crack. Marcel had to help me from the inside of the boat in order to get the bolts for the new dolphin striker mount aligned properly. It was difficult to line them up, but we managed to get it done and sealed. The other crew members were busy hauling canisters of water to fill up our tank. It was April 29th. In the afternoon I carefully listened to the local weather forecast. For Thursday, April 30th, it said: "windy, waves 7 to 9 feet (2.1 to 2.7m), wind SE 20 to 25 knots". For Friday, winds were supposed to turn to the South and drop. It sounded just right for us. A bit at the extreme end of our wishful thinking for good weather, but we decided to go anyway. The Barometer at 4 p.m. stood at 1015. It all looked promising. We stowed our heavy 32kg (70lb) anchor below deck, tied everything up with extra care, and I checked that all the technical things were shipshape and in good working order. Everyone was busy doing last minute clean-ups and writing some long overdue letters. I tried to listen in to the weather from Herb but with no success. By then we knew that we would be on the water for quite a while. Anisha wrote in her diary:

April 30th. Today we will start our four-week crossing of the Atlantic Ocean. Mammy is going to take a shower over at our friends' place. I am excited but scared. I have to get back to my last minute cleanups!

The crew of Ishka, whom we had met in Marsh Harbour, was also ready to leave, and we agreed to travel together. For as long as possible we would keep in contact over the radio. It was about 8 o'clock in the morning. We took an extended last hot water shower at our friends' place. They then brought us to the boat and said farewell. We pulled up our dinghy and secured it safely to the dinghy supports on the deck. I lashed it down with extra care. We knew that it would not be needed for a while. The bike chain and other parts were sprayed with oil. It was then time to leave.

Everybody took some seasickness pills, except me. I knew that after 2 days I would be fine, with or without the pills. The logbook read 11 a.m. when we pulled up the anchor. As with the other anchor, we stored it below deck and thus had few moving objects above deck. The chain locker's caps were taped with duct tape but that turned out to be of little use. We found out that duct tape does not stand up to saltwater and its glue quickly dissolves.

Out on the Sea of Abaco winds were about 20 knots and in the far distance, we could make out Ishka, just North of Man-O-War Cay and sailing towards the channel leading to the Atlantic. We were then in contact by radio and confirmed our sighting. The normally blue sky was covered with dark gray clouds. The wind was from the SE, and we had an easy passage. Once past the protected waters of the Sea of Abaco, however, we were out on the Atlantic and faced waves of up to 3m (10 feet). It did not take long until I got seasick. There was nothing I could do but wait it out. We set our autopilot to a course of 68 degrees and the sails were set to get optimum performance. There was not much else to do other than to hold on and enjoy the ride as much as possible. We were out on the open ocean, and there was nowhere to run aground.

We made 260km (137 nautical miles) on the 1st day. That was quite good for our boat. Unfortunately everyone else on the crew got seasick too. Morale was down. Most of us felt best when up in the cockpit and that's were we spent most of our time. We each knew how best to deal with the situation. Anisha took her place under the saloon table, a spot where the wave action was felt the least and also where she would not roll much to the sides. The V-berth in the tip of the boat was too uncomfortable in such seas. She goes on to write in her diary a very brief message:

May 1st. Day 2: "Very seasick. Still in touch with Ishka."

On our 3rd day out the winds abated in the early morning hours, as forecast, and all that was left were the big waves. It made for a very uncomfortable ride while travelling at 2 knots and rolling to all sides. We had to charge the batteries and were glad to switch on the engine. The sails stayed up and with the increased forward motion, the boat became much more stable. The first thing that my tummy did not refuse was a grapefruit. The Raman soup (some dried noodles and broth) also stayed down, and soon the whole crew was starting to love eating that soup. Other than that, no one had much appetite for a full meal.

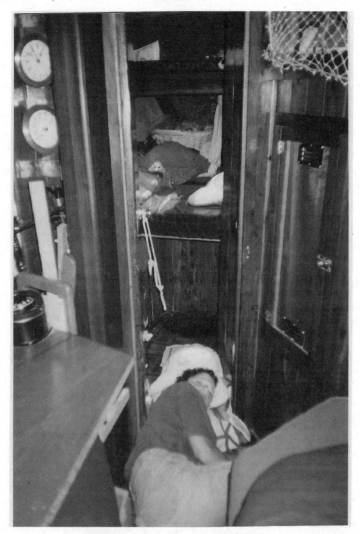

Anisha, sleeping on the floor

According to Herb's forecast, last night, a storm centre would be arriving in Bermuda on Tuesday, with gale force winds heading in our direction. We motored most of the time in the hope of passing Bermuda before Tuesday and avoiding the worst of the storm. We covered about 203km (107 nautical miles) with very little wind, but the waves were still between 1.5 and 2m (5 and 7 feet). Herb's advice was to head to N28 degrees, W 68 degrees before Monday evening. That was about 452km (238 n.m.) away from our actual position. It looked as if we could achieve that by using both motor and sail. We had not, however, intended to burn so much fuel right at the beginning of our journey. I pondered this while sitting in the cockpit on my watch. We had the watches set up so that I would do the one from 4 p.m. to 8 p.m. (and 4 a.m. to 8 a.m. respectively), Chäberli from 8 p.m. to midnight, Marcel from midnight to 2 a.m. and finally Anisha from 2 a.m. to 4 a.m. On the previous night Chäberli had wakened up in the morning at 3 and found Marcel fast asleep in the cockpit. He was supposed to have done his watch till two in the morning and then awakened Anisha. Everyone had difficulties in adjusting to the new rhythm this life demanded. For the kids it must have been very hard. They did not take it seriously enough. Further changes in the watch schedule brought some improvements. It was particularly difficult for Carina who was only 11 years old. During the daytime we sometimes exchanged watches but the responsibility always remained with the Captain.

It was early in the morning, and I was lounging on the starboard bench of the cockpit. From time to time my eyes scanned the horizon. The view was captivating but clouds hung over us, making for poor visibility. I had not yet adjusted to our new schedule and felt tired. The wind had picked up over the last couple of hours, and we were sailing at a good rate of 6 knots. It was difficult to be sure but either I must have become used to the rough seas or the waves had actually lessened. Just as I thought about checking again for other boats along the horizon, I heard the low roaring noise of diesel engines, just behind me. At first I thought I was dreaming. I looked over my right shoulder to verify that there was no noise from that direction. I could not believe my eyes. Just a couple of boat lengths from us I was looking up at the two big smoke stacks of a freighter. It certainly got my attention. The freighter was on a converging course with us and it looked as if we were about to crash into each other. I quickly stretched my left arm out to turn the wheel in order to avoid this imminent danger. At the same time my eyes were following the freighter, trying to make out exactly where it was heading. For some odd reason the steering wheel did not want to turn. When I used both hands, to get a bit more leverage, the wheel felt as if it were locked in position. I quickly took my eyes off of the dangerously close freighter and glanced at the wheel; I had been trying to turn the handle bar that was mounted just above the wheel rather then the wheel itself! I sure was desperate to make a change in course but, so far, nothing had happened. I kneeled behind the wheel and could see that the freighter was moving in almost the same direction as we were, coming closer with every second. After a few seconds of observation it looked as if the freighter would pass, less than a couple of boat lengths, ahead of our bow! The name Quintino flashed past my eyes as I scanned the bow, and it was registered in Rio de Janeiro. I could easily make out some people on the bridge. By then the back of the freighter was just about to clear, so I abruptly turned the wheel to starboard in order to cross the freighter's bow wave at as acute an angle as possible. What a wake-up call that was. During my watch I had, obviously, not looked back very often to locate boats from that angle. This one had just about run over us. I wonder if they had wanted to scare us or if they had even seen us? In our log book all there was to read was: "6:45 a.m., position N28 degrees 07.7 minutes, W73 degrees 16.1 minutes, winds from the South at about 12 knots, seas 4 to 6 feet (1.2 to 1.8m), Quintino from Rio passed just in front of us."

The winds slowly increased to about 15 knots, and we recorded 7 knots over the ground on the GPS. This was unbelievably fast for our boat. With the wind turning towards the south-east, we were sailing on a beam reach, with the wind blowing from the starboard side. We were, most likely, getting the benefit of an ocean current which sped us along our route.

It was in the late afternoon when another freighter, Nagatino, from Spain, passed fairly close to us. This time we were ready, and with the built-in compass in the binoculars we could see if we were on a collision course or not. Our motor pushed the boat at a rate of about 6 knots with waves of only about 1 to 1.5m (3 to 5 feet). We hoped that we would escape the worst of the approaching storm.

We continued to get information from Herb, but the weather patterns seemed to be very inconsistent and nothing was very sure. It was Sunday, our 4th day, and I could see that we would not reach the waypoint we were headed for in time to miss the storm. We changed course to sail further north in the hope of getting more wind. I thought we should, however, avoid going higher than 30 degrees north until Thursday. With a course pointing to the Azores, of about

74 degrees, we should have been able to do just that and have the wind almost abeam. My seasickness was gone, and I enjoyed a good cup of coffee in the morning.

The waves continued to subside and, by 6:15 a.m., I was convinced that the seas would be calm for some time to come. I climbed the mizzenmast, using the bosun's chair. During one of our manoeuvres with the sails, the topping lift of the mainsail had got caught in one of the wind generator blades and broken it. I had only 3 spare blades and started to worry about how quickly we would need more. Anyway, up I went to work. To balance myself against the action of the waves was quite tricky, and I had to hold on well. It took me 1.5 hours to finish the job! In the meantime we had motored for over 12 hours at full speed and another 5 hours at 1400 rpm. I hoped for some wind or we would soon be out of fuel. My appetite was enormous now, and I enjoyed sharing a coke with the kids. For supper we had mashed fresh potatoes with cream of chicken soup and cabbage salad or coleslaw as it is called. The coleslaw I knew from the restaurants never tasted as good as the one with the home-made salad dressing. Chäberli took over the watch and set her wristwatch to ring every 10 minutes in order to keep her awake. We thought this to be useful and followed her idea.

May 2nd. Werner was on watch and, at about 6:50 a.m., he called out in a scary voice: "a freighter!". He had not paid any attention until it was almost too late. The memories come back about the bad experience on the first trip on the open water, while crossing the Gulf of Mexico, where I wanted to quit altogether. But by now I have gained enough strength to cope with situations like these. Maybe next time around I would certainly prefer an aeroplane ride instead. Anisha and Carina both mentioned last night that they were scared. Carina had to throw up again this morning. With her and Pascal's body weight so little I am worried about them getting dehydrated. But then I know that the first 3 days at sea are always the worst when it comes to deal with seasickness, and later on both ate and now feel better. I cooked pasta with Parmesan cheese and corn for supper. Ishka called us, and according to the position they gave, we figured that they are about 18 n.m. ahead of us.

From The Diaries

Monday, May 4th, 5th day out. The sailing is slow. We have almost no wind and travel at 2.5 knots unless we use the motor. The morale of the crew is low. Marcel is teasing everybody, and I am grumpy because we are trying to head east, but the boat just bobs along over the unusually high 4 to 5 foot waves. Climbing up and down waves does not make for speedy travel. Last night I tried hard to set the sails in order to take full advantage of the light winds. From midnight until 3:25 a.m., I tried all kinds of sail combinations that might yield a bit more speed. Eventually the wind died off completely and the autopilot could no longer steer the boat. I gave up and used the engine to gain steerage way. When the wind blew from the east, I motored SE. When the wind changed to SE, I motored ENE. In this manner I could sail as close into the wind as possible and gain what little advantage the wind offered. It was a real struggle so, eventually, I just set the autopilot to 75 degrees, towards the Azores. I revved up the engine to its full output of 2000 rpm. We then travelled at close to 5 knots. Finally, at 9:25 a.m. the wind picked up and we were able to sail at about 3 to 4 knots. At 14:30 hrs the wind dropped to a trickle of about 5 knots. We again sailed at 2 to 2.5 knots.

Moving over the ever-new bumps, appearing from nowhere, makes it difficult for the autopilot to keep a straight course. Setting the autopilot to a medium sea state seems to give it the best chance to cope with keeping course. The sun, at least, is out although it is very hazy. There was dew on the boat this morning. With the speed we are travelling now we will not be able to get to 68 degrees West in time to avoid the storm. I have been forced to steer lower in order to use the wind from ESE. We are at N29 degrees already while only at W68° 47'. All the weather forecasts have promised SSE winds of 20 to 25 knots. We have seen nothing like that. The winds are supposed to be stronger at N30 degrees or more, so I hope we will soon find some wind. The forecasts tell of a storm system moving this way, expected to arrive on Thursday. A low, approaching Bermuda from the North, will also reach us on Wednesday, with winds to 35 knots north of N30 degrees. It is very frustrating to hear these forecasts with nothing happening. It was much easier to travel without any forecasts while crossing the Gulf of Mexico. We just took whatever weather there was.

I learned that Murphy's law is one of the most enduring facts of life on a sailboat. You try to set or change sail in the dark of night by using a harness to secure yourself to the boat. The line, however, constantly gets tangled up. It gets caught between the dinghy mount and the dinghy, on the genoa sheet, on the top or front rail, and to go to the other side of the boat is not to be recommended. It takes, for example, 5 minutes to get the winch handle, or the genoa sheet undone. I get stuck, most often, just a foot short of where I need to reach. Murphy has great skill in tangling up lines, such as the topping lift in the wind generator, the bosun chair's end of the line between the stay and the mast and so on. I have given up using the lifeline for now, until worse conditions arrive, when I can see that it would be useful. At least I am living my dream. The dream, however, did not include the hardships that I encounter such as 2 days of hanging over the rails being seasick and then being weak for another 2 days, before gaining my sea legs. The kids don't have it any easier, and Carina has the hardest time. It is a fact that fear must play a great role in getting seasick. So do smells such as the one from the kitchen sink that does not drain properly due to the listing of the boat to that side. Rotten eggs are a great smell in comparison. I think the dream becomes enjoyable only if you live every moment and pay no attention to the time frame. Listening to these weather forecasts urges us to go faster in order to escape the storm, but the wind does not cooperate. This builds frustration.

May 4th. I can't wait till it's my birthday. Mammy said she would make a cake in the Azores. I guess I didn't sleep enough last night, because I am pretty grumpy. I looked for my watch strap but all I found was the pin and now I lost it in the cockpit. We have been on the Atlantic for 5 days and I am feeling good enough to write in my diary. Today we had sweet and sour. Yesterday I caught somebody's toilet paper while fishing and today I haven't caught anything. I bought 2 boats in Marsh Harbour and I tow them behind our boat. The motorboat I pulled already since Man-O-War Cay. Since I can't

*wait for my cake, I am going to write down the position. It is N29°
47', E67° 58,3'. I read other things from the GPS, such as the speed,
distance travelled and all kinds of things. It says that it is using
6 satellites, the speed is 3.1 knots, the average speed 4.8 knots and
the track is 39° and bearing 77°. The distance remaining to travel
shows as 3819km (2010 n.m.). Some things I feel are a bit out of
whack.*

*May 6th, 7th day out - Atlantic - I am still feeling pretty
bad but, if I think of something else, I forget about my
seasickness. I usually think of what I will do when we are
on solid ground again. Ishka, the other sailboat, is going
to the Bermudas. (note by the author: they had torn one
of their sails and had some leaking hatches which they
wanted to repair.) We are still heading for the Azores. We made up
that whoever gets to the Azores first makes a chocolate cake. When
we were talking to them on the VHF last night they said that they are
going to look forward to the cake. They are faster than us, but since
they are stopping, we might get there first. I don't think I will ever
cross the Atlantic (or any other ocean, for that matter) again. I will
simply refuse to do it. I will take the aeroplane. We have no wind
right now, but we have 2.5 to 3m (8 to 10 foot) waves. It is raining
and Daddy just came in from a shower in it. He is listening to Herb
right now. Murphy is working hard on us. All our vents are leaking,
and so the V-berth is very wet. The doll that I made and my beanie
babies are soaking lots of it up. I'm glad that this boat does not leak
much, I hate being constantly wet, and that is why I am not sleeping
in the V-berth. I am sleeping on the ground under the table. We have
rivers (salty rivers) rinsing our hatches. Pascal just figured out the
V-berth is wet. He always wants to play game boy, but there are no
batteries in it.*

*May 7th, 8th day out. Just 11 more days till my birthday. I
think I don't want to write the position and all that stuff
down anymore. Daddy just found out that the plug for the
GPS had shortened out and blew a fuse. Just right now I
reefed the main with Anisha and we are probably going
to take down the genoa and put up the small one. Today I
cleaned the cockpit and we dried lots of things. Carina walked*

around in her pyjamas and she didn't want to put her clothes on. We are having soup with potatoes and beans. Pascal is complaining. He does not like it. For supper Dad wanted to have a beer but couldn't find it in the fridge and then he almost dumped it after that.

May 7ᵗʰ, 8ᵗʰ day out. The sun is shining! We put all wet pillows and blankets on deck for drying and Marcel cleaned out the cockpit. The bridge was covered with soil from the flowerpots resting there. Some of them had tipped. The kids seeded beans, peas and rye and observe how it all grows. Most of the plants died. One pea, which was planted by Anisha, survived. The parsley and chive are also doing fine. At noon we got more wind and everybody ran to pick up their wares to save them from getting blown off or sprayed by the saltwater. Today Werner wished for fried eggs with bread for lunch. We still bake our own bread. All the work involves extra energy and takes double the time, especially when the kitchen is leaning to one side.

May 8ᵗʰ, 9ᵗʰ day out - Atlantic - It is raining again. I guess yesterday was just a dry off day. It's pretty calm right now. We are going about 3 knots. We are still 1813 n.m. away from the Azores. Daddy is looking for his hat and cannot find it. Everybody has to get out of his way when he is looking for something. I am safely out of his way, but Carina sure isn't. Pascal is whining for a bread with brie (cheese) on it. It is very annoying when he does that. Mommy is doing a watch right now. Marcel is reading "Left On The Labrador", Carina is lying down (as usual), Daddy is sleeping (I think he found his hat) and Pascal is saying he is bored and has nothing to do. I am reading the book "Anne of Green Gables" again. I have read almost every book on this boat. The wind is picking up again I think. I have to lie down again now, I am still not feeling very well. Sometimes I wonder what it is like not to be seasick.

May 8ᵗʰ day out. Today I finished "Left on the Labrador" it is a good book but the people in the book talk funny. Today Daddy can't find his hat, and we are all very tired and grumpy. I just woke up from a nap but I am still tired. Daddy got mad at us and changed the watches so that

Carina does from 8 p.m. to 10 p.m., Anisha 10 p.m. to 12 a.m., Dad 12 a.m. to 2 a.m., I do 2 a.m. to 4 a.m. and Mommy 4 a.m. to 6 a.m. I don't know how long we are going to keep that up. Today I put up the staysail and mizzen all by myself. Daddy is grumpy, and he is making everybody grumpy too. We had "wershtly" for supper and rice (note by the author: this expression by Marcel comes from the Swiss and English he sometimes mixed together, calling it a new language "Swinglish". So "wershtly" means sausages). *I wish we were in the Azores already, because the trip is getting worse and worse. I have to brush my teeth and go to bed soon. I wish Daddy would find his hat. We charged the batteries during the calm this morning.*

May 8th, 9th day out. We are east and about 100 miles south of the Bermudas. Things are getting desperate. I cannot find my favourite blue cap. I've been looking for it since about 10 p.m. last night. The wind dropped off to nothing again. Chäberli was on watch, but I could not sleep so I took over the watch. Sometimes I could get 2 knots out of the sails, but with the waves still 4' to 5' they stopped the boat and made the sails flop. I used the reefed mainsail to cut down the sideways movement a bit by tightening it and pulling it to the centre position. This helped somewhat but the remaining wind turned to the east then and died off completely. When the wind turned, of course, the boat tacked and I had to bring the fouled up genoa to the other side. We were then headed almost due south. I tried to get back to the other tack but, with the little wind, it would not work. In order to get back to the other tack I had to "fall off" the wind completely and bring the boat all around. I did get it to the other tack like that but, even then, we could make only about half a knot. It got to the point were I set the staysail to a heave-to position with all other sails down. By then it was 4 a.m. and time to wake Marcel to do his watch.

May 9th, 10th day out. I was quite grumpy yesterday as I had done a 6-hour watch and then could not sleep through the day. Marcel was constantly bugging someone in order to make him/her scream. It felt like a mad house. Hopefully no one will turn insane. Today started out much better. Everybody is happy to see the wind pushing us forward. The patch we had placed over the stitches along the bottom of the jib sail came off again. We put it on while the sail was still a bit

moist. We will have to do it again. At 1:25 p.m. we got tired of rolling and steered a new course of about 80°, which will bring us to N33°, W55°. The midpoint of our crossing is still about 931km (490 n.m.) away. (*The following text was written at the end of the above entry and it refers to Chäberli.*)
"And if it isn't glue
That made the dream come true
It's you"

May 10th, 11th day out - Atlantic - We have gale force winds right now and we are not feeling very well. It is 8:03 a.m. The wind generator is making very funny sounds. Our batteries are getting charged all right! The cockpit is all wet so we are all down below. It is raining. We have about 35 to 40 knots of wind. We are still 3059km (1610 n.m.) away from the Azores. We do not talk with Ishka anymore, because we cannot reach them. They are probably still in the Bermudas.

May 10th. This morning, at 2 a.m., the wind picked up to about 20 to 30 knots and Daddy and me took down the white gooseneck sail. When I woke up this morning we had gale force winds till about 9 a.m. I am using a pen because I couldn't find my pencil. After the strong wind passed it was pretty calm and we (Anisha, Marcel) took down all the sails and when the main came down all of the sliders came out too. I noticed that one of them was broken and we fixed it. We are 2985km (1571 n.m.) from the Azores. My watchstrap broke again. Today we played with the Legos and there was lots of screaming. For supper we had ravioli and salad.

May 10th. Carina fell asleep during her watch and I woke her up at about 10 p.m. It was time for Anisha. When Werner had his watch the wind picked up and the gooseneck sail was taken down. There was the staysail and the mainsail with one reef still up. When my time for the watch came the wind was already pretty strong. We went at about 5.5 to 6 knots. At 6 a.m. the wind was even stronger. I was afraid that the boat would get knocked down. That, of course, would have been almost impossible, with our heavy boat. But it was very uncomfortable and I woke Werner up. He took the mainsail

completely down. The wind was blowing over the deck at about 25 knots. The wind kept increasing in strength! The wind generator sounded strange and the whole boat vibrated. That was our first experience with gale force winds. The water was foamy all around us and the waves were very high. I didn't like it at all but Werner did! He thought it was more entertaining than going to the movie to see a storm. I went down below, around 6 a.m., to pick up the logbook. A big wave rocked the boat, and I hit my head and back on the shelf above the bench. Ow! It hurt. It lowered my already low state of energy and I was ready to call it quits. The longer we travel, the less I can understand why someone would enjoy sailing like this! The gale force winds held up till 9 a.m. and then dropped to nothing around noon. Then a heavy rain set in. The children looked out of the hatch once in a while but spent most of the time playing with their Legos down below. They are not impressed with things such as this anymore! They often lie down, because they get sick. Pascal has to throw up almost every morning when the weather is like this. After 10 days I took a shower using the sun shower bag.

Sunday, May 10th. I played my guitar last night and made a tune up, called "The Bloody Waves". We sure got our share of waves over-night and even now in the morning. We started the night with just the staysail and one reef in the mainsail. In the early morning the wind was so strong that I had to take down the main. It was raining and the saltwater spray blew over the deck. I held tightly onto the mast and undid the halyard to the mainsail in order to lower it. I had two sail ties ready in my mouth, hanging out like long whiskers. By the time I had them lashed around the sail and to the boom I was soaking wet. Even then, with just the staysail, we maintained a steady 6 knots. I sometimes referred to the staysail as a *diaper.*

The winds piped up to at least 40 knots and water was flying everywhere. Chäberli, who did the watch, was not very happy. I enjoyed the moment, marvelling at the forces of nature and the strength of our boat. There are only minor problems with Kristy Nicole. All the vents leak in heavy weather. They are the dorade-box type ones. With so much water they are not able to drain fast enough and the water runs inside. This is annoying, as one likes to keep the inside of the boat dry. I had, already, replaced 2 out of the five vents

Mountainous waves were left behind by the gale

with just clear lids and they worked well. There are no other leaks, except the spills we create. I was ready to enjoy a cup of coffee, which I had prepared with great caution. I was just about to sit down and sip it when a big wave pushed the boat away from under me and my coffee cup was then only half full. I attempted to set it down in the sink in order to clean the floor when another wave emptied the cup to a third full. I decided to gulp down what was left and then clean up. To prepare a slice of bread, topped with jam or some similar substance is another story. Mine landed on the now clean floor before reaching my mouth. Needless to say it landed face down and stayed there (fortunately you might say).

The wind generator was kept busy charging all the batteries, including the re-chargeable Ni-cads, using the 110-Volt battery charger. With that kind of weather the energy balance was well maintained. This was the first real gale force wind we experienced on open waters. It sure felt and looked impressive and a bit scary, but by then I had learned what sailplane to set for the wind strength we got and how to compensate for when they were from abeam or slightly ahead. I had recorded them all in the diary.

More Excerpts From The Diaries

May 11th, 12th day out - Atlantic- We have washed our floor in the saloon with many different things. First, we washed it with coffee, and that did not work, so we spilled some cooking oil on the ground, and then coffee again, and today we washed our pillows with black tea. I am not feeling very well. We are 286km (1510 miles) from the Azores still. I have just finished reading the book "Left on the Labrador". It was a good book.

May 11th. We are sailing almost down wind. This morning Pascal woke me up with a plop onto my bed and then he wanted to play Legos with me. Today I can't write very long, it's getting dark. I caught a fish and it took all my line and now I lost all my strong 55kg (120lb) line, and I hurt myself while I was at it trying to hold back the line.

May 11th. I put out the fishing line but no fish were biting until the afternoon. Marcel wanted to take in the line and took it off the winch. As he was winding in the line a fish bit. It must have been a big one, because Marcel could not hold the line and it unwound through his hands. The line is gone and both of Marcel's hands are ripped open. It hurts him a lot and at the same time he is upset to have lost the line. He is crying. We laze around the whole day. Werner has a headache and lies in the aft berth. Today even he is complaining about the "bloody waves"! Besides lying around, which I find pretty boring, I stitch up Werner's jacket, bake bread and prepare a soup. For supper we eat beef stew. We move along fairly well averaging about 4.5 to 5 knots. Soon we will reach the halfway point.

May 11th. It would not have been as hard to stay put in the boat during the gale, if the floor had its normal surface. However, for some "Murphy-reason" salad oil got spilled onto it and we now live on an ice rink! The only way to hold yourself is by bracing against the walls, etc. I am glad the boat is small so there is always a chance of holding on to something. Yesterday we sailed 255km (134 n.m.), quite a distance. We are making up a bit for the calm days we had.

We are still a day or two away from the half-way mark. I feel weak. The constant balancing takes a lot of muscle power. I eat lots but am still hungry. This morning I woke up with a headache. It is better now after some more rest and a yarrow tea *(the tea was harvested and dried at the farm in Enderby and carried along. It helps to lessen pains.)* We are sailing at about 5 to 6 knots. Where are the Azores? I cannot remember the waypoint and have to look it up. It is at about N38° 30' and W28° 38'. There is still a long way to go. I get quickly run down and feel tired even though I sleep or, at least, rest a lot. The kids hold up unbelievably well and, I think, Pascal has, finally, got over his seasickness. Presently we are on a downwind course due east. I hope the wind will turn to SW or S again. The downwind course is very uncomfortable, to say the least.

May 13th, 14th day out. Today we changed our wrist watches to 1 hour ahead. We also passed the halfway mark, so in about 13 more days we will be in the Azores. It is already day 14. I can barely believe it. I am reading the book "Rainbow Valley" for the second time. I have not read the book "Nancy Drew and the Hardy Boys" yet, but I don't really like the Hardy Boys. I will read "The Twenty-One Balloons" after Marcel has read it. I definitely need a shower. This morning when I was combing my hair, I made it go flat against my head! It is pretty yucky if you ask me.

May 14th. Carina is playing with the Legos. She makes dogs out of them and is pretending they are circus dogs, like always. She is making a parade with them. We are going to have rice for supper. We are still 2101km (1106 n.m.) away from the Azores. I wish we were closer. We are going 4.7 knots. I have finished reading "Rainbow Valley".

May 1st. Yesterday I was talking to Anisha and Carina after it got dark and I couldn't write. We had macaroni for supper with applesauce and "brösmeli" (a Swiss word for fried bread crumbs) as Pascal calls it, and cheese. Yesterday I had to get up at 6 a.m. to take down the gooseneck sail. And all except two hanks came lose. I finished the book called "The Twenty-One Balloons" and today I finished "The Message", which is part of the Animorphs Series by

K.A. Applegate. Today for supper we had rice and salad. Mommy is having a hard time to get Carina to brush her teeth. She is just crying.

Thursday, May 14th. We are 2 weeks on the trip and have passed the half way mark. This morning it was foggy and moist. Visibility dropped to about 1 mile for a while. Anything that was still dry inside the boat is now moist to the touch, such as the bed sheets, the sleeping bags, pillows and so on. We still do not see the sun come out, and drying anything is impossible. Taking a shower would be a freezing opportunity and everybody seems to prefer the sticky hair and smelly body over the freezing experience of a shower.

The waves have subsided a bit, to about 1.2m (4 feet) on top of the large drawn-out swells, and we are travelling quite comfortably. We are able to do things without having to constantly brace ourselves, except for a "once-in-awhile big wave" just to keep us on our toes. It looks like we are making good mileage, as our average speed shows 5.7 knots. Of the 40 or so grapefruits which were stored in the aft cabin cupboard only 4 have gone bad. Not too bad a loss. We can still enjoy half a grapefruit every day, the only fresh fruit we have. Presently the boat is on a course of 87° magnetic, pointing towards the Azores. Winds have predominantly been from the S to SW and, according to Herb, we should keep these winds until Saturday or Sunday. We will see what changes we get today.

We had a good lunch, as usual, this time baked sausages wrapped in pastry. Delicious! I just had a good power nap, and when I wanted to go up into the cockpit for a while there were already 2 people comfortably stretched out there, both reading. It is uncomfortable to sit up in there, and I chose to retire back to the aft cabin. When it is bumpy I cannot read without getting a headache. Twice in the past on this trip I had a headache after reading, so I may as well just lie down and dream.

Later during the day I was listening to what Herb had to say about the weather. Our position was N33° 32', W50° 36'. The following information was entered in the diary for positions and winds of different boats near us.

Sealoon: N28° 18', W55° 55', winds from the S at 18 to 20 knots
Caledrion: N28° 25', W55° 49', winds form the S at 18 to 20 knots

Shadow fax: N27° 37', W54° 42', winds from the S at 18 to 20 knots (Note: above names were taken via radio signal and may not be spelled correctly)

Chäberli has stopped writing into the diary for now. She does not feel motivated to do so. I had not noticed that she was at a low point. She continued to prepare excellent meals and did not mention anything about her feelings. The trip went on as described with the following entries in the diaries.

May 15th, - Atlantic - I have figured out what to give Marcel for his birthday, although I'm having second thoughts if he deserves a present at all! I am crocheting a little woollen bag for him to put his game boy into. We are still 1862km (980 n.m.) away from the Azores. That is about 10 days if the wind keeps up (which I hope it will). We are going to have baked potatoes for supper, and tuna salad. Marcel is in one of his teasing (bugging, I mean) moods.

May 15th. Today I don't have much to say. We are having tuna with rice, as usual, and potatoes "uh". I was going to put out my thinner fishing line but I don't want to lose the line. Anisha said she has a present for my birthday, but I don't think she does. Carina is boasting that she is teaching Pascal good stuff. She said that I only teach Pascal bad stuff, but that is not true. I was reading "The World of Ben Light Heart". It is a book about a boy who learns to live with blindness. Anisha and Carina have a secret about something.

Friday, May 15th. Still over 1900km (1000 nautical miles) to go! We had about 4 hours of no wind at night, and it started again to lightly blow around 2 a.m. I un-reefed the main and we moved again at about 4 knots gradually going faster. The wind in the late morning was about 15 knots, a pleasant ride, with acceptable waves that were, however, building steadily. According to Herb another front will pass us on Saturday, with strong winds at our waypoints and even stronger winds further north. We should make good progress. The crew is calm and mostly involved in reading. I played my guitar for a while. Even this is hard as the strings always jump away from me. I again recorded the positions aired by Herb of other sailboats near us.

Sealoon: N29° 32', W52° 59', winds from the S at 20 knots

Caledrion: N29° 31', W52° 58', winds form the S at 15 knots
Shadow fax: N29° 21', W51° 15', winds from the S at 18 to 20 knots
Papatilly: N31° 52', W52° 10', winds from the S-SW, 20 knots

May 16ᵗʰ - Atlantic - I have finished Marcel's birthday present. Last night I didn't do a watch. I didn't do one because Carina did not wake me up properly for my watch. Carina's watch is before mine, and when she wakes me up she just shakes me until I make a sound, and then goes to bed. She did not wake me up properly and I just slept. My watch is from 10:00 p.m. to 12:00 p.m. and then comes Daddy's. Around 1:00 a.m. Marcel woke up and noticed that there was nobody up in the cockpit. We figured out that we had been going 3 hours with nobody on watch!

May 16ᵗʰ. Mammy was trying to make bean salad for supper but the beans seem to always land on the ground. Right now it is pretty rough weather. We have about 20 to 30 knot winds. We still have 161km (852 n.m.) to go to the Azores. Tonight we are having spaghetti and, ah, I don't know what. Mom gave us an Animorph book and I said it was mine, Anisha and Carina disagreed. Today I read a book called "Monkey Trouble". There was a guy in there and his name was Sorty and he was pretty funny. I want to practice my hand writing but it is sort of hard when the boat wiggles. Our position is N33° 29.3', W45° 00.7'.

Saturday, May 16ᵗʰ. The anticipated low from yesterday moved west and stalled. We are going along very well now, having steady winds of 15 to 25 knots, from the S-SW. We record an average speed of 7.1 knots, measured every two hours. Over night we reefed the main and took the mizzen down. We recorded average speed this morning of 6.4 knots, a fast course with the wind slightly from behind and on our starboard side. Kristy Nicole bashes through the 2.4 to 3.7m (8 to 12 foot) waves, heading almost due east. We are following the 33.5° line of latitude. There is a low north of us and a newly forecast gale further west off our path.

There is always the odd 15 foot, or higher, wave surging underneath us and making things a bit uneasy. On May the 11ᵗʰ Papatilly covered almost 9 degrees longitude while we covered more than ten. We definitely are moving faster, maybe because we are a bit further north and have stronger winds. I think Kristy Nicole is a fast offshore cruiser, and she can carry a whole lot of weight.

The weather is still very depressing, as it is cloudy and we experience some rain showers or mist. Pascal just thought he needed to puke again but nothing happened. He just ate some breakfast and is now lying down.

The wind generator can provide power for some of our requirement but we still, for the most part, need to run the engine. When the winds are at least 15 knots the generator puts in about the same energy as we take out. With the larger waves the bilge pump needs to come on more often, as water comes through the lid of the lazarette, and if we do not have the front bilge pump on, that water also runs into the bilge. It enters through the chain locker lids which we had taped up, but they let in some water every time a spray comes over the front deck.

I estimate the autopilot uses about 2 to 3 amps or 50 amp hours (Ah) per day. The fridge uses about 35 Ah, the navigation lights about 24 Ah plus the cabin lights, radio, VHF and bilge pump about another 20 Ah, for a total of 129 Ah. We need to charge about 155 Ah. In a constant 15-knot wind the generator produces 120 Ah per day, so we are still short some energy, which we replace with the engine.

I am presently reading a book (I picked it up in a second hand book store) about how to find a job. It sounds like a circus. I need to cut my hair, put on a 3 piece suit and shirt with tie. Then I have to arrange interviews and play a stereotype person to please the interviewer. First impressions, according to the book, still seem to be important, but in what field do I really want to work? In tourism as a tour guide? Then I had better pick up some French. Or in the publishing area, in the computer area, in the training of people, in language training?

It is 4:19 p.m. and the weather has turned nasty again. Humidity in the saloon is at 94%. We have 30 knot blows from the South and had to take the jib down. We still move 6 knots with the reefed main and the staysail up. At 6 p.m. our position was 33° 29.3', 45° 00.8'. Winds were still strong at about 30 knots. So far we can call ourselves part of a 16-day milk shaker, now at full speed! Brigitte just spilled a can of beans which were intended for our supper. It's all on the floor which has certainly had its fair share of cleaning up.

Climbing a wave, at a fast pace

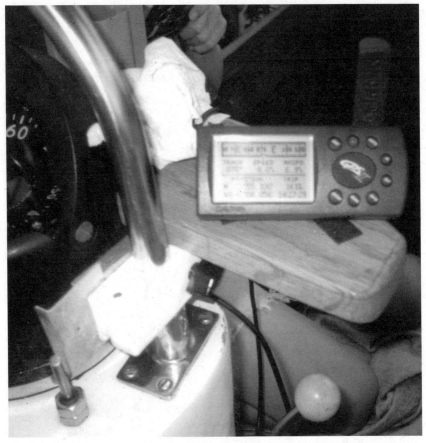

Bottom left shows the rudder indicator rod in central position.
Centre shows the GPS on its little table.

Land In Sight Soon?

While sailing over the open waters, I wanted to reflect upon our journey. Reading the entries from the diaries may give a clear record of how the days passed but there were underlying currents that were not mentioned. I don't remember having much intimacy with my wife. There was just no feeling of wanting to be closer together. I was not sure if Chäberli felt the same. She did not say much. Routine kisses were exchanged but that's about it. Her thoughts were, most likely, focused on other things. The constant worry about survival may have had something to do with it!

Looking back I can see that I had a lot of expectations about how the trip would be. I had expected to be travelling over the waves, with a smile on my face, all the way across. I envisioned myself as being much more in tune with the elements around me. I had hoped that the endless universe would join my limited way of thinking and that it would inspire me to find new understanding. In actual fact, it turned out to be a constant fight against the elements, and I did not have much time to ponder the big question. It was more a fight with nature to keep the boat afloat, upright and on top of the water. At the other extreme we had to learn to wait, sometimes in agony, for the much-needed wind.

Certainly, there was that feeling of being able to go anywhere in the world. A feeling of power and freedom. This was counterbalanced, however, with the reality of having to work hard for any goal which we wanted to achieve. After all, even now that we could have gone to any place in Europe, we had, first of all, to choose where we wanted to go. It was a feeling of being rich but not being able to make use of all our riches.

The environment we found ourselves in was, certainly, invigorating. We could look around and see the endless mountains of water, marching off over the horizon. Each time we saw different things, especially in a storm. The waves approaching from different angles, the foam spraying over us, the clouds moving, the light changing and reflecting on the water's surface. Sometimes the waves were dull for a while and then changed to all kinds of dark blue, gray, white and so on. At such moments the sheer scope of things captured my soul. I was trying to comprehend the idea of a limitless universe, but no clear answer ever appeared. Maybe I was expecting too much. I can't explain exactly what it was that I felt I should have been discovering. My mind accepts the knowledge that there is a limitless universe so why should I have had to find any further explanation?

Part of the problem was, I believe, that it is difficult to connect with waves which are constantly on the move. I thought of life on the farm were I could sit in a field of all kinds of vegetables, inhaling the different smells, watching them move ever so gently in the wind and almost hearing them grow. There I talked to the plants in the hope that they would grow more robustly. I certainly was connected to the food which I grew and ate like that. Life afloat was quite different. The imminent danger of losing my life or, more seriously, the lives of my whole family, kept thoughts tied to what was happening around me. Talking to the waves would have been difficult. First of all because they did not hang around to be talked to and, secondly, I would have had to scream at them in order to overcome the noise of the wind in the rigging. I could not find a connection with my surroundings because of the almost constant struggle to survive, and the fear of drowning. I tried to overcome such thoughts and feelings, but with no success. The harder I tried, the lesser I felt to be part of the whole.With those thoughts churning through my mind I carried on the job as a skipper and concentrated on the things that were real, such as my love affair with the barometer. It was always a great satisfaction to be able to know, ahead of time, what kind of weather was coming. With the barometer I could do just that. It was almost like clockwork; two hours after a one-millibar drop of the needle and the wind would pick up. Things like that made life a little bit predictable and much more bearable.

The evening weather forecast sounded as if the worst was yet to come. Papatilly reported that they had some very strong winds of up to 69 knots the previous night. It had damaged some of their sails. Another boat to the south, Kelly, positioned behind us at N31° 57', W49° 42' reported 35 to 50 knot winds. I wondered if our estimations of wind strengths for the previous night had been on the low end of the scale. We certainly had moved along nicely. The boat Sherycan (note: boat names are spelled as they sounded on the radio), which was located about 114km (60 n.m.) behind us and to the south, reported winds of from 20 to 25 knots.

I also had to make plans for what we would do once we were in Europe. It was clear that we needed to replenish our dwindling capital, in order to be able to continue travelling. Our only chance to do that would be in Switzerland; where I would not need a work permit. Marcel and I had talked of doing a bicycle tour through England. In the fall we would sail the boat to the warmer climate in the south before settling in Switzerland. I was still keen to continue our trip back, via the Canaries and the Caribbean, to the farm in BC. We also thought of selling the boat in England and buying a car to travel in Europe. The idea of selling the boat would have been a good way to deal with the tight budget situation. It would, however, have been difficult, for me, to part with Kristy Nicole. I guessed that we would reach Switzerland about mid July.

Meanwhile, aboard the boat, the crew felt well and everyone had settled into a certain routine. Despite the humidity all our equipment had performed well but everything was sticky to the touch. Visibility was poor. In the afternoon the GPS revealed an average speed of 6.7 knots, calculated over a three-hour period after lunch. Kristy Nicole seemed to sail well at speeds of up to 7.5 knots. Anything faster than that and she started to sway into the wind and slow herself down by burying her bow in the oncoming waves. This brought lots of salt water in, over our rails. Our current course produced flooding of the port side scupper. The water then ran along the deck where it drained, through the various scuppers, over the side and back. Some of the water, of course, found its way into the lazarette, flooding everything in it before ending up in the bilge.

On Sunday, May the 17th, at 7:23 p.m., when listening to the weather forecast, I heard another boat which was on the same journey as we were. The name of the boat was Symphonia, positioned about 20 miles to the north and 180 miles behind us. I marked it down in the diary, besides other boats whose names I could not decipher. Then I heard the name Ishka. They had just left Bermuda and were heading towards the Azores. They had stayed there for 10 days to fix their boat and to hope for better weather. We had stitched our jib sail, as best we could, while still under way. We also fixed the hanks on the gooseneck sail, which had only been held in place by its corner cleats. It looked strong again, but we decided to work with the jib only and to keep the gooseneck sail as a spare.

May 17th, - Atlantic - I have finished wrapping up Marcel's present. This morning we saw a school of dolphins. There were about 50 of them at least! They were only about 1.5 metres (5 feet) long, but they jumped very far out of the water, about 1.5 metres (5 feet). They were the first animals (not counting the birds) that we have seen on our trip across the Atlantic.

May 17th. Tomorrow is my birthday and I am very excited. I like writing with pencil more, because my writing is nicer. Today we are having mashed potatoes. Right now I'm listening to Weird Al while I'm writing my diary. Before that, Pascal and I were listening to Weird Al together with Fabian's Walkman. Carina let me use her new headphones. I got an egg carton from Mom and I made egg carton air planes. This morning we saw dolphins. They were about 1,4 metres (4.5 feet) long and the babies were very cute. They were swimming with us for about 30 minutes.

The logbook read: 5 a.m., big school of dolphins, water temp 21°C, salinity 1026. It was a great sight to see these big creatures jumping all around you. Some were going fast and jumping with big white splashes, while others just swam in the bow wave of our boat. They are always a welcome sight for our children, especially now as they have not seen any animal life, so far, on this trip. Later on in the morning we got a brief stroke of sunshine but soon new clouds moved in.

Now it's my turn to comment on our first leg of crossing the Atlantic. I stopped writing in my diary after some days because I did not feel like writing every day about what we had to eat. That was the kids' job and they did well at it. I also didn't want to tell about all the mishaps; the others did well on that too, and I must say it is quite funny to read about it later. Although it was not always funny when it happened. I just lived from day to day, did my jobs like cooking, cleaning up, taking my turns on watch and looking after the kids, if

they needed me. I also took my place under the table with Anisha to sleep, it was the most comfortable place when it was rough. I did not feel too scared while under way, but I did not stop feeling seasick all the time we were on the open water. It was not that I had to throw up; I just did not feel well at all. I was not able to read; that would have made me dizzy. I couldn't cross-stitch either, so I just had to sit around, something I don't like doing. It felt almost boring, but that would be the wrong word. I had lots to take care of but never had the drive to do more than just the bare necessities. The routine on the boat started to feel as if it would never end. Rather like a turntable that is stuck in the one track and you wonder if it will ever come to an end. Occasionally I would peek outside, in the hope of seeing something other than just water.

There was, at least, hope and I knew that Werner would get us to our destination as quickly as possible. It is certainly a strange sensation when you feel that time is standing still. I felt that we were in the same spot each day. The only difference was in the size of the waves

Dolphins, some of them showing off with back flips

and the odd time, when there was a break in the clouds, that gave us hope that we would be able to dry the boat out. It was not leaking anywhere but, with Werner coming into the cabin soaking wet, after doing a sail change or other work on the deck, things slowly got that sticky feeling. It was the salt that made things feel wet, even though they were not. There was moisture saturated air everywhere and the linens, cushion covers and towels were taking it all in.

Each of us looked after our assigned tasks. Otherwise we tried to jam ourselves between parts of the boat in order to find some rest. Werner spent most of his time in the cockpit but, when it got really rough, he sat on the bench near the companion way. He had his watch set to beep at 10 minute intervals to remind him to climb up the ladder into the cockpit to do another scan of the horizon. It was tedious and, at the same time, uncertain. Our field of vision was, at times, not more than a few 100 metres(300 feet). When Werner was dressed in his full rain gear I don't think he was very comfortable.

On one occasion Werner said that he had seen a boat, travelling at a speed of about 16 knots, about 15 minutes travel distance from us. At that time visibility was good but the 15 minutes would not have given us much time, if necessary, to have made a sail change. On other occasions, because of poor visibility, we would not have had more than 2 minutes to change course. Basically I did not feel safe and tried to divert my thoughts by concentrating on my duties. On the other hand I would not have been happy to sit in the cockpit for most of the day, constantly turning my head to look for something which might happen. I was, however, sure that my prayers for a safe journey would be answered.

A Celebration And Another Gale

Monday, May 18th. Today is Marcel's birthday; it is 5:30 in the morning and 1266km (666 n.m.) more to go. Marcel is one happy boy. He enjoyed getting all the Animorphs books. Yesterday, in the evening, I was listening to some classical music. I sat on the bed in the aft cabin, watching the ocean on either side going up and down while the music smoothed it all out. Every movement of the boat and the elements outside, were transferred into a smooth and calming motion. For supper we had my favourite dish, mashed potatoes with gravy and beef. What an excellent highlight. There were also some beets with it, and it took 3 servings before I had to refrain from eating any more.

The winds kept up, blowing at around 10 to 14 knots throughout the night, and we had all sails up. This morning I reefed the mainsail as it was getting to be a bit bumpy. I also changed the course to 77° magnetic. The barometer dropped a bit. We then had a following wind and were running the motor to charge the batteries. That gave us a speed of over 7 knots. The average speed for the past 17 hours had been 6.8 knots. Not a bad average for Kristy Nicole.

We were expecting a weather front to pass us, as predicted by Herb. There were supposed to be some strong winds north of 34°, and we were just about to reach that area. Our present position was N33° 40', W40° 35'. We hoped to arrive in the Azores on the evening of Sunday, May 24th. That would reflect a nice, fast trip. Hopefully the weather would be nice as we intended to stay there for about a week. I was keen to read all the E-mails which should have piled up in our "In Box". I wondered if the phone system would be any better than it had been in the Bahamas; otherwise we would have to wait until our arrival in England.

It was still hard to believe that we had travelled all that way by our own means. It had taken some patience and a lot of adjustments in terms of cleanliness and other factors. The boat was filthy, with dust everywhere. The bed sheets smelled from sweat and other odours better not mentioned. All was moist and sticky. I still got tired quickly and ate more often then usual. I was starting to miss fresh food, especially apples, and was looking forward to what we would find in the Azores; maybe some bananas?

Because we had made a fairly quick trip, our supply of drinking water would be more than sufficient. We had not had to gather any. That would have been difficult with the high seas and the resulting spray. To create a fast and simple way to catch rain, I had prepared a hose system to catch water from the reefed mainsail. Unfortunately we had not had any downpours to test its efficiency.

My handwriting has become much better as a result of making daily entries in the diary. I seem to get a better flow in my writing, and I even like how it looks now. Another Swiss "damage" I had to endure as a youth was being forced to write with my right hand when I entered grade 3. After leaving school it took years for my left hand to regain its dexterity.

With things more or less under control on the boat, my mind had time to wonder about things in the "real" world. Would I have to register for military service when I started a job in Switzerland? How was our housekeeper in Canada making out? Was the house still rented out? Now that spring is there and all in bloom the place must look nice. I hoped that the house sitter was continuing to prune the berry bushes and fruit trees, and to pay rent.

We had to double reef the mainsail when the winds started to gust to 25 knots. The mizzen was still up and so were the stay and jib sails. The wind generator was pumping electricity in spurts. With the wind more from the back and gusty it made the mast, and generator, swing a lot. I was trying to recharge 8 rechargeable batteries for the Walkmans. Each kid had one.

In the afternoon I listen to classical music. We had some really great cookies for desert with chocolate cream on top. The gale force winds had not yet materialized as predicted. They should, however, last through the night. We would get an update on them in the evening. We had to change the time on our wristwatches again, in order to stay in touch with daylight.

In the evening, I listened to Herb's weather forecast. Most of the previously named boats were reporting winds of around 25 to 30 knots over the past 24 hours. The boat Symphonia was closest to us at about N34°, W41°. I could not hear the minutes of their position. We were at N34° 13', W39° 18', or about a day's sailing ahead of them. Herb's warnings were clear and there was no escape from it. Strong gale force winds were forecast to reach us in the morning.

May 18th - Atlantic - Today is Marcel's birthday. Carina did not have a present for him so she just gave him a card. He did not pay much attention to my present, not that there was much to pay attention to, but he sure paid attention to Mammy and Daddy! He got the Animorphs series up to book 10. I have read them up to book 4. He also got Mel the Koala, a beanie baby. I knit 30cm (1 foot) today on my knitting. We are still 1113km (586 n.m). away from the Azores. We are going to have sweet and sour for supper with macaronis!

May 18th. Today I almost forgot to write my diary. For my birthday I got a pouch from Anisha. She made it to put my Game Boy into. I got the rest of the Animorphs books up to book 10 and Mel the Koala from Mommy and Daddy. I read book 3 and part of book 5. Pascal made a very nice card. Mommy made sort of a cake and we each got a whole can of coke.

May 19th, 20th day out - Atlantic - It is 10 p.m. and I don't think I should be using light. We saw whales today. I don't know what kind.

May 19th. Here I sit on my bed in the evening, next to me a well-protected coke-rum cup so that the waves, the bloody waves, can not take away my little pleasure by spilling it. The whole day was a disappointing and frustrating one. Early in the morning I had the hatch (to the aft berth) opened just a small gap to overcome the smell produced by the galley sink. The rotten egg smell travels along its path to the aft cabin and it is very disturbing. Anyway, some time later I got a salt-water shower and the whole bed and sleeping bag was wet. I did not have much sleep, and it was a grumpy start. Then I had to go up and take down sails as the winds started to build. Eventually we just sailed with the "diaper" (staysail). We had gale force winds for most of the day, a very bumpy ride and no way to sleep. Then it started to rain and spray kept the cockpit wet. Finally the front passed and the wind came from the west. I thought it would turn to NW and tacked to sail with the wind abaft to do some "northing". The wind turned back towards SW and, eventually, we had to tack back and settle on a 95° magnetic course. Because the waves were still big, it was an uncomfortable ride with lots of flapping of the jib sail. The sky cleared in the evening and we had some sunshine, just as the sun set. "WHALES"! I called out. At about 6:30 p.m. we saw about 10 or 15 of them trailing behind us. From a distance, their body colour appeared to be plain gray. This was the first time we had seen whales. It was quite exiting. Our position was N35° 14', W37° 08'. The water temperature was at 20° C with a salinity of 1026. That day would have at least one excitement, whales. I hoped that the waves would soon subside to make it a bit more comfortable and less stressful on the sails and rigging.

Herb's 7:30 p.m. message was disturbing, to say the least. The boat, Symphonia, which had been a day's sail behind us yesterday, had troubles with a torn sail. Herb relayed a message from the coast guard confirming a MOB (man overboard) on Symphonia that morning. The rescue team could not locate the man but had found a life jacket and a ring. Most likely the boat would have been only 100 miles behind us when the strong gale force winds swept through to cause such havoc.

First sighting of whales

Things Improve, Weather-Wise

We had been out on the Atlantic for more than 20 days. This was the only time that the sun had stayed out for the whole day. We were able to dry out some of our things. There were hardly any waves and, obviously, no wind. We moved at one knot or just sat there in the water. I took the opportunity to enjoy a wonderful hot water shower with the sun-heated water. That was something I had been looking forward to for some time. We had to patch the jib sail again, this time further up on top. The staysail had a short rip of about 25cm (10 inches) along its foot and the main needed some patching up around the top batten pouch. The batten had disappeared sometime in the past few days. The 5cm (2 inch) wide piece of fibreglass had cut a hole at the end of its pouch and slipped out. This had happened before and we carried replacement material with us. We had managed to come through that squall with little loss and were looking forward to a bit of a rest. It was good to notice that this time the forecast was right on the ball, and we were able to prepare well. During the rest of the day we had some good wind and a lovely day's sailing. There was the odd 6-foot wave that jiggled the boat a bit, reminders of the past gale, but, for the most part, it was plain sailing.

Thinking of the man-overboard scenario it seemed obvious that, once a person was overboard, there would be little chance of being saved. There were too many odds against a safe rescue. The rough water, the temperature, the poor visibility and the constant spray all worked against the rescue team. It certainly was important to wear a life jacket, something the person on Symphonia, presumably, had not done. Wearing a harness tied to the lifeline in such bad weather is an absolute must. I had often complained about how uncomfortable it was but, if I had fallen overboard during a gale, the chance of being rescued would have been slim. On several occasions in the past I had not strapped myself to the boat while on the forward deck in bad weather. This was to avoid the awkward safety gear but, in retrospect, was rather short-sighted. With no one else on deck my absence could have gone unnoticed for some time. Marcel would have been able to steer the boat, but where would he have looked for me? The line which we pulled behind the boat in bad weather would have been my only chance for survival. Fortunately we never had to find out if it would have worked.

It was difficult to put this matter out of my mind. While gazing over the surface of the water in the early dawn, I started to hallucinate. Suddenly I saw a bush of blond hair floating on the surface. At first I thought it was a person's head. Squinting my eyes I toyed with the idea that it was just a coconut but, right beside it, I saw an orange object which looked like an emergency beacon. I thought I could see the man who had fallen overboard and was already on my way to loosen up the mainsail, to stop our boat. When I turned my head again to look at the spot, all the things I had just seen were gone. I went back to where I had been sitting but nothing unusual could be seen. For a minute I had been absolutely sure that I could see a man in the water. Then I was starting to question my state of mind. I sat down and tried to compose my mind, trying not to think of the above experiences.

The following day, May 20th, brought another sighting of a whale. This time we were almost sure that it was a pilot whale. I measured the salinity of the water to be 1024 at a temperature of 21° C. I had it in mind to send all this information to a whale watch organization but never got round to it. We knew, at least, that the water had warmed up a bit. The whale slowly crossed in front of our boat. I watched it blow water out of its spout, in short spurts, until it was too far away to make out the details. It had been a great experience and something to remember.

With a fair bit of spare time on my hands I had a tendency to daydream. On one such occasion, as I enjoyed the fresh sea air, I designed a clean air helmet for pedestrians. Thinking of these poor people, trapped in smog and auto fumes, I thought that a helmet, with a built in solar collector, would be a welcome addition to their attire. A fan could filter and recycle the air in the helmet and a hint of pine scent might be added. Now that cyclists have been persuaded to wear helmets can pedestrians be far behind? On rereading the diary I am not sure if this was a genius at work or the hallucinations of an under-employed mind.

There were still 627km (330 n.m.) to go and the winds, over the past couple of days, had been on and off. We started to motor sail again.

During the past few days my stomach had developed some kind of trouble, producing excess gas and causing lots of cramps. I had to dispose of a lot of wind. It was very inconvenient for all of us, and I was invited to spend most of my time on deck. I could not pinpoint the cause and thought that it might be connected to the lack of physical activity. I tried to eat more selectively and to chew things longer. I longed for apples. Memories about our life on the farm came to mind. I would go down to the root cellar on an almost daily basis and select one of the many varieties of apples stored on the shelves. Even at the end of winter, there were still several varieties available such as red- and golden delicious, winter bananas and belle de boskoop. The last is a sour apple and used, mostly, for cooking. I would have given a lot now for any one of these. We had run out of apples within the first 10 days of our trip. They might have lasted longer but, with the price for them being as high as they were, we had not bought a lot. For the time being, we would have to make do with grapefruit. Up until then only 10 had turned bad. They had started to taste very sweet and, apart from Chäberli and me, the crew did not like them much. We also had dried plums and dried apples with us but they could not replace the taste of a fresh apple.

We enjoyed a couple of days of calm weather and pushed ourselves smoothly through the water, safe in the knowledge that we had ample fuel to get us to the islands.

May 22nd - Atlantic - We will probably be in the Azores tomorrow (Yupee). I still do not like sailing any better than when we started. We only have 200km (104 n.m.) to go. Pascal just learned how to draw dolphins, so his next few pictures will be filled with dolphins.

May23rd - Atlantic - I am doing a watch right now. It is a night watch and since we have the motor running (because there is no wind) and are charging the batteries, I am allowed to use the light. My watch is from 10:00 p.m. to midnight. Today we saw some more whales. I took 2 pictures but I think they were too far away. We also saw dolphins again. They had yellowish sides so I think they were common dolphins. We are now only 119km (62.4 n.m.) away from the Azores. We will be there by noon tomorrow, I think.

I used the VHF radio to contact a large, striking looking sailboat, called Truly Classic, which passed to the south of us. It was a 19m (63 foot) ketch and the crew reported their average speed to be 8 knots. They had experienced the same strong winds as we had a few days ago. They had managed a rate of 18 knots, under two fully reefed sails. Ship traffic increased as we got closer to the islands. Yesterday a tanker had passed and, during the night, a 61 foot sailing yacht, called Paladin, had passed us on our starboard side. We were all looking forward to our arrival in Horta the next day, Sunday, May 24th.

Up to the last day at sea my tummy had acted strangely. Maybe it was the home baked bread made with spelt that I could not digest. Whatever it was it was most uncomfortable. A drink of coke seemed to help, especially when thinned with rum.

We passed about six more whales with some of them coming fairly close to us. We tried to change course and approach one of them head on. We had no chance. It quickly noticed and disappeared, just as we tried to steer towards it. After a few minutes it resurfaced, on the other side of our boat. I tried several times to motor towards it but without success. After a while I gave up and resumed course.

We had plenty of fuel and, because there was no wind, used the engine to move us at 4 knots. I confirmed a waypoint with another sailor near us who was also approaching the island of Faial. His waypoint was slightly to the Southeast of ours. Everything was ready and we were eager to see land.

At around 10 p.m., the entry in the logbook read "61.3 n.m. to Horta". There was no wind at all and barometric pressure was rising. At two o'clock in the morning Marcel wrote into the logbook; "fog, still see ok". When day broke, we tried to find signs of land but could see only white clouds of mist. Only when we were as close as 8 n.m. could we make out two faint bumps on the port side of our bow. Land ahoy! We all shouted. By then it was ten in the morning.

We raised the Portuguese flag, as a courtesy, as well as the yellow quarantine one on our starboard stay, a procedure used to signal officials of our status as a new arrival. Out of the mist came the island of Faial, green and lush, with steep sides. In some places we could make out buildings and roads. The town of Horta was around the tip of the island, on the other side. How impressive it was to see this island appearing from nowhere, out here in the Atlantic Ocean with nothing but water around it for hundreds of miles. The mist still hid the neighbouring island. Slowly we passed the outermost southwestern tip of Faial and the town hove into view, with its large seawall. To the back, the houses making up the town were set into the lush green of the trees. Flowers could be seen on some of the hillsides. It was an inviting view to say the least.

The engine had purred steadily for nearly 24 hours. We tied up to the seawall at about noon, reading the position as N38° 20.2', W28° 37.7'. We had made it! Out of the 90 gallons of fuel we had started out with we still had 140 litres (40 gallons). We also had about a quarter of our 700 litres (200 gallons) of drinking water. We were safely tucked in but it still felt as if we were out on the Atlantic. We were happy to know that, for the moment at least, we wouldn't have to suffer the tortures of unpredictable weather.

It was really a bit more than exhausting, all this shaking and rolling around. All in all I was glad to see land and to know that I would soon have some good solid ground under my feet. Most of the time on the trip across the Atlantic I just slept, ate a tiny bit, puked, and repeated. I got used to all the moisture but still did not like it at all. I don't really remember much of what happened on that trip. I know it was long and boring, and didn't want to do it again. Daddy said that we still had to make some more passages on the open sea. That didn't help me feel any more enthusiastic, but I didn't have much of a choice. The only positive thing was that the next part of the trip was only going to be half as long. I wondered why we didn't just take a plane and get it over with.

I made only one entry into my diary during the 23 days at sea. And even that one did not sound like it was exciting. The most exciting thing to look forward to was eating. Mom still had some good tricks up her sleeves when it came to food. She could prepare something out of nothing. I liked the noodle soups best as they also came up the easiest (if I still got seasick). At one time, when I was watching Mom making the noodles, I ticed the stove gently moving back and forth, balancing the hot pan with the water in it. Sometimes a bit more, then less, just as the waves were slushing past the little round window behind and to the side of it. There was a kind of pattern to the rocking of the stove and the heaving of the waves. Daddy mentioned to me once, that usually every 7th wave would be a larger one. To me they all seemed to be too large as it was. It looked really weird. Everything was solid, just the stove moved, almost like magic. My observation got diverted when the pan started to rattle and the lid released some steam. Mom added the noodles to the hot water and placed the lid back on. It seemed to stay on pretty good, from time to time releasing more steam but I could not notice any spills. However, the windows above became fogged up from the escaping steam and it got even more moist inside the boat than it already was. I thought, who cares, I was just glad I'd soon have some noodles in my rumbling stomach. With the sea not rocking us too badly just then, the chances were greater that the noodles were going to make it all the way to my bowl. We had other batches that went on the floor, because of a big wave just at the wrong moment. There was also parmesan cheese and canned tomato sauce. For all of us to sit down at the table and eat, we had to squeeze around the small table and try not to fall off the seat while the boat was moving us up, down and side to side. Mom had to sit at the end and didn't have as many things to squeeze between or hold on to, except the post next to her. Many times she would almost fall on the floor. It must have looked funny to see us all sitting there around that table munching on our food, bracing ourselves against the boat's structures and at the same time clutching at our plates like they were treasures.

Arriving in Horta was a great relief. Now finally I could use my feet again and walk. I wobbled and swayed a bit for a day before I lost my sea legs and felt comfortable on land again. On one occasion we were invited by an association of sailors to attend a bread-making party. It was a beautiful place. They had a large stove, heated with wood. All us kids were lining up around the edge of a very large drum full of dough and pushed our little fists into the mixture of mostly flour and water. Slowly the consistency changed from the fluffy white mass to a solid heavy mud-like texture. It took a long, long time before we finally could sit down and eat. But wow, was it ever good. There was a lot of different kinds of salads and breads to eat and we dug in with a vengeance. There were other kids too and we made friends with a couple of boys from *Windekind*, a sailboat sailed under the Swiss flag by their mother. I was very impressed that she was the captain sailing with her partner and her two kids. We ate dessert on her boat and later went to play along the piers with the two boys.

We were docked on the outer sea wall of the harbor and as such, we had to walk all around the harbor to get to the other boats. Along the walk we could see hundreds of street paintings of boaters that visited the place. It was a custom to paint the boat's name as well as the crew's names onto some part of the harbor walls or floors. Dad gave us some paint he'd used to touch up the hull of *Kristy Nicole* and asked us to do a nice mural. Anisha, Marcel and myself got to work. We did get the job done but at the end I felt like I had as much paint on me as there was on the wall. Nevertheless I felt it came out quite nice and we all signed our names to finish the job.

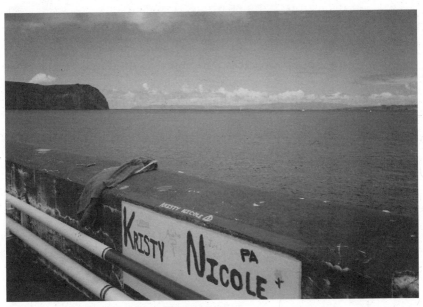

Our mural in Horta, Azores

Storm

1. The perfect storm some would say
Who really wants to go on this way
We still have to continue for another day
All we can do is wait and pray
All we can feel is something turning like a wheel

Ref: And the waves came from the front
And the waves came from the side
And the waves came from everywhere
And the captain didn't care

2. So we all do go down below
Hoping the weather wouldn't follow
Escaping the screams of the wind
Bracing us just as if pinned
All we can feel is something turning like a wheel
Ref:
Solo: G/Am/G/Am improvisation
Ref:
3. All we were thinking, thinking about
was, how we could get, could get out
Out of an endless looking mess, and everyone under stress
With winds at 60 knots more or less
It's a wild ride with the boat on its side
Ref:
Last line: And we did no longer care

A CD with colour pictures and songs can be ordered.

Horta

I was supposed to be the first and only one to go ashore. The kids, of course, could not wait and stepped on land anyway. They laughed at me because I was walking like a drunk, but they had problems themselves. It was a real challenge to cover the half mile to the office building, just to find out that it was closed. Naturally, they did not work on Sundays, but I had not thought about that until I noticed the sign on the door. The banks were also closed so I tried to withdraw some cash from a cash machine. For some odd reason my debit card was not accepted. That certainly gave me something to think about. The ATMs had always given us such great and reliable service. I knew there were enough funds in the account. The machine was refusing my card right at the start of the transaction, when I keyed in the password. The password seemed to be the problem. I always used a word as a password because I could remember words more easily than numbers. After all it was called a password not a pass-number. I had tried twice now and was not about to do it again. These machines let you do it wrong only three times a day and then the card gets barred from further transactions. I was sure that the machine was at fault but could not find another one to test that theory. We would just have to wait for the stores to open the next day.

On the way back I took a stroll along the main street and stopped at the local bar, Peter's Café Sport. I had a few dollars with me, enough for a beer, before returning to the boat. On the return journey my walking seemed to improve. I did not know if the one beer was responsible or if it was just the sea legs wearing off. Along the seawall, just a few boats ahead of us was Symphonia. It was a big and modern boat with a very tall mast. You could not miss it. There were still pieces from the torn sail on its deck and some hanging down from the front stay. I would have liked to talk to one of the crew members but had other things to do. I particularly wanted to start with the cleaning out of our boat. We retired early that day and had one long, well deserved rest.

A telephone call to Canada brought light to the mystery of my banking card's refusal to work. The letters assigned to the numbers on the handsets in Horta were not the same. In Canada the letter A was assigned to the number 1 and so on but, throughout Europe, it was the number 2. As I always keyed in letters rather than the numbers, the code was now completely different and the bank machine promptly rejected my card. Once I used the related numbers things worked fine.

The weather was a mixed bag of rain showers and sunshine. We did manage to get most of our things dried. More important was the washing and drying of all the bed sheets and clothes. There were all the facilities at the marina, including showers, which we enjoyed taking. We had not planed on any particular length of stay but were keen to leave as soon as possible. As soon as the boat had been taken care of, we would be on our way. The marina was no cheap place to stay when compared with our life at sea or at anchor over the past few months. When we left we paid about Can $120 for the 10 days. That was actually reasonable. The officer had kindly given us a lower rate; reasoning that we had to stay at the seawall. I had a short list of things to do. The most important I felt was to fill in the hairline cracks along the sides of the hull. I had not fixed them up well enough while in the Bahamas and it now showed. There were red stains oozing out through some of the cracks, as the salt water started to corrode the iron rods inside the cement hull. I had to make sure that the hull was perfectly sealed in order to preserve it.

The harbor was big but no boats were allowed to anchor in the middle. Most boats were tied up north of the fuel dock. There they were tied up 3 beside each other in order to make the best use of the available space. I had not wanted to squeeze into that maze of boats. With our limited steering and the heavy boat I was afraid of getting into trouble. We were just fine along the wall that protected the harbor area from the waves. It was a good step up to reach the pier and we had to install our boarding ladder to enable us to climb ashore. This part of the harbor was actually designed for larger ships and freighters. When I first checked-in the officer wanted me to move but, after some discussion, agreed to let us stay put. People were friendly and most courteous.

Now that I had to relate to life on land again I became aware of not having my watch. Time was valued again. The watch had been lost at sea, during one of my night watches. Following Chäberli's idea I had it set to sound a "pip" every 10 minutes, just in case I might fall asleep during the watch. With the wind and other noises around it was, however, sometimes difficult to hear the "pip" so I rested the watch on my chest, closer to my ear. On one occasion I had to do some changes on the sails during the night. Half asleep I got up, without remembering that the watch was still on my chest, and that was the last time I had any contact with that watch. It must have stuck to me long enough to get to the railing and then dropped overboard. I wonder if that incident was a message to tell me not to take time too seriously?

Shopping for fresh food was the next big need on our list. Finally apples could be purchased at a reasonable price as well as fresh vegetables. We even bought a bottle of wine and chocolate. Things became very pleasurable and cozy again. The crew eased up too and with the great food Chäberli prepared, we soon forgot about the hardships we had just shared.

There was even a place to check our e-mail. It was part of a private school. I spent a few afternoons there, updating the homepage. During our stay in Horta, we met up with a couple from Switzerland. They had just returned from a trip to the Caribbean, on the sloop called Windekind, and were about to leave for Spain. The Captain was just the right person to ask about the coast of Spain. She helped us get an idea about the harbors and the costs of living, just in case we might be heading that way. I also received a book from her about the English Channel, an excellent help to navigation. She wanted to know about how to use e-mail, so I set up an account for her with Hotmail, one of the free services on the net, and showed her how to use it. They had two boys along with them. Our kids were glad to socialize in the Swiss German language and to share their stories. We had a great time together during our stay in Horta and met up several times later on during our stay in Switzerland.

The children had started to paint a mural along the seawall, a tradition followed by sailors when arriving in Horta. We agreed to a design using the colours of our hull and then Anisha, Marcel and, to some extent Carina, went to work, busy painting. It looked beautiful when finished. The kids were really proud to know that their name had been permanently marked on the wall.

I went shopping and bought more chocolate to take on board. Everyone seemed to like it. We had not had many treats on the first leg of our journey, and it seemed that we should try to compensate for that. While we were loading up the boat with fresh food, an elderly man had been watching us. After some time he had started a conversation and was very keen to know what exactly we were doing there. He showed a lot of interest in our activities and invited us to a dinner, with his wife, at one of the restaurants in town. We were overwhelmed about such an honour and accepted the invitation. What a fancy place it was. The restaurant was all decorated in the renaissance style. We sat at a large, round table covered with a white tablecloth in one of the corners in the dining hall. Crystal glasses and silverware were placed in front of each of us and the menu handed out. Our children were not quite used to this kind of eating out. However the couple seemed to enjoy every minute of our conversation. We told them about our life and the crossing of the Atlantic. It was already late when we left the place, all of us grateful for such a memorable evening.

I had taken care of the major items that needed attention and we were ready to resume our journey. Our next destination would be Falmouth, England. Although the weather was not cooperating, I decided to sign out the next day, June the 2nd. Indeed, the weather did not look good at all. At one time, we had 25 knots of wind in the harbor. We sure hoped for better weather to come. We pulled over to the fuel dock, to refill with diesel and water, and stayed there for the remainder of the night. We were tied up, side by side, with two more boats.

During one of the last days along the seawall I had taken the opportunity to talk to a crew member of Symphonia. He explained how the captain had fallen overboard. It was at night when the genoa had torn apart. He had tried to control the sail by hand, after the motor driven sail winch had stopped working. That was when he must have fallen overboard. The sail was built from very strong material. We were given some of the torn material. It made a solid cover for the bicycle and we stitched some of it together to make bags for storage which we still use today. Symphonia was a luxurious boat. There was a lot of instrumentation spread along the bridge and the inside was spaciously arranged. It looked as if they were living in a hotel.

There was a dark sky above us, on June 2nd, as we prepared to leave. The crew was not very happy. I left the boat to check out with customs and to exchange the remaining Escudos for Can\$. It took a long time at the bank. There was a queue and things were moving slowly. Eventually I had just a few coins left. I spent them at the next corner store on vegetables. I made a quick stop at the school to notify my sister in St. Erth, Cornwall, of our departure. I asked her to start looking for us should she not hear anything within the next 20 days.

On the 10-minute walk back to the boat I reflected on the good memories we would have of this short stay in Horta. It would be a long time before we returned. I took a last glance at the mural on the seawall, just above our boat, before stepping aboard to ask the crew to make ready to leave. No answer came. All were lying around like dead flies. It was drizzling and everything on deck was wet. I was determined to leave and asked them what the reason was for not wanting to leave. They all said that they were sick. It took a while to make them understand that I had every intention of leaving. It was a tough stand to take but, to wait for good weather, may have meant to stay there forever. I was anxious to get under way. A crew member from Symphonia had given me a package of pills against seasickness, called Stugeron. He said that they worked quite well and suggested I try them on our next trip. I took one now and the rest of the crew followed suit. After some food, stitching the canvas to the cockpit in a couple of places and cleaning up, we handed the lines and set off at 1:15 p.m. By that time it was raining and fast-moving clouds hung over Horta. We all knew that things might not be ideal out in the open water. Winds got stronger, first from abeam but soon on the nose. Eventually we had gale force winds on the nose and only the staysail up, going about 3 knots. Everyone had to throw up. I did it four times. As the seas were about 3.7 to 5m (12 to 16 feet) high mountains only four pukes was not too bad. The crew was all upset with me to leave at such a bad time.

There was a feeling of happiness in me to know that I sailed so far over open waters. For me this was an important fact and I was proud of it. Now of course I was very happy to be able to step on land again. I was warned by Daddy not to talk to any person, because some may want to find out when the boat would be without crew, in order to steal things. Now in a country with a culture I had not experienced before, I could not tell the difference. Horta to me looked like another city. There were houses and lots of trees. The roads were full of cars and everybody looked busy, just like in a City. At one time an elderly person was watching me working on deck, removing some rust spots that had formed along the rails. He was starting a conversation with me and was very interested how a little boy like me would take a trip on a boat like this. I was very happy to talk to him and eventually he asked if he could talk to my dad who was below deck. I called him and the two had a good conversation. The man actually wanted to know if we would be able to get together with him for supper, in one of the very fancy restaurants in Horta, and talk about our adventures. I did really enjoy that meal. I can still remember me taking some French fries and then eating them with my hands. Of course I was not supposed to do that in a fancy place like this. Daddy quietly made me aware of that. The two elderly people had such a good time and we were keen to tell them of our adventures. I was very happy to share my experience with them.

Phone booths did not seem to work very well. One time I went along with Mom and she wanted to make a call. However it took her forever just to figure out how it worked and once the phone rang no one on the other side answered it. She wanted to call her parents while I was waiting outside getting bored. I wanted to explore the city and see the different shops. Finally Mom gave up but tried again, later. Then it was time to do some shopping. It was a nice clean place but I could not understand the people talking. I had never heard this language, and it sounded rather strange and loud. When Dad went to see the crew at Symphonia I was allowed to go with him. The engineer showed us all the interesting stuff. The generator room to produce all the energy for the boat was so big, we could stand in it. The motor was a huge thing too. Our little 3 cylinder Yanmar was just a toy in comparison. I liked to see all these technical things. But the boat had other nice features, a large kitchen, a hot tub, washing machine and drier, several rooms and a large corridor with shiny hand rails leading to the next level. The back of the boat was carrying a large motor boat to go exploring. It was all very fancy and luxurious, and I was puzzled to know that someone had fallen off this boat. We left with some large pieces of sail material that they had no use for. They were waiting for a new sail and had to do some other repairs to the boat.

The day came close when we were leaving. The weather never was very inviting but that day it was outright miserable. I was down below in the saloon lying down to relax. I felt seasick just by thinking of going out at sea again. Mom was sleeping in the back and the girls were quietly reading in the V-berth. All our bedding was nice and dry again. We had washed and dried it all ashore. We aired out all the cushions, and it was a cozy place again, just like a house. I could not understand why someone would want to destroy all this peace and leave this safe harbor. When Dad arrived and announced that we were leaving, no one really cared. Mom was not at all in agreement, and I tuned in with the same statement: "the weather is so bad, we cannot go now". Dad got somewhat upset having to deal with a crew not following the requests of the skipper. He argued that it was agreed earlier that we had to leave this place soon, that it was expensive to stay, and so on. Furthermore, Dad had made all the arrangements to leave, and he was not willing to stay any longer. We became all very grumpy and only disagreeably followed his instructions to untie the boat. I remember very well receiving the front line from the engineer ashore, who gave us the send off and threw the line over, for me to tie up. The boat was free and ready to go. However the crew was not. Dad had some new pills against seasickness, and we all took one. I think that was the only sensible thing to do.

Another drawing of Kristy Nicole by Pascal

On The Atlantic Again

An hour after our departure the logbook read: "waves choppy", and at 3 p.m.: "storm, 50 knots". By that time we had left the wind shade provided by the island, and the wind had turned from South to Northwest. It was right on our nose, and we were pounding into the waves like a seahorse. I reduced sails quickly to be ready for the worst, but the strain on the rigging was already tremendous. Sailing with the staysail into the wind yielded 3 knots, and I could feel how the boat tried to push its way through the choppy waves, being pushed away from its desired path and with that losing momentum. The present speed was just enough to maintain our course. The waves had no pattern and the noise and vibration of the wind generator blanketed the sound of the ocean and the whistling in the rigging. Water that was washing over the front, driven by the wind, was trying to carry off anything which had not been tightly fastened to the boat.

We had to maintain our course and head as much as possible to the North at first. One reason for this was the prevailing winds.

Leaving Horta in bad weather - Photo by Skipper of Windekind

According to our guide books, they should be more from the north, further into our journey, and then we could use them to head east. We also had to make sure to stay away, as much as possible, from the opening to the Bay of Biscay (France). Thirdly, and of much more pressing importance, we had to stay clear of the islands on our starboard side. The first would be Sao Jorge and, later in the night, Graciosa. At the time I thought the latter didn't deserve its name at all, sitting right smack in our preferred direction of travel. We would be on a lee shore and uncomfortably close, even if we were able to maintain our set course. We had to keep sailing into the wind as much as possible in order to avoid running into the island and hope that the wind would not turn to the north within the next 8 hours or so. With the weather as it was, navigating by sight was out of the question. We had to rely on the chart and the readings from the GPS.

Entries into the diaries were rather short and revealed some of the crew's thoughts.

June 2ⁿᵈ - Azores - We are leaving Horta right now. We have just cast off. I feel sick just to think about it. It will take about two weeks. I do not want to do it.

Tuesday, June 2ⁿᵈ. In the morning I quickly called my parents to let them know that we, most likely, would leave today. The children and I don't actually want to leave, due to the strong winds, but Werni thought we could use the wind. As we become more exposed to the elements, the winds turned into gale force. Despite the fact that we all took pills, everyone was seasick. Werni, however, felt much better than he would have without any medication. I am a bit upset about him taking us out into a storm.

The storm continued to blow full force during all of the night. We cleared Graciosa Island around 10 at night, according to the chart. We could not see anything. All I hoped was that the photo-copied chart was accurate enough, and I checked the position several times to make sure we had not drifted. Not seeing any lights was better than seeing them too close, I thought. At around the same time Seastar, a freighter, called us on the radio. They were not sure if we were ok. We confirmed our position. They gave us a brief outlook on the weather and the seas ahead of us. It did not sound good at all. They let us know that they preferred to go another way.

June 3ʳᵈ - Azores to England - I am very seasick. We are in a gale. We have to keep the bathroom light on so our batteries will not overcharge from the wind generator.

Winds stayed northwest till noon today. We had to change course slightly to the East, set the jib again and one reef in the mainsail. Everything looked fine. Some of the blows during the night must have been in the 60 knot range. The wind generator, which usually displayed a red light on the bottom of its belly, to signal that it was charging, showed no sign of light at all. Had it broken down? I checked the A-meter in the aft cabin and noticed nothing different. There was a steady current of about 7 to10 Amps coming from it. That was more than we needed, but I did not want to switch the generator off. With the autopilot using its share of power and the fridge running, plus a few other things, a fairly good balance was maintained while keeping the batteries charged. When day broke we took out a reef in the mainsail to gain some more speed.

During the later afternoon we decided to put the second reef into the mainsail again, to be safe for the night. As we lowered the sail we noticed that the sliders were leaving the track half way up the mast. The mast's track was assembled with two profiles making up the whole mast's length. These profiles were held in place by rivets. For some unexplainable reason the rivets to the lower profile, which was usually flush to the upper one, had popped out and the profile had slid down in its groove, inside the mast. This had created the gap that allowed the gliders to slip out. We were in a dangerous situation, unable to move the sail either up or down. Something had to be done quickly. We could not afford to leave it like that. In the event of more bad weather we would have to be able to lower the mainsail altogether or we could be in big trouble.

We released the main sheet to take the wind pressure off the sail, enough to make it just flap slightly. We still had enough forward movement to keep the boat heading through the water with a more-or-less predictable rhythm. With a little luck, I was able to get the escaped gliders back into the upper track. The next step was to pound the lower track back up to come flush with the upper one. It would not move freely. I had to hold a wood block between the hammer and the track to avoid damage to the aluminum track. I swung my right arm around the mast in order to secure myself to the boat and held the wood block over the end of the track. With my left hand I tried to guide the hammer so that it would hit the block straight on. It took a long time before I was able to do this. Fortunately, once flush with the upper track, the lower one stayed in place. The wind was still blowing at about 30 knots or more, and some waves continued to make it over the deck. I was soaked to the bone and still clinging to the mast. The constant moving of my muscles to balance the body kept me warm, and I wore a safety harness tied to the starboard lifeline. Whenever I had to move I clutched onto whatever solid object was within my grasp. My vision was badly hampered by wearing glasses covered with raindrops and at times fogged up from the warmth of my body. My feet became cold and numb.

Below deck, Marcel had wired up an extension cord from the 12V/110V converter located in the aft cabin, leading to the hatch over the galley. We had hesitated about buying the converter in Melbourne but it had become an essential part of our tool kit. Once everything was set up, he handed me the end of the cord through the hatch, trying to have it opened for just a brief moment. Below deck Chäberli had to constantly clean up any water which entered through the gap created by the cable. Marcel climbed up to the cockpit to hand me the drill, rivets and the tool to mount them. Clumsily I crawled the few feet back to the cockpit to take the items. With my body turned against the weather I tried to protect the drill from the water coming over the deck. Most waves broke over the forward port side, emptying over both sides before reaching the mast. Ever so slowly I moved forward to the mast again. It was clear that I could not mount any rivets high up the track. Conditions just would not allow for that. If I could, however, drill two holes in the bottom of the track it would, most likely, hold it in place. That's all we could hope for. My right arm was wound around the mast again while I reached for the loose ends of the two power cords in order to plug and tie them together. It was difficult to keep the drill away from the constant spray and rain while dealing with its cord.

I crouched in position to drill the first hole and shielded the drill with my body. It was only a question of time until the drill would quit working because of the spray constantly hitting it. The first hole was under way when a large wave rocked the boat. Instinctively I turned my head away from the weather, still holding the drill in its place. Water came right over the port side and then like a waterfall gushed over the drill and me. With all the other noise around I could not hear the motor of the drill but the vibration of its housing told me that it was still running. I kept on working. The weakness created by my seasickness did not help in this matter. I was amazed to notice how much more energy was needed to do the job. Every now and again I had to bend over to protect the drill from the water while at the same time trying not to loose my balance. It felt as if I had been standing there the whole day before the first hole was finally done. I stuck the drill inside my jacket and started to mount a rivet. The rivetting pliers had been bought at the start of our trip, in Texas, and was now a key survival tool. Fortunately the rivetting process was straight-forward. Another lengthy drilling procedure followed for the second hole before I finished the job successfully. The tools were handed back through the hatch. With some luck and by waiting for a favourable break in the pattern of blowing spray and water, I was able to pass these items down below without allowing too much water into our quarters.

I must have been out on deck for at least a couple of hours. There had been no possibility of hurrying things up. The pace was dictated by the elements. My tension eased up only once things were back in place. The sail was reefed as planned and the main sheet pulled tight to fill the sail on a close hauled course. By then I could not feel my toes and my clothing could not have become any wetter. I had a final look-around before going below. The sea surged past our boat in great, white-crested billows. Close by I watched the white water flying over the tops of the waves in all directions, making a great contrast with the black sea just below. Looking forward, I could watch the boat climb the hills of waves, a reminder of the previous night's storm. Kristy Nicole would heel a bit more to starboard until she reached the top of the wave and then gently glide into the trough between waves. It wasn't always as gentle, though. Some waves came so close behind each other that the boat dipped its nose right into the top of the second wave and pushed her way through it. The hull shook for a moment due to the impact with the water and the auto pilot kept on course as best as it could. In the distance the dark waters mixed with the almost black sky into a seamless horizon. It felt as if water was all around us. I carefully made my way back to the cockpit and climbed below deck to warm up. Chocolate came as a great treat and with a change into dry clothing I warmed up quickly and was ready for some sleep. Looking back I regretted not having taken pictures of me out there hugging the mast. But at the time my thoughts were completely centred on the task at hand.

 *June the 4ᵗʰ - Azores to England - We are listening to a story-tape called "Kasperli".* (note: Kasperli is one of the famous fairytale figures in the Swiss German area of sagas.) *The wind is pretty strong. I have a headache, so I have to lie down now.*

Two more freighters crossed our path during the past night. Around noon the barometer dropped by 1.5 millibars over a two hour time period. We prepared for some more strong winds to arrive and soon they materialized. We took down the jib and mizzen. Sailing with just the staysail, we made good way. At 2 in the morning winds were strong at 40 knots. It was not until around lunch time that I could raise the jib and still make 5 or more knots. My diary starts with a rhyme and reads:

Friday, June the 5ᵗʰ.
She is like a lady and gives you a hand
When you least expect it and brings you to land.
Finding a place to sleep on this highly mobile boat is quite a challenge. Chäberli is sleeping in Marcel's bunk. I had used it when off watch because it is the most stable bunk on the boat. Marcel has moved to the short, starboard bunk but cannot stretch out in it. Carina sleeps on the floor between the starboard settee and the table, but half way into the V-berth. Anisha sleeps in the V-berth. Pascal sleeps in his own spot in the aft cabin, a nice cozy place indeed and a good seagoing berth. In order to keep from rolling off the port settee, I had

come up with the idea of using the centerboard from the dinghy as a lee cloth and it worked perfectly well.

On my early morning watch I reclined on the port bench with my legs braced between the bench and the post holding the table. My head was resting on a pillow, held in place by a bungie cord. Every 10 minutes I went up to the cockpit to look around for traffic. I hoped to see something before it hit us, but it was like looking for a needle in a haystack. Every time the boat tipped hard to one side, the bilge pump came on, briefly, as the switch got tripped. I hoped that the motor would not burn out. Pascal got up and checked on his Mom, who was still asleep, so he went back to bed. It was then 7:50 in the morning and everybody was still asleep, so I made myself a good coffee and ate a piece of white home-baked bread.

June the sixth was not a good day. The wind died down completely and the waves kept bouncing the boat about like a toy. We had to motor for a few hours until the wind picked up from the south southwest. I then had some time to reflect on the situation we were in. Taking off from Horta a few days ago had definitely been a rough start. It had been a tough decision for me to make. We all knew that the weather was not good, but we might have had to wait in Horta for a long time. It was a rough start with stormy winds and stress on everything, and it had stayed like that till the 6th. The staysail halyard had been badly chafed and needed replacement. The line holding it to the stay was about to break. It was not just the strong winds but the continuous stress over a long time that had made it very uncomfortable. Even though making coffee was a balancing act in the real sense of the word, I needed coffee to help me balance my feelings. After all I had to bear the responsibility for having led the crew into this mess. I looked forward to being in England and socializing with my sister Therese and her husband Paul.

I was seriously rethinking about what to do with the boat. Should we try to sell it for a good price in England or should we try to navigate the French canals? I studied all the books we had but could not find an easy answer.

The day ended with a nice sail into the night and the good weather held for the next day. In the evening we talked to the 3rd officer on the freighter Envy, which was about a half a mile away from us. The

Envy was run by the company International Star and registered in the Philippines. They had a load of soybeans to deliver. It was a great feeling to talk to someone other than our own crew.

 *June the 8ᵗʰ. Today we are stuck out on the ocean for the 7ᵗʰ day.* We got pooped (means to have a wave come over the stern from abaft) *and got water in and down the companionway. It made a big wet mess. I am getting tired of sailing but I know that when I get off the boat for a while I will miss poor Kristy Nicole. When we were in* the Azores, we made a painting on the wall. Every boat is supposed to make a painting but lots of charter boats don't. It has been rough weather since we left the Azores. I am reading a book called "Martin the Warrior". It is a funny book. It has been very hard for everybody to sleep. The crew is talking when you try to sleep, or the boat is rocking so hard that you can't sleep.

Tuesday, June 9ᵗʰ. I got some long overdue sleep in Marcel's berth. The back cabin is useless in a downwind course as it lifts you head to toe, very unfriendly. Today the winds picked up around 2 p.m. and I had to reduce sails again from the jib to the staysail and a reefed mizzen. That works well for winds such as these, 30 to 45 knots, and gusty. The waves are big now and we got pooped. I got the brunt of it because I was sitting in the cockpit. The waves reached at least 4.9m (16 feet) in height. The spray got us wet while on deck even though the sun was out for most of the day. I did not know if we were still in the same gale as the previous day, but the wind was favourable, from west-northwest. Two more lows, above 50-degrees north, were forecast by the officer of Envy. I'm sure that we will feel them here too. They are both moving north. This, hopefully, will give us better weather for crossing the English Channel.

I missed out on Herb's weather forecast last night. What I could get was that we should not go further north than 47 degrees on Wednesday. Our position was N46° 11', W15° 26'. The wind generator swivels around its supporting post when it gets into the wind shade of the mizzen sail, but still produces lots of power, even though the base light is not working. The whole boat has had a thorough testing. Last night the tri-colour light on top of the mast quit working so we now use the anchor light to make us visible to other ships.

Wednesday, June 10th, I turned on the tape from the Beatles with the songs such as Norwegian Wood and Dizzy Miss Lizzy. It takes away the noise from the wind and boat. The gale force winds kept blowing all night and turned to a more westerly wind. With diminishing winds we can move about 4 to 4.5 knots, with large waves pounding from the side. If Herb is right we will be keeping the gale winds until we reach the English Channel. I hope that the low on Thursday will be well off to the north. Sleeping under these bumpy conditions is difficult. For most of the time I just lie around. I make the odd repairs and try to clean up some leaks caused by the vents. Water has found a way into the boat, even through the bathroom vent and the fan above the stove in the galley. The barometer went up 2.5 millibars in two hours. It looks as if we should get a short break in the weather.

June 11th. We are listening to the "Fire House Dixie" jazz tape. Yesterday and today Pascal had to throw up. I do watches from 6 to 8 in the evenings and 2 to 4 during days and nights.

From June 11th until we arrived in Falmouth, England, no other crew member made any entries into their diary. It looked as if we were becoming used to the pattern of having one gale after another. According to Herb's weather forecast, another storm with gale force winds was building up ahead of us. Our course was taking us right into the storm, and June the 12th was another rough day. Winds built during the night. On that night, about 280km (150 n.m.) to the northeast of us, another boat was out at sea. I found the following information on the Internet. The Pen Duick had left Newly, near Penzance, at noon with winds blowing hard from the north but turning south. They cleared Lands End in the evening, heading north. Their captain, the famous Eric Tabarley, (described as the father of yachting in France), was lost at sea during that night. The crew reported swells of 3 to 4 metres (13 feet) and repeated rain squalls. We heard about the tragic event on our arrival in Falmouth.

June 13th, at 7:30 p.m. a rough voice called on channel 16 about a sailboat being on collision course. Now that we were in the English Channel ship traffic was much more evident. I had not checked our position for some time, and we had not seen any sailboats on the water during the past watches. The radio had been quiet during the whole day. It was obvious that this call was addressed to us. I acknowledged it. The captain was irate and asked us to alter course immediately or else we would be in danger of colliding with him. His grumpy voice did not make me feel at all comfortable, but I acknowledged his request and jumped off the seat to reach for the ladder to the cockpit. On the last watch no boats had been sighted, but now I could faintly make out a shape in front of us and it sure looked like a big freighter. It certainly looked as if it was moving fast and it would have been impossible for such a huge vessel to alter course at all. The weather was miserable, and I was not able to guess either the distance or the direction of the freighter but had no wish to run into it. We decided to change our course from East-Northeast to South-Southeast. This was easier said than done. The wind was blowing at around 30 knots. During our downwind course, the reefed main was set to starboard, and for security was tied down to the deck to avoid an accidental jibe. Changing course could not be done quickly. I untied the safety tie to the sail and went back to the cockpit to pull in the sheet of the main. I was prepared to see the sail come around and bang to the other side. The trick was to get it pulled as close to the centre as possible before it crossed to the other side. I left the autopilot on the downwind course. That way it could only move a short distance and not put a strain on our boat. The mainsail swung over to the other side, with a bang, when I had it sheeted in about half way. We tied it down in its new position and established the new course on the autopilot before settling down. The whole manoeuver had taken us about 5 minutes. Through the rain and mist we could see the huge tanker passing safely on our port side. I could not read its name and did not feel like calling them up again. I quickly established our position on the chart and noticed that we were just entering the main shipping lane around Lands End. That was not what I had intended to do. The currents must have carried us north faster than I had expected. I could understand the captain's grumpy voice. The course change had been more than due! We certainly did not want to travel in one of the main shipping lanes.

Marcel's entry into the logbook reads as follows (note: no spelling corrections applied):

"Cange corse because of a bloody friter."

With the wind still from behind, we continued a rolling ride through the bumps of the sea. Watching the waves catching up from the back was an amazing thing to see and something totally alarming. Some white crested ones looked as if they were just about to bury our boat. But, just when they were a bit too close for comfort, the back of the boat would move up, ever so gently, onto the top of the wave and the white crest would disappear. It was a fascinating and scary pattern to watch. I have read in books that sailors would pour oil over the back of the boat to make the waves smooth out. Sometime they would pull something behind to break up the wave. I thought, however, that the waves would have to be bigger before that would have become necessary.

The winds continued to come from the west-northwest until our 10 a.m. arrival in Falmouth. We tied up at a pier which we thought was the public one, before settling down to reflecting on our journey. Oddly enough, there was not much to reflect on. We were just happy to know that we had arrived safely. Longing for showers and clean clothes was much more on our minds than thinking about the past few days. The "real" world had again captured our minds and us.

When I noticed that we tied up on a pier belonging to one of the more expensive marinas in Falmouth, money became the first issue. The staff were very helpful and allowed us to stay at a reduced rate for the day. We sure used their facilities to the utmost and got everything that was washable, washed and dried. It was still drizzling for the rest of the day. We felt that we had gone to heaven when we were able to sleep in dry bedding, tied to a pier and not having to fight with the waves any more. I felt great and was able to drop all the tenseness that had built up during the last 12 days. Nothing, I thought, could interrupt my sleep.

I was very happy to have arrived safely in England. The last 12 days had been very hard on all of us. The crew all left Horta being mad at the skipper, and I did not feel happy with him all the way. He had gotten us into such a bad mess; why could we not have waited a bit longer? I don't think it would have mattered that much. The worst for me was the first night passing among the other islands. I was not

able to sleep right, always looking out to see if we passed far enough away. When I took a peek through the aft cabin's port hole I saw no lights at all but knew that, if there were any, they would be hidden by the blowing rain. The boat never really gained a lot of speed as we sailed into the wind as much as possible, slow and with a strong listing to the starboard side. The waves hit the bow straight on and from time-to-time a short wave would make the bow split right into the following wave with the hull resonating and making a hollow sound like you would when hitting a big drum. It was impossible to find a place where you would not be thrown about. Even under the table you would bounce between the leg of the table and the bench on the other side. It was just being in a big washing machine. Werner kept me up-to-date with the course we were on and mentioned that it would be a close call to pass the island ahead to starboard. And as a matter of fact, after some time there was a dim light visible. We assumed it to be the tip of the island. The course plotted on the chart was leaving a fair bit between the land and us. That was the only check we had. The chart was a photocopy of the whole Atlantic Ocean, nothing too accurate to go with. However the depth sounder's reading made it clear that we were in deep water. Keeping an eye on the light was certainly a relief, and we could see it slowly pass to our aft and eventually disappear. At the same time, I noticed the winds picking up more momentum. We were now exposed to the full extent of the elements, having no land to divert the winds. Werner was pretty tense. He knew that we were all mad at him. Nothing could stop him now. I was looking forward to getting the last troubling leg behind me.

And now we were in England. We had done it. We went all across the Atlantic ocean! But I don't want to do it again. If Werner wants to go sailing on the open water again, I will not accompany him. I have had my share of sailing across oceans. I don't mind if he wants to go again with somebody else, maybe one of the kids, but not me. I certainly liked the travelling in quiet waters or as long as you could make out some land.

But we were not quite finished yet. I definitely enjoyed the showers every time we got into a harbor. It was one of the first things we did and then of course wash the clothes. And walking on land again was

Tying up in Falmouth, England

always a funny experience, it took a while to get used to it. We all had lost some weight, not that that was bad for me, but the kids were already thin to begin with. The constant moving and using our muscles, even when sleeping we had to brace ourselves, was like doing exercises in a gym.

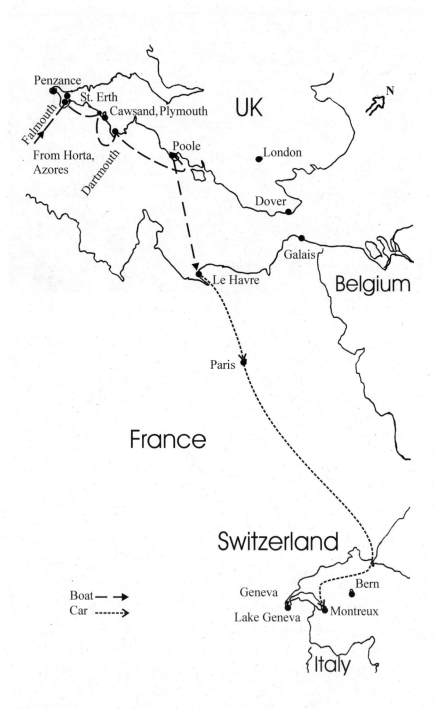

Europe And Another Island

It was a strange feeling, to walk on land and not have to worry about the weather or the boat being in danger. Sleeping well at night, however, was another matter. Every so often I would wake up from a dream with tall waves and a boat that was moving up and down. Pictures of freighters, passing close by, came to mind, even during the day.

Life on the land brought other priorities, such as looking for a reasonable place to put our boat and to calculate how to continue our travels, with the meagre funds we had left. First on our agenda, though, was to get in touch with my sister. Therese and Paul had invited us to visit them when we reached England.

We remembered Falmouth from our visit back in the seventies. To us the city had not changed much. The cobble-stoned streets and old buildings lining the main section of town appeared as inviting as they had then and so were the many piers for ferries, boats and other services. It certainly was a town oriented towards boats. Everywhere people were friendly and were proud of their places, making them look nice and neat. Along the water, there were always hundreds if not thousands of seagulls around you and, if you were the chosen one, you may have ended up with one of their blessings right on your head or shirt. I noticed this on one occasion and was glad to be wearing my hat.

Around Falmouth was a lush, green countryside, begging to be visited. With so much to see and do in this area we decided to stay for some time, before continuing on our journey. When I checked with the harbor authorities, I found out that we could have anchored the boat there. The only stipulation was that the boat had to be manned at all times, in case it had to be moved. That would have cost less but was not possible for us, so we chose to tie up at one of the many, more expensive, buoys. It was certainly cheaper than the dock. What we really missed was the freedom to anchor at no cost. Our budget had not been made to include fees for docking or similar expenses. It was one of the first things we had to accept: boating in Europe would not be inexpensive.

During our stay, several things on the boat had to be taken care of in order to continue our trip safely. The things I had written down in my diary added up to a list of some 23 items. Fortunately the only serious one was repairs to a sail, and we had all the necessary supplies on board for all the repairs.

We were lucky to have found such a great boat and to have got off so lightly cost-wise. The only drawback with Kristy Nicole had been trying to manoeuver her in tight corners. She was heavy and the motor's output was at the lower end of the necessary horsepower. We gladly took these drawbacks in return for a roomy, cozy and safe boat. We had put a lot of money into her upkeep, and she had become like a very close friend, someone we could trust. The thought of selling her made my tummy grumble, and I did not like to think about it. However, financially, it was a fact that we could not continue much longer if we could not find ways to cut costs. I had to get over my mental blockage and accept that my friendship with the boat would have to end, sooner or later. During our stay in England I did approach a broker with the request to put her up for sale, but he was not interested in listing the boat unless it was left in his yard. His position came as a relief to me! It gave me some more time to stay with the boat. I quickly dropped the thought of selling and started to plan a continuation of our trip.

When I contacted my sister we arranged to be picked up later during that week. It was a great feeling to see all of her family again and to share our past. They still lived in St. Erth, about an hour's drive from Falmouth, and for two weeks we were their guests. Their place was very inviting and felt much like home. It was more than that and at times; I felt I was being treated like a king. They were very supportive about our travels too. I felt that Chäberli had found her own self again, which strengthened our relationship. Maybe it was the combination of things such as socializing, living in a house, travelling on roads rather than water and of course, a bed that didn't rock. It was a terrific time with trips to the beach, sightseeing and visits to Paul and Thereses' two daughters, who lived nearby, whom we remembered as children. We made several journeys to visit old friends in the nearby town of Penzance. The harbor with its many boats was like a magnet to me. I enjoyed looking at boats and watching the activities along the piers. And there was always a place to get fish and chips. I came to like that stuff. I still enjoy walking along harbors when we are in a seafaring town.

We had finally made it across the Atlantic Ocean! The trip from the Azores to England was horrible. Sometimes we had to keep the light on in the head, in order to consume the extra power produced by the wind generator. We could, at least, sometimes listen to our Walkmans, but most of the time was spent feeling incredibly seasick. I remember when we finally arrived in the marina. It was so nice to be able to have a hot shower and put on fresh clothes. It felt great. But it got even better. Dad's sister and her husband came and picked us up, and we were allowed to stay at their place! In a real bed! I remember their beautiful front yard, all laid out with flowers, on both sides, and green bushes everywhere. At the far end there was a huge tree which Marcel and I climbed many times. The branches were nice and thick, and I could sit way out on them. I could look down on the neighbouring farmer's field, which bordered the place, with its many colourful wildflowers along its edge. That brought back memories of the farm.

Sometimes I joined Marcel, who watched TV a lot, but we also played a lot of badminton. Another thing I remember doing a lot of was playing the piano there. I loved piano, and it thrilled me to stay in a house where I could play the few songs I knew. Unfortunately, I got sick a few days into our stay there, and had to stay in bed for some time, while the others, except Daddy, went sight-seeing. It was terrible to be stuck inside now that there were so many new things to see. Just like back in Canada, I enjoyed the long evenings again. It would stay light out until about 9:30 p.m., and I was able to do a lot of reading. I also took some time to actually do some schoolwork. I did almost all of my subjects, excluding math. It was still not my subject of choice. History was a bit more interesting. Daddy mentioned that I might go to a school in Switzerland for some time. I hoped to be able to be ready for the grade I would go into, but I was also a bit nervous that it would be in a different language than English. I wasn't sure if it would be German or French. I concentrated on the French, and wrote a letter to one of my friends back in Canada explaining all of this. She spoke French at home, and was also home-schooled. We were close friends when we left. I did a lot of letter writing when we finally made it to England, catching up with all of my friends back home. I didn't really get much mail from anybody anymore, though. It made me feel a bit homesick. I longed for the fun of going horse riding again with some of my friends.

I got better after a few days in bed, and could join in on the sight-seeing outings again. We actually found a store that sold beanie babies, and I got Mystic the Unicorn at one of the visits to town. Soon we moved back to the boat and celebrated Mommy's birthday there. It was funny, we all got presents.

After some more visits to Falmouth, we found a nice park called Kimberly Park, where Mommy showed me how to make wreaths out of the little flowers growing in the grass. We spent hours there. I had taken some of my beanie babies along, and all of them got necklaces and wreaths on their heads. They looked so cute, and the day went by much too fast. Over a month had passed when we left the place and took a short sailing trip towards Plymouth.

Parting with our relatives and friends was not easy. We did not know when we would see each other again. We carried with us memories of the great days spent along this stretch of the English coast and the hopes and dreams for a future visit. We were off with a sunny day and great wind. Plans were to sail to the nearby town of Fowey, halfway between Falmouth and Plymouth. The weather was so nice and the wind with us so, around midpoint, we decided to go all the way to Plymouth. The search for an anchorage did not take long. As we sailed towards Plymouth, we saw to the left a large bay and sailboats could be made out at anchor. We decided to explore the bay and headed towards the boats. We found a spot not too far away from the shore. According to our chart the town that spread along the shore in front of us was Cawsand. The twin, conjoined, villages of Kingsand and Cawsand, known to locals simply as Cawsand, is not very well known to the tourists. Cawsand is, however, popular with a large number of people from Plymouth. On summer weekends they board a ferry to sail across Plymouth Sound to the village beaches as a Saturday or Sunday treat.

Anisha enjoys the view from the mast

Cawsand attracted us due to its view from the water. Most likely anyone who was looking for a landfall at Plymouth would be seduced by the sight of the village in the lee of wooded Penlee Point, itself providing a calm, green, tree-reflecting mooring. Cawsand has an air of deliberately turning its back on the mainland, and its face to the waters of Plymouth Sound. This is understandable when one knows that its commerce was with the sea, either through the naval and mercantile tradition of the great port of Plymouth, fishing or that most traditional of local past-times, smuggling. Until the late 18th century, the border with England ran through the centre of the village, thus giving it two subsidiary parts, Kingsand in Devon, and Cawsand in Cornwall.

On one day we took a hike of about 6.4km (4 miles) to reach the Mt. Edgcumbe Estate, a well laid out old stone mansion, with a huge garden area stretching down to the water formed by the river Tamar, which leads to Plymouth. The place was built in 1547 and at one time incorporated a deer park. The remains of a gun-battery were visible, built to protect the waterway entering Plymouth. It looked nice. The walk itself was enjoyable, following the coastline, passing through fields and forests made up, mostly, of deciduous trees.

With the boat anchored in the wide-open bay, waves created by large vessels passing by created some uncomfortable swells. At least that was what we thought to be the cause. Our boat never seemed to be at rest. It made the crew uneasy. We escaped the uncomfortable situation and explored the town of Cawsand some more. One of the residents invited us to see his house, built in the 1500s. It had a small floor plan but was 3 stories high, accessible by narrow stone steps. The place was decorated with many ancient artifacts. His predecessors had been living there as fishermen, and most of the treasures on display related to that fact. We were fortunate to have met this person. It was nice to see how people arranged their houses to make them friendly and cozy places.

We had intended to stay another day but, with some bad weather in the forecast, we decided to leave the open anchorage and sail to Dartmouth, about a 9 hour trip. The girls were reading during most of the time. The winds were in our favour for the whole day, and we arrived in the evening. We were relieved to be in a more protected anchorage. The new day broke with gusty winds, some up to 30 knots, even in the anchorage. I decided to set two anchors. There was a strong current flowing with the direction of the tides.

I spent some of my time reading "Redwall" books. The kids thought I would like to read them and it was indeed entertaining. Every day the harbor master came by to collect the harbor fee, about $15.00. A steep price to pay for anchoring I thought. After a couple of days on the boat the weather improved, and we could use the dinghy to safely go ashore. There we enjoyed the hot showers but, of course, had to pay $1.25 for 4 minutes of hot water. Three minutes of waiting sometimes feels long, but the four minutes of the hot shower sure didn't. I took the shower together with Marcel and Pascal and managed to work it all with two coins. We would have to get used to that kind of life. Even the tourist city map was only available for a charge. There was a nice park close to the harbor. We purchased some food and, while the sun was out for a while, sat there and munched on French bread and slices of cheese and meat. Returning to the boat we had a great surprise. There sat a bag of cookies with the name Ishka written on it. We were overwhelmed to know that they had found us here. We remembered them starting out with us in the Bahamas. What a small world we live in. Later in the day I noticed their boat in the anchorage and we made a visit. They both had a terrible cold and did not feel well. We arranged to see each other again the next day. There were many memories to share and a lot of stories to be told about the crossing of the Atlantic. It was one more great feeling to hear about their adventures and to know that they had made it safely.

We could not afford to stay any longer and decided to use the improved weather to sail on towards the east, along the coast. We hoped to arrive in Pool before dark.

We started out at 5:00 a.m. Marcel and I were busy getting under way. Marcel, however, did not remember that we had two anchors down. He was on the wheel while I was pulling up the first anchor. I then signalled him to pull forward for the other anchor (I thought). He thought that the signal was to go ahead and leave the harbor. As we passed over the second anchor I realized that he had not understood my sign. He was already starting to turn, in order to pass the boats that were anchored in the centre of the anchorage. I gave the line a free run. There was little time left to hurry to the cockpit, before the chain would all be out and tangled up with the boats at anchor. That would have pulled us all into a messy bundle of boats. Arriving in the cockpit I grabbed the accelerator stick, set it to low rpm, switched the gears into reverse and revved up the engine as much as possible. The boat came to a stop just before the chain started to wind itself around the boats at anchor. Fortunately there was enough room to turn Kristy Nicole and proceed with the task of pulling the other anchor up. It was pure luck that we had managed to stay out of trouble. All this exercise warmed me up enough and, once we were under way, I found the time to have an early morning coffee. It was high tide and an easy exit from the harbor and out into the ocean. The ride was comfortable with enough wind to keep going.

It took us the whole day before we saw the entrance to a big bay, Port of Poole. A wall had been put up to protect the bay. A sailing regatta was under way, and it made for a pleasant view, even though the weather was a mixed bag of mist and light rain. We were in a protected place, but the bay was so big that its waves alone still made for an uncomfortable night. The boat never came to rest, as the wind was blowing across the wide-open bay. Our last day in England had arrived. It was time to reflect on all the places visited and enhance the memories of our adventures. The summer had passed quickly. I missed the sunny days and the warm weather of the Bahamas. It now felt as if we had no summer at all. On July the 19th, at 6 p.m., we set our course towards Le Havre, France.

We were about to set sail again. The stay in Falmouth was great and I got my feeling for the land back again. It was actually exciting when I realized how far away we were from our home in Canada. I slowly came to recognise and, to a certain degree, appreciate the fact that we were actually travelling through the world, carrying along all our pots and pans. It was a great experience. The visit at my Dad's sister's place was absolutely beautiful. I fell in love with the quaint English villages and the air of mystery which hung over my aunt's garden. In the countryside long stone walls bordered fields and roads, and looking out the window of the car when we

were driving was like following a long path with nothing on either side but rock walls. There were walls for miles and miles interspersed only in short sections by bushy hedges. It was a funny feeling going along these narrow roads. They were not wider than one lane of the road leading up to our farm in Canada, but here we seemed always able to pass oncoming traffic, sometimes slowing down and hugging the side as close as possible.

Sailing along the coast of England was enjoyable compared to what I'd been through just a while ago. The waves were small, and I saw no imminent danger of getting water splashed over the side of the boat. I didn't mind the sailing at all anymore and had plenty of things on board to play with. The boat was dry and we got the odd days with sunshine. Hikes to points of interest along the trip made it interesting, but I have already forgotten most of it. I could not find much additional information in my diary until the time when we were in Switzerland. Boat life was too exciting, I couldn't be bothered to write in my diary. It became second nature, like stepping into a car to go somewhere. There was still the convenience of having all our things along while travelling. It was a great way to go places, but for me I had almost had enough and did not want to go anywhere anymore. I can still remember the crossing of the English Channel. The winds were calm and we motor sailed most of it leaving Poole in the evening. There was a lot of ship traffic and lights from other boats, ferries and freighters were visible all around. Dad thought it would be easier to do it at night and then arrive in the morning, at first light. I watched some of the fast ferries, a good distance away from us, go across. Some were hovercraft type boats and they moved along rather quickly. I soon went to bed and woke up when we were safely docked on a pier in Le Havre, France.

 In retrospect I think that this trip was a very good experience but it was at times both stressful and difficult to cope with. I did, however, enjoy the reunion with my parents, after the long voyage. Sailing along a coastline is one thing but I have no desire to be out on the open water again. Living together with 5 other family members in such a small space and for such a long period of time was probably the most challenging part of the whole expedition.

Preparing food in a tiny galley (kitchen) provided challenges of a different nature. The fact that the counter tops were often slanted tended to make things move as they pleased. Because the sink was on the starboard side it was fairly easy to cope with by just leaning onto the side of it when the boat was tacking to port. A starboard tack was, however, a real balancing act. I always had fresh bread ready if anyone was hungry, especially for the people on watch at night. The oven was tiny so I could bake only two loaves at a time. The kitchen utensils were all close at hand and easy to get at.

Most of our meals were prepared in one pot because that was the easiest approach. For salads we had cabbage and carrots most of the time. These are the vegetables which stored the best. When we were anchored we had more elaborate meals, just as we would have had at home. Shopping for goods was always possible, but sometimes we had to walk quite some distances to do so.

If Werner wants to go sailing again, and that is what he intends to do, the children, now grown up, will most likely be his crew. I will choose to fly to the places they will be sailing to and join them there in order to enjoy the calmer waters at anchor or short island hops with predictable weather forecasts.

Family Reunion, Parting From Kristy Nicole

The crossing of the channel was for the most part done under power through a pitch-dark night. As the current was going, more or less, in the same direction as us, we still managed about 7.5 knots over ground. We could make out the lights of other boats, maybe ferries, some of which were moving much faster than we were. It took us 12 hours before we reached the harbor, early in the morning. The sky was a gray colour, almost sure to drop some rain. Not a soul was to be seen, so we decided to berth in one of the many empty spots in the marina and take a rest. Later, during the day, we checked with the marina but, as expected, it would not be cheap to stay there. We inquired about a place where we could stay for free and indeed there was such an option. It soon became apparent that our French was very limited. Fortunately one of the people in the marina explained, in his broken English and in a bit more detail, how to get there. It didn't appear to be easy to get there, no matter how much French we knew, but we certainly did not want to spend $20.00 for a day at the marina. The staff were extremely nice and helpful. They called the customs people and announced our arrival. That was all that was needed. We could take the yellow flag down. It was actually not even needed. For a year the European Union had made things easier that way, at least for those who belonged to it. In the EU there was no longer any need to check boats in and out of participating countries. Boats from outside the EU could stay for a maximum of one year only; after that an import tax would be charged on the boat. We had got a stamp in the Azores and our year would be calculated from that date. We had already been 3 months in Europe. Time just seemed to fly past.

According to the directions of the staff from the marina, we had to wait till the tide was high. The difference was about 5 metres (16 feet), the highest we had experienced on our trip. The lock we had to go through was able to operate at high tide only. We had to wait till later in the afternoon and approached the lock, calling the lock operator on the VHF. My French must have sounded funny so he responded in English. I thanked the bridge master for this kindness. I had often met French speaking people who were not willing to talk English. 30m (100 feet) down from the lock was a road bridge. It also had to be opened for us. We then entered a small basin from which yet another opening road bridge led into the "Bassin Vauban", our destination. The railway station and grocery store were just a 5 minute walk away from our boat. A public swimming pool was located nearby.

Along the seawall we could make out a boat yard and further down a few boats, most of them in a desperate state. We were not sure if we should turn around and leave. However, just next to the opening bridge was a boat with someone on it. We inquired about where we could put our boat, and he pointed to an empty spot just behind him. It was a bit tight but it worked. Just behind us was the boat yard, all fenced in. On the shore side was the tower house for the bridge tender. Across the basin, which measured about 100m (320 feet) in width, we could make out a busy road. After introducing ourselves to our neighbouring sailor, as much as was possible with our rough French, it was time to get some French francs and look for groceries before settling down. We were warned by our boat neighbour not to leave the boat unattended. There were many people around who would steal things. We made sure that someone would stay on the boat at all times. It may have been a bit of a handicap, but it was certainly cheaper than the marina.

A nice sunny day arrived, and I decided to take the bike off the boat and try to get it working again. All the pieces looked very rusty. The chain did not turn at all nor did the handle bar. I sprayed oil onto the parts involved. With brute force I got the handlebar turning again. The chain took a bit longer. It was, of course, a messy job. The back brake cable was completely seized, and I left it like that. The front brake seemed to work fine though. After some time I got it to the point where I could ride it again. I took a quick trip around the area to the east. On my way back the pedal suddenly started to idle, not engaging with the back wheel, which it was supposed to drive. All was turning well, except the gear on the back wheel, which was turning without the wheel. That was something new to fix, and it did not look like an easy job. I pushed the bike back to the boat. Once there I immediately got at it. I took all my hand tools out and started to undo the nuts on the back wheel. Marcel came and asked me if I would like to come with him to see a boat which had just arrived in the boatyard. I joined him, leaving the bike resting on its handlebar and saddle, with all the tools around it. We had a good look at the beautifully-crafted wooden sailboat that lay on the pier before turning back to get on with the work. There was, however, no need to do any more work. The bike was gone. Fortunately, all the tools were still there. How could someone steal the bike in such a hurry? The poor guy could not even ride it. We broke out in laughter as we joked about how the thief must have felt when he found out that the thing did not work at all. In a way we were happy to be rid of the bike. It was not much good to anyone. It was a good warning. We would have to guard against people who might steal things off our boat. When we looked at all the boats along the seawall further up the road, we noticed that many parts had been taken off them. These boats were not attended to at all and looked very much abandoned. It looked as if some people certainly were in desperate need to get anything. It was sad to know that it was so.

When we arrived in Le Havre, on July 20th, I did not realize that this would be our last voyage with Kristy Nicole. I was still sure that we would continue up the Seine to Paris. However, our financial situation just did not warrant any further trips. Staying in Le Havre was not an option either. The place could hardly be called a holiday paradise. There were all the amenities we needed, but it was located in an industrial part of town. We were downwind from the ferryboats and their big stacks; this area was constantly sprinkled with the remains of burned up diesel fuel. The weather was getting colder too. We would have had to go more to the south to enjoy warmer climates during the winter. I slowly understood that we were stuck here and needed to make some changes to our plans. With less than $3,000.00 left in the piggy-bank, it seemed impossible to sail south.

I thought about buying a car, but looking at the advertisements for used cars I soon realized that I could hardly understand what was being offered. There were so many cars which I knew nothing about. Talking to people, face to face, yielded some results, due to the fact that I could use all the gestures ever invented for that kind of conversation. It was, however, impossible to get that kind of message across on the phone. We looked at one car, a 2CV, but it was obvious that it was not a car we could use. After that experience we abandoned the idea of buying a car in France and decided that I should buy a ticket to Switzerland and look for a car there. Then I would come back and pick up the family. We would put the boat in the boatyard, for safety. It would cost about $250.00 per month but the chances of finding it there, when we returned, would be much better.

The arrangement with the boatyard to sell our boat had not yet borne any fruit. We had signed a contract for 3 months, but there was no sign of a sale. I didn't mind. There was so much sentimental value attached to Kristy Nicole that it was difficult to make any decision about her future.

My shoulder-length hair was, mostly, dark brown, but some gray was starting to show at the temples. I had not noticed it at first, but it was becoming quite pronounced. I asked Chäberli to cut it short. There on the ground, beside Kristy Nicole, were the remains of my long hair. We had decided that this would be the best in order for me to fit into Swiss society. Long hair, even then, was still regarded as something only for a hippy, a street person or a layabout. We thought it would be easier for me to find work by adapting more closely to the normal customs.

A week later I was on the train to Switzerland and visited Chäberli's parents in Montreux. It was a happy reunion, and they could not wait to see their daughter again. The last time they had seen her was when they had visited us in Miami, shortly after the purchase of our boat.

Fabian, the younger of our two sons in Switzerland, took time off from his work as a cook in Zermatt to make the long-awaited reunion with him possible. The small town of Brent, part of Montreux, was nestled above Montreux, about a 40-minute walk, mostly up hill. There were maybe 50 houses in that part of town and one belonged to Chäberli's parents. It had once been used as a children's summer home. It had since been remodelled and rented out as an apartment building. Our future home was to be the ground-floor apartment. We stayed there for some time.

I frantically searched through the many newspapers for a suitable car. This time I had the help of my father-in-law, who spoke French fluently. He must have become tired of my constant begging for clarifications of abbreviations in the advertisements. After a few days we found a Renault Espace, sold by an American couple leaving Switzerland. Espace in French means space and that it did provide. The car was in acceptable shape but 10 years old. With the financial help of my father-in-law, I was able to finalize the deal. The most important feature the car sported was its 6 seats. With the mini-van type arrangement, there was enough room for our whole family.

The 1st of August is the Swiss national day. It felt odd to celebrate this just as I returned. Traditionally, fires were lit everywhere to celebrate the founding of Switzerland in 1291 by the 3 original Cantons, Uri, Schwyz and Unterwalden. Free sausages and wine were available.

The next day we were on our way to Le Havre, an 800km (500 miles) trip to pick up the rest of the family. Fabian joined me on the trip. Chäberli's father also came along with his car, in order to load up some of our most needed possessions to settle down in Montreux. It was a lovely reunion for us all. The last task at hand was to prepare the boat for a longer stay on its own. All the canvas was removed and stored below. Plenty of fenders hung on the sides and everything was locked up. We were preparing for a life on land again. It was a sad day for me, but a happy ending for my wife and children. We were all looking forward to celebrating the reunion of all the family members. Not much later, on August the 15th, Thomas, with his girl-friend, came to visit us in Brent. We were all together as a family again!

The broker in Le Havre had not come forth with any sales. It looked as if he was not interested in having a quick sale; the boat generated good income while berthed at his marina. I put an ad on one of the Internet sites and soon received an email from a broker in St. Augustin, USA, who offered to sell the boat, for a commission. We struck a deal and in April the next year a prospect from England, presently living in the Netherlands, showed interest. I forwarded as much information as possible and, after negotiating the price, a sea trial was arranged. The boat was sold on April 22nd. The broker kept a portion of the sale and the rest I received by cash. I still remember leaving the barrister's office in Vevey with a briefcase filled with

$100 bills. The struggle for financing our lives was over. By then I was working as a computer consultant and, later on, took on a teaching assignment.

When I look back and read the stories that came from the kids, some time after the trip, then I feel that Carina must have had the most challenging part in her life on the boat. What makes me think that she still liked it, however, was the fact that, sometimes after we arrived in Switzerland, she had a birthday gift for me, one of her so beloved beanie babies. It was a small teddy bear that said "Thanks Dad" on its apron hanging over its belly. I felt this to be a very nice little sign from her, and I think she did mean it. There went along a little story about the bear and at the end of that story she wrote: "I'm doing fine, the chapter you wanted me to type out is not typed out, and I'm having a good time teasing you about it. Ha Ha!!" Needless to say, the book printing got held up due to her dragging on with handing in her chapter.

Pascal, of course, does not remember much of the travels at all. But, when he sees the pictures, he can, sometimes, put together some stories about the places seen.

The trip, for me, was an exceptional experience, something that really did build my confidence and at the same time gave me a different outlook on life, namely to put time aside, if in any way possible. Furthermore I learned a whole lot more about sailing and off-shore navigation by simply reading and then doing it. When the time came to sell Kristy Nicole, about a half a year after our arrival in Le Havre, it was an emotional task for me to tackle. More difficulties followed as we tried to survive in Switzerland in order to regain some of our material needs. This will, eventually, become part of a future story. What I never expected to happen was that I would spend more than 7 years in Switzerland. Finding a position as a science teacher at a private school gave me a very fulfilling task to deal with and still provided the opportunity to spend about half of the year at home in Canada. It was this combination that allowed me to put the infrastructure into place to generate additional funds and continue publishing this book.

The book has, finally, come together, with substantial contributions from the crew members. I appreciate that. It is needless to say that I enjoyed putting this story on paper and reliving the adventures, even the scary ones. At several times the project came almost to a standstill. In spite of that it has been completed, and I hope that the reader will enjoy sharing the experiences with us.

Whenever I mention to anyone that I lived on a sailboat for a year-ish, I often get an exclamation of some sort, such as, "Wow, that's awesome!" or "WHAT? You're crazy! ...are your parents hippies or something??" (to which I always answer yes, he he), and then quite the bombardment of questions, such as, "How long? Where? WHY? What did you do? How long were you out at sea for at a time? How did you manage to live in such close quarters with your family for such a long time? You must all be really close...or hate each other now! Were you ever scared? Were there big storms? Did you see lots of sea life? How did you go to school? What did you do with yourself when you were out at sea? What was your favourite part? What was your least favourite part? Would you do it again?..."

I'm not going to go into all of those questions, because they normally take quite a while to address properly, and you've probably read the book, so you likely know the answer to some of them already. The most common question that I get asked is what my favourite part of living on a sailboat was. I've answered that question in so many different ways by now, though, that I can't honestly say that I have just one favourite part. There were so many things that I remember doing that make me so nostalgic to think about, such as sailing the dinghy in Annapolis with our friends from Cool Change and Aquila; making cork boats out of wine bottle corks, with a nickel for a keel, a toothpick as a mast, and piece of paper as a sail, and having little regattas with them with our friends from Lindsay Kristine in Melbourne; meeting all of the people that we met everywhere we went; swimming in the ocean - especially in the beautiful clear aquamarine waters of the Bahamas; visiting the Smithsonian Museums in Washington, DC - especially the Museum of Natural History; watching schools of dolphins swimming along with us, playing in the bow wake; watching the plankton light up and sparkle as the water ran alongside of the boat on a night watch - which made the watch a little less tedious and helped to keep me awake; seeing sunset after beautiful sunset on the ocean (I was usually still sleeping for the sunrises, but I'm sure they were lovely, too!); ...the list goes on and on. It was truly an amazing experience.

Of course, it wasn't all sunshine and flowers, though. I think the main ticket item that I disliked was being seasick. Then again, who does like being seasick!? To quote what Pascal used to say when asked how he liked living on a sailboat, "I like sailing but not the seasick." Also, storms scared me. I used to hide out under the "V" insert of the V-berth, hugging my Teddy, when it got really scary out with strong winds and huge waves and an irritated Dad who had somehow managed to lose his hat or watch overboard again, or was bemoaning the fact that the weather forecast hadn't forecasted this particular storm or weather pattern, and therefore it was not supposed to be happening! As far as living with my family in such close quarters went, it really didn't bother me that much. That's probably because I was already used to travelling with them in a van across country, where we had limited space, too. Granted, in that case we could go for a walk if we wanted to get away, but it was good practice! I think it brought us closer together, if anything.

Looking back now, I think that it was one of the most amazing experiences of my life so far, even if I didn't fully appreciate it at the time. There were many, many times during the trans-Atlantic crossing that I fully could not wait to get to Switzerland and finally have my own space, with a closet to put my clothes in, and a desk that I could sit at, and bed that I didn't have to share with my sister, but all in all, I absolutely loved it. I really don't regret anything about it at all, and would do it again in a heartbeat. This time around, though, I would like to explore the Pacific Ocean.

Arriving in Falmouth was a great relief. I was happy to know that I had travelled all the way to England by boat. It sure took us a long time but we made it. The last part was absolutely terrible. We were tired and soaked to the bones when we arrived. I had not slept much during the trip. A light drizzle greeted us, this did not make it any better. "Typical England," was the comment from my Dad. The people at the marina where we stopped were very kind and happy to

see people arriving from Canada. We could use their facilities and I had one long shower.

In the harbor of Falmouth our boat was tied to a buoy and safely secured. There was no danger from the elements, and I could sleep without being shaken up every so often. The harbor was large and several times during the week local people had regattas. It looked really cool. There were no people living on most of the boats around us; we were the only ones in that part of the harbor. There was a small area with a dock, where we could tie up the dinghy when going ashore and we could take showers nearby there too. There were also some boats anchored out next to the dock. This was all right in down town Falmouth. I enjoyed walking through the narrow streets between the old houses. I was not used to such cities in Canada. The buildings in that part of town along the water were mostly old ones, with fat walls and small windows. Everywhere there were seagulls. Sometimes I took the dinghy and went sailing to explore the shore. It was made up mostly of walls from buildings. I saw a lot of ducks and swans along the pier. Sailing was easy in there. There was always a bit of wind going. It was fun to pass close to the walkways where people were watching. I had such a good time. Sometimes I had to watch out for people ferries or other boat traffic, but that made it all the more interesting.

The trip along the coast of England was pleasant but the highlight was the visit with Dad's sister. We stayed there for some time. I remember very well our visit to Paradise Park in Hayle. They had hundreds of birds and animals there, from all around the world. I received a little paper with a quiz on it and enjoyed hunting for the right answers. You had to know the capital city of several countries. Then there were questions about animals living in these countries. There was nothing about Canada, but China, Australia, USA and more. Of course England wasn't missing. With the help of the displays I got all the questions right and I received a badge. Next we were offered some sweets and a coke.

Some of my time I spent with Dad to split a large pile of wood from a tree that had to be cut down at his sisters house. It was a lot of work but fun and we piled it up neatly beside their garage.

A visit by bus to Penzance was another fun thing to do. There was a parade with all kinds of strangely dressed people parading behind large scale, scary looking puppets that were carried on sticks or pushed along the streets. After the parade we went to hear some bands play. One of the bands was astonishingly good, and I enjoyed listening to them.

Arriving in Le Havre brought with it two very distinct changes in my life. First of all I did not understand a word of French. This lack of knowledge took a year or so to correct. As a matter of fact I stayed for more than 3 years in the French-speaking part of Switzerland and then moved to a German-speaking one. This alone could be another book, so I stop here.

The more serious change was that this seemed to be the end of our sailing trip. No more fun with the boat, the sailing dinghy, the fishing line, the excitement along the trip and on and on. It was to be a life just like the rest of the people. In a house, going to school, doing homework, how boring. The feeling of having your own little world on the water was to be put into the past.

I am certain that it will stay vividly in my memory for the rest of my life. Nothing more exiting than this adventure had ever happened in my life. All this made it bearable to look forward to going to school and to adapt to the everyday life of an adult. Who knows, I may one day set out on my own to do another trip on the water. I sure wouldn't mind.

Family Reunion: Marcel, Thomas, Carina, Pascal, Brigitte, Werner, Fabian, Anisha

Floor Plan For Kristy Nicole

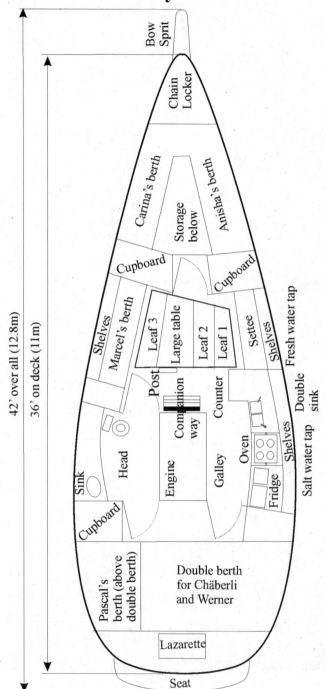

Floor plan for Kristy Nicole

Boat Specifications

1983 cutter rigged ketch, centre cockpit, full keel, ferro-cement
Construction: Hull built by a crew of Samson
Measurements: LOA 42', LOD 36', LWL 32', beam 12', draft 6', displ. Approx.
14 tonnes (18 tonnes gross), colour green, max. height above water 49'.
Steering: Vetus hydraulic wheel inclusive Benmar auto pilot.
Engine: Yanmar Model 3QM30, 30HP, salt water cooled, fuel: diesel, Gear box:
Yanmar Drive to prop: 2.5:1
Electrics: 12V with outlets and lights (plus 2 fans) throughout the boat, Battery
charger 110V, Wind generator type Airmarine for battery charging, Alternator
90A driven by engine for battery charging. Charging controlled by Mariner
Alternator Controller, A-meter and V-meter.
Numbers of deep cycle batteries: Bank 1: 2x6V in series (220Ah), Bank 2: 3x12V
parallel (240Ah), Bank 3: 1x12V starting battery and dinghy motor. All banks
controlled via two switches for individual use/charge. Shore power plug-in, wired
for 110V with outlets throughout the boat.
Tankage: All tanks made out of fibreglass. Two fuel tanks at 45gal each, deck
filled. One fresh water tank 200gal, deck filled. One holding tank 6gal, (mandatory
for Florida, US) incl. pump out connection and Y-valve for direct discharge. Water
system: Hand pump for fresh water in galley and head, foot pump for salt water
into double galley sink.
Rig: STA-lock fittings on both ends of SS wire. Spar is aluminum. All standing
rigging is SS. Size 3/8" for main stays, 5/16" for Mizzen and side stays. Running
rigging, also SS and Nylon ropes/lines.
Sails: Reefing: Mainsail 2x, mizzen 2x, stay 1x.
Main, 150% genoa 34' x 24', jib 34'x16.5', stay, mizzen, storm, all
tanbark-coloured and made by Lee. Jib spare, high cut white, 26'x17'
Barlow winches: Genoa, 2 times model 25. Mizzen model 16, halyards 2x model
23. Stay, model 1. Ground tackle: 70lb Danford, 55lb Delta, 35lb Danford, 20lb
Danford. Chain 3/8" 60' and 100'. Manual windlass type Lofran for chain and
warp. Warp 3/4", 150' two times, 5/8" 300' one time. 280' spare line.
Accommodations: No. of berths: 5 adults, 2 children. Cooking facility: Force 10,
propane, 2 burners, one oven. Fridge: Adler Barbour, Headroom: main cabin 74".
Garmin GPSII, Windex wind direction indicator; one VHF fix mount, one small 2
Watt hand held Uniden. 8 man life raft type Viking, 8' fibreglass sailing- rowing-
or motoring- dinghy. Outboard electric motor 27lb. thrust

Reference to literature mentioned in text

-Harmonic Farming: A Love Style, Werner M. Gysi
(page 8 and chapter 9-95)

-Martin The Warrior,   Brian Jacques (Redwall books)
(chapters 8-89/32-290)

-Maiden Voyage, Tania Aebi, Bernadette Brennan (chapter 13-132)

-Waterway Cruising Guide (Florida, etc.) (chapter 15-149/153)

-Lassie And The Secret Of The Summer, Dorothea J. Snow
(chapters 18-179/22-216)

-Guide to Abaco, Bahamas, Steve Dodge (an excellent guide and
reasonably priced, chapter 21-204)

-Anne of Green Gables, L.M. Montgomery (chapters
21-205/26-244)

-Left On The Labrador, Dillon Wallace (chapters 26-244/27-249)

-The Twenty-One Balloons, William Pene du Bois (chapter 27-250)

-Rainbow Valley, L.M. Montgomery (chapter 27-250)

-Nancy Drew and the Hardy Boys, Marvin Heiferman, Carole
Kismaric (chapter 27-250)

-The Message, K.A. Applegate, Animorphs Series (chapter 27-250)

-The World of Ben Lighthart, Jaap Ter Haar (chapter 27-252)

-Monkey Trouble, David Martin (chapter 27-253)

-"Kasperli", fairy tale figure in Swiss stories, Globi Verlag
(chapter 32-288)

-Fire House Dixie jazz band, sound tape (chapter 32-291)